CLINICAL SUPERVISION

A Practical Guide To Student Teacher Supervision

CLINICAL SUPERVISION

A Practical Guide To
Student Teacher Supervision

W. Scott Hopkins
Cameron University

Kenneth D. Moore
Wichita State University

WCB Brown &
Benchmark
P U B L I S H E R S

Madison, Wisconsin•Indianapolis, Indiana
Melbourne, Australia•Oxford, England

Book Team

Editor *Paul L. Tavenner*
Developmental Editor *Sue Pulvermacher-Alt*
Production Coordinator *Karen L. Nickolas*

**WCB Brown &
Benchmark**
P U B L I S H E R S

A Division of Wm. C. Brown Communications, Inc.

Vice President and General Manager *Thomas E. Doran*
Executive Managing Editor *Ed Bartell*
Executive Editor *Edgar J. Laube*
Director of Marketing *Kathy Law Laube*
National Sales Manager *Eric Ziegler*
Marketing Manager *Pamela Cooper*

Advertising Manager *Jodi Rymer*
Managing Editor, Production *Colleen A. Yonda*
Manager of Visuals and Design *Faye M. Schilling*
Production Editorial Manager *Vickie Putman Caughron*
Publishing Services Manager *Karen J. Slaght*
Permissions/Records Manager *Connie Allendorf*

Wm. C. Brown Communications, Inc.

Chairman Emeritus *Wm. C. Brown*
Chairman and Chief Executive Officer *Mark C. Falb*
President and Chief Operating Officer *G. Franklin Lewis*
Corporate Vice President, Operations *Beverly Kolz*
Corporate Vice President, President of WCB Manufacturing *Roger Meyer*

Cover and interior design by Carol V. Hall
Copyedited by Jane Dowd

Library of Congress Catalog Card Number: 91–77138

ISBN 0–697–13012–6

Printed in the United States of America by Wm. C. Brown Communications, Inc.,
2460 Kerper Boulevard, Dubuque, IA 52001

10 9 8 7 6 5 4 3 2 1

Contents

PART 3. THE FUTURE

Preface

The demands placed upon teachers are changing. No longer do school systems want teachers who view their primary responsibility as doing what they are told and following directions. If our society is to have teachers who are capable of making decisions, encouraging higher order thinking skills, and evaluating their teaching in the light of student learning, the preparation of teachers must provide these experiences. Student teaching, the zenith of any teacher's professional education coursework, is often a traumatic experience wherein the student teacher attempts to make adjustments from the university to the public school classroom while trying to please a cooperating teacher and a university supervisor.

If our school systems expect to have teachers who are self-motivated and interested in self-improvement throughout their career, their first total immersion in the teaching process should focus on the skills deemed desirable to success as a teacher. Clinical supervision, with its focus on reflective teaching, involves the student teacher in evaluating the effectiveness of instruction while still providing the necessary support.

The structure of clinical supervision focuses on the instructional acts within the classroom and determines the effectiveness of the teacher's instructional strategies. The basic structure of clinical supervision, with its total involvement of the triad (university supervisor, cooperating teacher, and student teacher) in determining and evaluating the content of instruction, can be adopted or adapted to fit many models of supervision without destroying the basic focus of supervision—the instructional acts of the teacher.

Teacher educators and administrators should examine the concepts presented in this text and modify them to improve student teaching and the total concept of supervision. If public education is to be improved, it will require more emphasis on the teaching act, the empowerment of the classroom teacher to analyze instructional acts, and the necessary modifications to improve student learning.

This book is for those individuals who work with student teachers in the professional application component of their preparatory program. Part 1 presents background information on the purposes and nature of student teaching. Human relations, communication, observation, and legal and ethical considerations as important ingredients in a successful student teaching experience are addressed. Part 2 presents detailed and specific components of the clinical supervision model. The clinical supervision model itself, along with application guidelines for all members of the triad, is the focus of this part. Part 3 focuses on the future of supervision.

Acknowledgments

We wish to thank the following reviewers for their insightful comments:

Andrew Brulle
Northern Illinois University

Floyd Coppedge, Principal
Oklahoma City Public Schools

Linda Coyle
University of Central Arkansas

Lonnie Fuson
Northeastern State University

Marsha Grace
Otterbein College

A. J. "Jack" Hytrek
Peru State College

Rose Khoury
West Chester University

John E. Merryman
Indiana University of Pennsylvania

Patricia Williams
Sam Houston State University

We extend our thanks and appreciation to the many student teachers and cooperating teachers with whom we have been associated. Their input has had a direct impact on the writing of this text. We also express our sincere thanks to Paul Tavenner; his expertise and sound advise have been invaluable.

We hope that this book will prove valuable to all concerned with the guidance and professional development of future teachers.

W. S. H.
K. D. M.

PART 1

ORIENTATION TO THE SUPERVISORY PROCESS

Those responsible for the preparation of prospective teachers are eager for reliable information on how they can be effective supervisors. The purpose of Part 1 is to develop a better understanding of the supervisory process. This orientation presents and discusses the history associated with supervision from the practical aspect to the research on working with student teachers. Chapter 1 focuses on the foundations of supervision. It looks at the purposes and objectives of student teaching, and, since student teaching and supervision have been an evolving process, it presents a brief history of the changing function of student teaching. Finally, chapter 1 explores and clarifies the roles and responsibilities associated with the student teaching experience.

Chapters 2–5 speak directly to the function of those involved in the supervisory process—to provide a helping relationship. Chapter 2 deals with the various relationships associated with student teaching, exploring student teacher relation-

ships with pupils, supervisors, school personnel, parents, and the community. The focus is on the establishment, pitfalls, and challenges associated with professional relationships.

Communication and the ability to collect accurate data are essential to the supervisory process. Chapters 3 and 4 address these skills. Chapter 3 looks at techniques associated with effective verbal and nonverbal communication, whereas chapter 4 focuses on various techniques for collecting viable student teacher behavioral information. The ability to communicate collected and analyzed information provides the framework for developing the helping relationship that is essential to the supervisory process.

Chapter 5 addresses the legal and ethical aspects of student teaching and supervision. The focus of the chapter is on the legal status of student teachers, pupils, and cooperating teachers.

CHAPTER 1

Foundations of Student Teaching Supervision

CHAPTER KEY CONCEPTS

Cooperating School
Cooperating Teacher
Coordinator of Field Experience
School Coordinator

Structured Observation
Student Teacher
Student Teaching
University Supervisor

Overview

Constant change and innovation have characterized and continue to characterize the process of student teaching. Recently, the function, goals, and responsibilities of this vital process have responded to forces from the community, professional organizations, public schools, state departments, and higher education institutions. Chapter 1 briefly addresses the purposes of student teaching and some of the changes that have taken place in this important process and looks at the need for change in the philosophy of supervision associated with student teaching.

Objectives

Upon completing your study of chapter 1, you should be able to:

1. Explain the purposes and objectives of student teaching.

2. Trace the changing historical concept of the function of student teaching.

3. Describe the contemporary student teaching experience as well as a rationale for this philosophy.

4. Outline school, university, and state responsibilities in a student teaching program.

5. Outline the criteria that should be followed in the selection of cooperating teachers.

6. Describe the benefits to public schools involved in student teaching programs.

7. Describe requirements and procedures for candidate admission to teacher education.

8. Describe the issues that state guidelines and standards should address in the establishment of viable state-wide student teaching programs.

9. Outline triad (student teacher, cooperating teacher, and university supervisor) roles and responsibilities that must be assumed for a successful student teaching experience.

For prospective teachers, the student teaching experience is a critical step toward becoming a professional educator. Even though the experience is not as realistic as being a certified teacher, it does give the beginner the opportunity to learn and practice the art of teaching. Indeed, it gives beginning teachers the opportunity to implement the theory, the ideas, and the skills of the craft. Essentially, the student teaching experience is foremost a learning experience with opportunities to learn from mistakes without an uncontrolled disruption in the learning processes of classroom students. It is an opportunity to grow in confidence and to strive for competence without doing irreparable damage to the clients.

Student Teaching Experience

Student teaching is more than simple practice. Rather, it is learning the art of teaching under supervision. In this context, supervision is defined as helping prospective teachers improve their instructional performance through systematic cycles of planning observation, and intensive intellectual analysis of teaching performances. Thus, the student teaching experience represents hard work with a definite and worthwhile purpose—instructional performance improvement.

Purposes of Student Teaching

Two compelling purposes support the desirability of a student teaching program. The first purpose is to help prospective teachers become skillful and creative teachers, depending less and less on direct supervision, in preparation for the first professional teaching assignment under limited supervision. Indeed, many states now recognize the need for some supervision during the initial year of teaching and require a supervised induction year before full certification is granted. Chapter 11 looks at supervision during the induction year in greater detail.

The second purpose of student teaching is to provide many opportunities for prospective teach-

Student teaching provides growth experiences for prospective teachers.

ers to raise questions, problems, and issues that should provide the basis for determining further needs and study. Thus, student teaching should provide growth experiences, with each experience furnishing the basis for the next step in the continual process of professional growth and development.

Objectives of Student Teaching

Superior student teaching should consist of a cross-section of realistic experiences in and out of the classroom. The furtherance of this goal suggests that student teachers be given the opportunity:

1. To become self-directive.
2. To construct a philosophy in terms of the experiences encountered.
3. To experience, under supervision, a variety of teaching-learning situations.
4. To gain experience in using methods, techniques, and instructional materials.
5. To experience and participate in extra-curricular activities.
6. To provide for individual differences found among pupils.
7. To become aware of and apply human relations skills when working with pupils, faculty, parents, and members of the community.

8. To experience a professionally supportive environment.
9. To experience the actual working conditions of public schools that should include acquaintance with school district and/or building policies, regulations, committees, records, reports, and other aspects of the school.

Indeed, the experiences incorporated into the student teaching objectives should serve as the integrative capstone of the essence of each step in a preparatory program. As such, it should be one of the most significant and important facets of a teacher education program.

The nature of the student teaching experience varies from institution to institution. However, the terminology should be consistent.

Terminology

Although some variance in student teaching procedures will be encountered, there are generally agreed upon terms associated with student teaching. Among the most commonly used terms are:

1. **Coordinator or director of field experiences.** The individual designated by the university with administrative responsibility for organizing and coordinating the university's total field experience program. These field experiences commonly include prestudent-teaching field experiences as well as the student teaching phase of the program.
2. **Cooperating school.** A public or private school that is not controlled nor supported by a higher education institution but provides opportunities and facilities for professional student teaching experiences in a teacher education program.
3. **School coordinator.** The individual designated by the school district with administrative responsibility for working with universities in providing field

experiences for prospective teachers. This individual usually works with university coordinators or directors in the placement of student teachers.
4. **Cooperating teachers.** A teacher in a cooperating school who is recognized by the public school and university as qualified to work with student teachers. This individual agrees to the charge of and guidance of the student teacher as the student teaching process develops. This person is referred to as the supervisory teacher or clinical teacher in some programs.
5. **Professional experiences.** Those contacts with children and youth (through observation, participation, and teaching) that were designed to contribute to an understanding of individuals and their guidance in the teaching-learning process. These directed experiences are planned, supervised, and evaluated.
6. **Structured observation.** Professional observations that have been planned in terms of the skills to be demonstrated, observation time, recording of data, and feedback.
7. **Student teaching.** The period of supervised teaching in which the university student takes increasing responsibility for the work with a given group of learners over a period of consecutive weeks. The student usually moves from "observation" to "part-time" teaching to "full-time" teaching.
8. **University supervisor.** The university faculty member who is responsible for supervising a student teacher or a group of student teachers.

While changes in student teaching reality require an equivalent change in the language about student teaching, knowledge of current terms should enhance the communication process that is so vital to a successful student teaching experience.

Chapter 3 takes a closer look at these important communication processes.

History

What is the aspiring teacher's place in the total organizational pattern of a school district? This is often a difficult question to answer since it depends on the specific school district and the concept of the function of the student teaching experience. This function has undergone several changes over the past years.

Changing Function

Clinical experiences have undergone considerable change over the years as knowledge has been advanced regarding the preparation of teachers. Student teaching has moved from (1) the apprenticeship era; (2) to the normal school era; (3) to the teacher's college era, and finally, (4) to the present day concept of student teaching. Figure 1.1 illustrates the changing era of student teaching.

One can say that the apprenticeship was the first technique for preparing teachers. Individuals were indentured to a school master to learn the profession. Although the apprentice did not receive a liberal education or study subjects in depth, he or she was required to do directed readings. The approach was essentially that of practicing the teaching craft until the candidate was deemed a qualified teacher. The apprenticeship gave way to the rise of the normal school in the era between 1829 and 1900. These early normal school programs usually consisted of a two-year course of study. The curriculum was much like the curriculum of the high school of that time. Students reviewed their elementary school subjects, studied some high school subjects, had a

course in teaching methodology, and did some student teaching in a model school usually operated in conjunction with the normal school.

Along with the advent of the normal school came the practice approach to teacher preparation. Prospective teachers were placed in the normal schools to observe, study, and practice teaching. The idea was to have the individual practice the art of teaching sufficiently to learn the necessary teaching skills. This practice concept was based on the premise that required teaching theory, obtained in the university classroom, only needed to be practiced in the normal school classroom until the application of that theory was acceptable.

In the early 1900s, normal schools with the practice concept led into the teacher college era with the emphasis on laboratory schools. In this era, elaborate on-campus facilities were developed to provide convenient access to classrooms. In effect, these classrooms were model public schools located on a teacher's college campus. Again, the emphasis in these laboratory school classrooms was on practice. Prospective teachers were shuttled in and out of these model schools as practice was deemed necessary for concept or skill development. "Practice" teaching often consisted of being assigned to a classroom situation for an hour per day with one classroom being shared among several practicing university students.

The teacher's college era gave way to the student teaching concept in the middle of the twentieth century. At this time, the view of the prospective teacher changed from the concept of "practice" to the concept that the prospective teacher was a student of teaching while in the classroom. This emerging new philosophy was

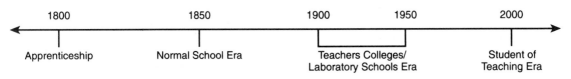

Figure 1.1 Changing concept of student teaching

based on the concept that the function of the classroom experience was to give the university student the opportunity to question, inquire, probe, and experiment. This new philosophy also eventually led to an extension of the student teaching experience. The experience changed to a few weeks, then to a half-day experience, and finally to a full-day experience for a term or semester.

The contemporary conception of the student teacher as a student of teaching requires a newer approach to supervision. The role of supervisors, cooperating teachers, and university supervisors must change to that of support and guidance toward an understanding of teaching with a corresponding shift in emphasis in role from judge to helper. Therefore, supervisors must become more analytical and more clinical in their approach.

It is assumed that most teacher education programs have endorsed the newer philosophy that undergirds student teaching. With this newer philosophy in mind, let's look at the present approach to student teaching.

Student Teaching Assignment

The student teaching assignment usually comes near the end of the undergraduate program for the professional and academic preparation of future teachers. Since most of the required university coursework has been completed, this organizational structure gives university students the opportunity to apply the theoretical learning to real classroom situations. Thus, student teaching provides the opportunity to implement ideas gleaned in prior coursework. Indeed, the experiences provide an opportunity to implement concepts, values, and skills as well as a place to grow professionally. The emphasis is on learning (that is, changing behavior) by doing.

The move from the university campus laboratory school to public schools has also resulted in two major changes in the student teaching experiences. First, longer assignments are now common. The increase in knowledge about learning and teaching itself requires longer training periods. Learning how to apply this knowledge with students of different backgrounds and cultures also requires more training time. To better achieve this latter purpose, institutions may require that the student teaching experience be split between two diverse sites. Elementary student teachers, for example, often complete a primary and an intermediate placement or an urban and a suburban placement, while secondary student teachers often complete a junior high and a senior high placement.

Second, there is more collaboration between public schools and universities in teacher preparation. Hundreds of public schools and thousands of teachers are now involved in the preparation of teachers. Indeed, these teachers often assume supervisory responsibilities for which they have little or no formal training (Morehead, Lyman, and Waters 1988). Moreover, in some special programs, public school personnel have assumed total responsibility for student teacher supervision (see chapter 11). Regardless of how a student teaching program is structured, the experience must be thought of as a viable partnership toward the future, a partnership whose success will be enhanced by proper preparation of all the partners to fulfill their roles effectively.

Partnership

Everyone involved in a student teaching program—the school, the university and the state—should share responsibility and support the development of a viable program. As such, clearly delineated responsibilities should be outlined for all involved in a student teaching program.

School Responsibilities

The primary priority of the cooperating school is the education of the children and youth entrusted to their care. However, the decision to participate in student teaching programs adds still another function to a school and obligates them to fulfill this function. The obligations include providing proper assignments, supervision, and opportunities for professional growth of future teachers. Thus, when schools agree to accept student teachers, they must be prepared to provide viable, effectively supervised assignments for student teachers.

One of the most important functions of the cooperating school is to assist in the selection of cooperating teachers. This selection process should be a joint effort between the school and the university. Because of the importance of cooperating teachers in the development of effective teachers, it behooves the selection team to select teachers based on their ability to work effectively with others and do the job of supervision well. Also, they should possess a philosophy of teaching that involves unselfish dedication and willingness to be useful in the preparation of future teachers. Among other criteria that should be considered are:

1. Academic preparation and standard teaching certification in the subject matter area.
2. Ability to work as an effective team member.
3. Academic competence and skill at successful teaching techniques.
4. Sufficient experience to guide the professional development and growth of aspiring teachers.
5. Evidence of a commitment to lifelong learning.

A cooperating public school must tacitly agree to accept some direction from the university regarding the structure of the student teaching experiences. For example, some structure items might include the need for release time for the cooperating teacher to receive preparation or the specification of minimal amounts of time that student teachers would be permitted to assume full teaching duties. Also, the school should provide materials such as a second desk placed in the cooperating teacher's classroom for the student teacher and teacher's editions of class textbooks for the student teacher. Further adjustments might be needed in the school requirements to give student teachers broad participation in the act of teaching. Thus, a school climate must be established that allows student teachers to be successful with a minimum of difficulties.

There are several advantages associated with school involvement in student teaching programs (Henry and Beasley 1982; Guyton 1987). First, the presence of student teachers in public school classrooms inevitably causes cooperating teachers to re-examine their methods, procedures, and management approaches. Thus, the opportunity for teachers to examine and improve their teaching performance can occur on an informal, voluntary basis.

Second, student teachers often bring new ideas and materials from the university to the assigned school, which enriches the classroom teacher's resources. Proper input from university supervisors can also enrich classroom instruction and procedures.

Finally, the presence of student teachers gives a district the opportunity to screen prospective teachers before they are hired. In effect, they can train these prospective teachers to be successful in the district.

Regardless of the type of agreement between the schools and universities, there must be agreement between the schools and teacher education institutions regarding the responsibilities of each function in the student teaching experience. This actual agreement can be in oral or contractual form. However, a written agreement is usually needed to satisfy accreditation requirements, often eliminating some confusion in communication and functions.

University Responsibilities

The number one priority of universities is to produce the best possible teachers for the children and youth of tomorrow (Moore 1989). As a result, universities need and desire the best possible student teaching experiences. To this end, certain responsibilities should be assumed by universities in working with the public schools. Among the responsibilities that should be assumed by most universities are:

1. Screen carefully candidates for teacher education program admittance. This screening process should include a screening interview as well as demonstrated:
   a. Commitment to the academic aspects of teaching through an adequate academic record (GPA).
   b. Evidence of adequate reading, writing, and verbal (oral) communication skills.
   c. Interest in teaching as a profession.
   d. Evidence of personal traits that suggest potential for working with youth, parents, and other constituencies in education.
2. Screen carefully students who make application for student teaching. Those who do not meet the established criteria should not be allowed to student teach until concerns and deficiencies have been identified and corrected.
3. Establish policies related to working part-time during student teaching and the taking of university coursework, ensuring that sufficient time is available to carry out the responsibilities associated with student teaching.
4. Provide necessary supervisory training for the personnel involved in the student teaching program. This training should include both public school and university personnel.
5. Provide sufficient structured supervision for student teachers.
6. Work with cooperating districts and schools to ensure the continued education of the children and youth entrusted to their care.
7. Provide communication links and leadership to all personnel involved in the teacher education program.
8. Hire and assign only faculty who are themselves models of teaching excellence and commitment to teaching.

Who should be admitted to the teacher education program? This is one of the most critical issues to be addressed by an institution. Questions regarding basic skills, academic qualifications, communication skills, personality factors, psychological factors, recruiting qualified minorities, and so on, must be addressed. However, many institutions are reluctant to face such issues because they fear legal ramifications associated with denial. Other than the establishment of grade point average (GPA) requirements, most universities have avoided many of the personality and psychological factor issues. However, this tendency appears to be changing with many institutions becoming more sensitive to the need for more adequate screening of teacher education candidates. In fact, some institutions now require an entrance interview and one or more personality and psychological tests. For example, Oklahoma statutes require that all prospective teachers be interviewed. Perhaps it is time to take a hard look at the criteria for admission to teacher education and address such issues as critical thinking ability, potential for leadership, open-mindedness, and reasoning ability.

Students preparing to student teach should again be carefully screened prior to being placed in the schools. Those students who have not met the criteria or demonstrated minimal professional skills after being admitted to the program should be offered a remediation plan or counseled out of teacher education. Of course, this is not always an easy task when dealing with determined students. But it must be accomplished if a program is to remain viable and a profession is to exist for teachers. Once established, admission criteria must be maintained with no exceptions.

Student teaching should be viewed as a job. That is, student teachers should assume the same schedules as their cooperating teachers. They should report to their assigned schools and remain at the schools according to district policy. This policy, of course, means that no outside employment or coursework should interfere with school policy or procedures. In addition, sufficient time should be available to plan and prepare for classes. Student teaching is not an eight o'clock-to-three o'clock activity.

Student teacher supervisors (cooperating teachers and university supervisors) must be competent to fulfill their function. A knowledge of content, methodology, management, professionalism, and interpersonal relations is essential to effective supervision. Thus, it behooves universities to be certain that supervisors receive the necessary preparation in content, pedagogy, and supervision. Universities should also provide supervisor orientation to program expectations. A supervision program should present instruction regarding student teacher planning, observation requirements, actual teaching by student teachers, and evaluation. A supervision course and a supervisor's handbook can be extremely beneficial in providing the necessary supervisory orientation skills.

If student teaching supervision is to be effective and helpful, it should be structured. As such, an occasional visit will not suffice. Each visit should be preplanned. The information and data collected should be followed-up with a discussion conference. Structured observations allow weak and strong areas to be identified. Follow-up work can then be planned to maintain the strong areas; remediation can be planned to improve the weak areas. For example, if a student is weak in the use of questioning and reinforcement, an appropriate source dealing with classroom teaching skills, such as that developed by Moore (1989), could be suggested.

The continued education of students in the public school classroom is a critical issue in student teaching. Cooperating teachers and univer-sity supervisors should cooperatively see that the overall function of the classroom is maintained. Generally, cooperating teachers assume subject matter specialist roles, and university supervisors assume the roles of specialist in the teaching-learning process and in teaching others to teach.

Successful student teaching programs require a partnership with effective communication links between cooperating schools and universities. Usually these communication links are best established when student teaching communication is channeled through one public school coordinator and a university coordinator of student teaching. The public school coordinator is the direct link to principals and teachers; the coordinator of student teaching is the link to university supervisors.

State Responsibilities

The State Department of Education has the responsibilities for setting student teacher guidelines and standards. These standards should address issues such as:

1. General guidelines for the student teaching program (academic preparation of student teachers, length of time, level, supervision requirements, and so forth).
2. Selection criteria for cooperating districts and schools.
3. Selection criteria for cooperating teachers.
4. Policy for remuneration to cooperating teachers for working in the student teaching program.
5. Use of student teachers in extra-curricular activities and as substitute teachers.
6. Establishment of a legal status for student teachers.

These standards, of course, should be established with input from both public schools and higher education institutions. Moreover, the standards should be somewhat flexible so that options can be exercised.

Many states have implemented special teacher requirements for serving as a cooperating teacher

Table 1.1
Responsibilities Associated with Student Teaching Programs

Responsibility	Public School	University	State
1. Establishing requirements	X	X	X
2. Establishing cooperating teacher criteria	X	X	X
3. Selecting appropriate sites	X	X	
4. Selecting student teachers		X	X
5. Coordinating placement requests		X	
6. Assigning student teachers	X	X	
7. Planning overall program	X	X	X
8. Training supervisors	X	X	
9. Directing daily responsibilities of student teachers	X		
10. Evaluating student teachers	X	X	
11. Providing professional consultation		X	X
12. Interpreting program to parents	X		

(Haberman and Harris 1982). Usually the requirements include some type of applicable coursework related to pedagogical skills, classroom management techniques, educational research, and supervisory skill development. In addition, some states have attempted to require a special supervisory certificate for cooperating teachers. These supervisory certification efforts have generally failed—primarily because they lack incentives associated with attainment of the credentials. Perhaps with substantial salary increments attached to these certificates such programs could be more successful. In fact, significant professional recognition such as being named "university clinical faculty" might be more successful and appropriate. Indeed, preparing classroom teachers and giving them university faculty status with access to university facilities can be quite effective incentives.

Joint Responsibilities

A successful student teaching program requires a close working relationship between the public schools and the teacher education institutions. Many of the arrangements that must be made are the joint responsibility of the public schools and

universities with each taking the initiative in its own peculiar areas. Universities, for example, initiate student placements while public schools make the final judgment as to the appropriateness of these placements. Table 1.1 indicates the responsibilities that each agency assumes in the student teaching program. The data in the table is not intended to suggest that one agency assumes complete responsibility for the indicated area, but rather the data indicates the agency that initiates the responsibility. As suggested in the table, many areas require joint cooperation to have a viable program.

A meeting of minds between the public schools and teacher education programs, within the constraints established by the state, is needed for a fully functioning student teaching program. Specific agreements must be reached regarding what is best for the public schools and best for the teacher education institution. As noted earlier, those agreements are often best established in written contractual form.

Successful student teaching requires a joint effort. Student teachers, cooperating teachers, and university supervisors must assume specific roles and responsibilities.

Triad

Student teaching is a team endeavor: student teacher, cooperating teacher, and university supervisor. The purpose of student teaching teams should be to develop the student teacher's full, creative potential as a classroom teacher and as a productive member of a school faculty. Therefore, the essence of student teaching is a collegial process involving the student teacher, the cooperating teacher, and the university supervisor in a triad. This collegial relationship is illustrated in Figure 1.2. Thus, student teaching must be viewed as a team affair with specific roles and responsibilities for team members.

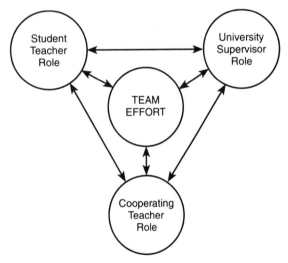

Figure 1.2 Collegial process

Student Teacher Role

Student teaching is the period in which trainees begin the gradual transition from students to teachers. Thus, student teachers must be given the opportunity to observe, participate, and teach.

Student teaching should be a time for making discoveries regarding the trainee's skill as a teacher. It is a time to implement the ideas and theories that have been accumulated in the university classroom, while a professional team stands by

to assist. It is a time to discover areas of strength and weakness and to be assisted with the improvement of skills. Finally, it is a time to be evaluated.

Student teachers, as key members of the triad, must assume various responsibilities. Chief among these responsibilities are:

1. To recognize the cooperating teacher and university supervisor as professionals whose functions are to guide and assist in attaining the status of co-teacher.
2. To become acquainted with rules, regulations, policies, curriculum, and facilities of the cooperating school.
3. To plan with the cooperating teacher and the university supervisor the steps to be taken in assuming the responsibilities in the classroom, realizing that more responsibilities will be delegated as readiness is exhibited.
4. To maintain an ethical and professional attitude toward all members of the school community.
5. To work as a professional and grow professionally in the ability to be effective in the classroom.

The successful fulfillment of these roles requires cooperative effort on the part of the student teaching team. To develop and refine competence in planning, implementing plans, evaluation, and so on, the student teacher requires support from both the cooperating teacher and the university supervisor.

Cooperating Teacher Role

The focal point for providing successful student teaching experiences is the cooperating teachers with whom the student teachers will be placed. Studies (Bennie 1972; Pfeiffer and Dunlap 1982; Guyton 1989) indicate that cooperating teachers are the most crucial factor in developing competent teachers. Indeed, cooperating teachers often determine the type of teaching done by student teachers once they obtain a job and, in fact, are even instrumental in student teachers' attitudes

Cooperating teachers should analyze the teaching act and identify teaching skills and techniques.

toward teaching and toward their students. There are numerous ways in which these cooperating teachers guide student teachers toward becoming highly competent teachers. Taking time to confer, formally and informally, with student teachers—before school begins, after school ends, and even on weekends and holidays—is only part of the total picture.

Other ways that cooperating teachers influence student teaching are through their involvement in such tasks as assisting in planning, selecting methods and materials, and evaluating learning; creating an atmosphere of warmth and sharing; help in analyzing teaching skills and techniques; and, finally, creating the opportunity to gradually work into the total responsibilities of a teacher. However, besides these concrete tasks there are also the intangibles; that is, understanding and assisting with concerns of inadequacies, respect for student teacher ideas and feelings, understanding and helping with personal problems, and general warmth and acceptance. This understanding and assistance is crucial at this point in the professional development of prospective teachers. It is obvious, therefore, that to meet these challenges cooperating teachers must have commendable skills—interpersonal and teaching. Thus, it is paramount that cooperating teachers be selected on the basis of a willingness and interest in work-

ing with future teachers. Those electing to become cooperating teachers should be willing to assume the following responsibilities:

1. To be willing to share knowledge, materials, and experiences with student teachers—yet look to student teachers for new ideas and approaches. For example, many teachers give student teachers copies of all their enrichment activities, and student teachers share the activities they have developed in their methods courses.
2. To encourage prospective teachers to try new ideas and join in the cooperative evaluation of the results. For example, student teachers can audio- or videotape their teaching and evaluate it.
3. To encourage prospective teachers to think for themselves, and provide freedom to accept or reject ideas.
4. To observe teacher candidates' attitudes, performance, and general attributes consistently and provide regular feedback.
5. To provide ideas, options, and suggestions for improvement.
6. To plan and hold informal as well as formal conferences with student teachers and university supervisors on a regular basis.
7. To provide guidance and counseling to teacher candidates in becoming a professional educator.
8. To critique themselves and invite student teachers to sit in on peer coaching sessions in which cooperating teachers are critiqued by other professionals.

There are rewards for being selected as a cooperating teacher, among which are the opportunity to: (1) refine and evaluate one's own teaching, (2) carry out new techniques and methods, (3) refine old and learn new human relations skills, (4) find more time to work with classroom students, and (5) work with universities for improvement in the profession. Thus, it takes time, energy, and perseverance to assume the role of cooperating teacher. However, the rewards are great in helping and watching future teachers grow and develop.

In the final analysis, working with prospective teachers gives cooperating teachers a welcome change of pace and presents a different type of teaching challenge. That is to say, it represents another opportunity to teach.

University Supervisor Role

The university supervisor is the joining force between the schools and the university. As such, the university supervisor is the university faculty member who is responsible for the specific student teaching requirements. That is, the university supervisor must see that the student teacher has meaningful student teaching experiences.

University supervisors must assume overall supervisory responsibility for student teaching (Bennie 1972; Pfeiffer and Dunlap 1982; Guyton 1989). Essentially, university supervisors have three important responsibilities. The first job is to orient student teachers to the placement assignments and to the university requirements. Student teachers should be aware of the program objectives, the type of activities that are needed to attain the objectives, and the general procedures to be followed in working with the cooperating teacher and university supervisor. In addition, the university supervisor addresses such requirements as lesson plans, conferences, the transitional steps involved in working toward acquiring major teaching responsibilities, and student teaching evaluation.

The second job of the university supervisors is to provide assistance throughout the student teaching experience. Strengths and weaknesses should be identified through observing the student teacher while teaching, conferencing with the cooperating teacher and principal, and conferencing with the student teacher. Some university supervisors require student teachers to maintain daily logs of their student teaching experiences. Such a record enables university supervisors to keep up-to-date with the student teacher's activities and areas of need. University supervisors should also keep a record of visitation observations and conferences with student teachers.

The university supervisors' third job is evaluative. That is, they assign the student teacher's official grades (letter grade or pass/fail) at the end of the student teaching experience. Assigned grades should be based on data gleaned by both cooperating teachers and university supervisors regarding skill attainment and promise as successful educators. In addition, university supervisors are often called on to write letters of recommendation for student teachers in their efforts to locate teaching positions.

University supervisors tread precarious paths. They must see that student teachers secure the link of experiences needed for preparation as teachers, yet supervisors have no direct authority over the classroom. Indeed, the university supervisor may, at the request of and in consultation with the cooperating teacher, building principal, and district student teacher coordinator, be called upon to terminate the student teaching experience when it interferes with the normal operation of the school. Chapter 5 addresses the termination of student teaching in detail.

Student Teaching Team

The student teaching team is often loosely organized. However, each member assumes an important part in the overall success of student teaching. In fact, if any one of the team fails to carry out assigned responsibilities, the experience may result in prospective teachers without the necessary skills to assume full responsibility in their own classrooms. Thus, the team should view the total supervisory picture and create the conditions for success.

Summary

Student teaching traditionally holds a vital place in the preparation of teachers. In fact, the very concept of student teaching has undergone much change over the past several decades. Initially, student teaching was viewed as nothing more than an apprenticeship that emphasized the practice of teaching theory until the prospective teacher was deemed ready to teach. However, today most states endorse the concept of the prospective teacher as a student of teaching and require a full term (usually 12 to 18 weeks) of student teaching prior to obtaining a certificate or license.

A viable student teaching program requires a collaborative effort on the part of a cooperating district or school, university, and state. A district or school should provide adequate qualified cooperating teachers as well as a desire to be an active participant in teacher preparation. The university should establish and maintain a careful candidate screening process for program admission, select and train adequate supervisors, and set up and maintain an effective communication network with the school district, school, and state. Finally, the state should establish program guidelines and standards.

Ideally, successful student teaching requires a good working relationship and team effort among the student teachers, cooperating teachers, and university supervisors. Such teams should guide and assist the trainees in making a transition from student to teacher. The trainees should be given the opportunity to study and practice the art of teaching. The full, creative potential of these prospective teachers should be allowed to develop and flourish.

Questions and Discussion Topics

1. Review the similarities and differences among various forms of school field experiences and student teaching? Are they the same in early childhood, elementary, elementary-secondary, secondary, and special education programs? Should they be similar?

2. Discuss the role of supervision in the student teaching process? What criteria should be used in selecting supervisors? Do supervisors need training prior to being appointed to this function? Should supervisors receive compensation for serving in this capacity?

3. What are the changing functions and advantages associated with the student teaching process for local school districts, for states, and for the nation? Should the student teaching process be controlled by the state? Should states have regulations regarding student teaching? Why or why not?

4. What issues are currently being faced in the student teaching process? Should states require student teaching of all prospective teachers; an apprenticeship; an induction year?

CHAPTER 2

Human Relations in Student Teaching

CHAPTER KEY CONCEPTS

Cultural Relationship
Friendship Seekers
Nonassertives

Psychological Relationship
Sociological Relationship
Workers

Overview

There are many functions carried out by cooperating teachers when they agree to work with student teachers. Essentially, they must be prepared to be counselors, teachers, and trainers.

One of the most demanding, yet essential, responsibilities that cooperating teachers must perform is to help student teachers establish effective and productive relationships. This chapter discusses techniques to help cooperating teachers establish such effective relationships.

Student teachers must develop working relationships with pupils, university supervisors, other school personnel, parents, and the community. Of course, it is also essential to establish positive working relationships between student teachers and cooperating teachers. The development of these relationships is not always easy and requires sensitivity, patience, and guidance. As such, the influence of cooperating teachers is often crucial to successful relationships.

This chapter focuses on student teacher relationships—their establishment, the pitfalls, and the challenge.

Objectives

Upon completing your study of chapter 2, you should be able to:

1. Describe the three levels at which relationships can be formed.
2. Identify and describe the problems and pitfalls that student teachers encounter in establishing relationships with pupils, cooperating teachers, and university supervisors.
3. Explain why student teachers often need assistance to establish a viable student teacher-pupil relationship.
4. Describe the adjustments that should be made by cooperating teachers when working with student teachers.

5. Explain the function and importance of university supervisors to the student teaching experience.
6. Explain why it is important that student teachers learn to establish good relationships with all school personnel.
7. Explain the reason for establishing good relationships with parents and the community.

Few would dispute that establishing positive working relationships is paramount to the success of the student teaching experience. However, such relationships do not "just happen"; the individuals involved are mutually responsible for the reality they create. This reality varies from situation to situation, and it is established by what is said and done as individuals interact. Moreover, this interaction often changes with time. An example of this is the differences in interactions between teachers and students on the first day of class versus that at midyear.

Levels of Relationships

Most individuals have relationships with a number of people at a variety of levels at the same time. For example, there are relationships with parents, friends, colleagues, and students. Relationships in each case are based on the information available and on past experiences. Generally, the relationship can be at three different levels: cultural, sociological, and psychological.

Cultural Relationship Level

Cultural relationships are what people have with the general public or with strangers. What little information that is available about individuals is based on past experiences (interactions with strangers, observation of strangers, what people have been told about strangers, and so on), immediate perceptions (how they look, what they say, and so on), and inferences made about them (such as their race, social class, occupation, and so on).

Cultural-level relationships occur upon first meeting other individuals. During this first meeting, information (accurate and inaccurate) is continuously received, and decisions are made on how to relate to individuals. As these interactions continue, the relationships may change or remain the same as more information is gained. Needless to say, initial perceptions can be deceptive, so people need to take care when they first talk and interact with others.

Sociological Relationship Level

Most relationships are between people who share a group identity. These relationships are at the sociological level (for example, students in a class, teachers in a school, and employees of a company). The relationship is based on similar and shared experiences; similar types of interests, hobbies, values, and goals are usually shared.

Behavior within an interacting group generally depends on an individual's perceived place in that group. In some group situations, the individual may view himself or herself as a leader, whereas in other situations he or she may feel like a follower. In short, one tends to analyze everyone's role in the group, which then determines how he or she interacts and shares information.

Psychological Relationship Level

A psychological relationship is intimate. At this level, one can predict another's thoughts, feelings, and behaviors. More than likely a person will reach this level only with a few individuals in his or her lifetime. Indeed, some individuals never reach the psychological relationship level because to do so requires that one take a risk with self.

Likely, most relationships among individuals within the school environment fall at the cultural and sociological levels. For example, with some school personnel (custodians, cafeteria workers, and so on), teachers operate at the cultural level and exchange only low-risk information, while with others (colleagues, student teachers, pupils) teachers operate at the sociological level and are more open. At the sociological level, the individual feels secure in sharing interests, abilities (or inabilities), and skills. This security comes from knowing the other person.

Student Teacher Personalities

According to Taylor (1983), student teachers will be one of three personality types: nonassertives, friendship seekers, and workers. *Nonassertives* show little enthusiasm for teaching and tend to be passive in practice. They are inconsistent in their management of the classroom and often have discipline problems. *Friendship seekers* want to be liked. They too often have classroom management and discipline problems because they don't want to be mean to pupils or be disliked. Pupils often take advantage of the friendship seekers. The *workers* tend to be effective in the classroom. They show initiative, react to needed improvement, and manage effectively.

The various personality types require different strategies for directing their experiences:

- *Nonassertive* student teachers ask few questions and generally do little unless specifically asked to complete a task. Nonassertive student teachers need more guidance than most student teachers. They should be given specific goals, along with completion dates. Supervisors should insist that requirements be met. Excuses for not completing tasks should not be accepted. Concise and specific written records of assignment tasks, completion dates, and results should be maintained and shared with the university supervisor. Concerns and suggestions should be written and presented to student teachers at scheduled conferences. With understanding and firm guidance, nonassertive student teachers can develop professional competence.
- *Friendship seekers* are often critical of other teachers because of a desire to be viewed as more understanding, fairer, and friendly. They often try to be one of the "guys" by talking, dressing, and acting like pupils. Friendship seekers are often inconsistent and give pupils unlimited freedom in the classroom. Friendship seekers must be given a great deal of assistance in establishing the proper relationship with pupils. They must be directed to establish an environment consistent with classroom procedures and priorities. Professionalism must be developed, sometimes at the expense of friendships.
- *Workers* are a joy to work with, direct, and supervise. They are self-starters, ask questions, produce creative units and lessons, and are energetic. Workers are eager for advice and welcome suggestions for improvement.

Personality assessment, a complicated, and questionable process, can sometimes lead to self-fulfilling prophecies and should be used with care. Personality is a developmental phenomenon that can be altered. However, since the different personality types require different supervisory techniques, it is crucial that supervisors know as much as possible about each student teacher.

Preparing for the Student Teacher

Along with the request for student teaching placement, the university normally supplies information about the student teachers. If it has not been made available, the personal information data sheet should be requested from the university individual in charge of placing student teachers. However, if this information is not received, the cooperating teacher may want to request that the student teacher complete a personal data sheet before the initial meeting. Figure 2.1 offers some guidelines for the kinds of information that could prove useful. Once the information is received, the cooperating teacher should use it to become acquainted with the background, interests, hobbies, educational background, work experiences, and characteristics of the student teacher.

```
Name:
Address:
Place of birth:
Graduating high school:                 Date of Birth:
College honors:                         Date:
Hobbies:

Travel experiences:

Areas where you have lived:

Experiences with children and youth:

Work experiences:

Colleges and universities attended:

Employment planned during student teaching:

Favored subjects, topics, and areas:

Least favored subjects and areas:

Career goals:
```

Figure 2.1 Student teacher data sheet information

Most institutions also require that student teachers schedule a short meeting with their cooperating teachers prior to the first assigned day in the classroom. This meeting should be informal and used to alleviate student teacher anxieties; essentially, it should be a get-acquainted meeting.

Once the cooperating teacher is familiar with the background data on the student teacher and has met him or her informally, an initial professional conference should be planned. This professional conference can also take place prior to or on the first student-teacher-assigned day. At this conference, the cooperating teacher should acquaint the student teacher with the school as a total social institution. This entails providing information about school procedures, the school calendar, students and their parents, the community, and the curriculum (explaining the school's preferred dress code; other teacher regulations such as smoking, chewing gum, and drinking coffee; and the time that faculty are expected to report to and leave school). The cooperating teacher should also discuss and solicit informa-

tion about the student teacher's ideas on how to relate to pupils, educational philosophy, and concerns. Finally, the cooperating teacher should discuss the worries, apprehensions, and concerns of the student teacher and try to alleviate them. The organization, procedure, and relationship of this first conference should set the pattern and ground rules for all subsequent conferences.

Student teachers need their own territory in the classroom. Such a space communicates a feeling of belonging and ownership. It is the cooperating teacher's classroom, but a small piece should belong to the student teacher. Therefore, to develop these feelings, the cooperating teacher should provide a desk or work area that belongs only to the student teacher.

Nearly every student teacher finds that first day of student teaching both exciting and frightening. Inside, there is some anxiety and insecurity. Such feelings are a natural part of becoming a professional educator. Indeed, student teachers who are not initially anxious about teaching probably lack the sensitivity and commitment to establish a working relationship with pupils and supervisors and to become an effective teacher. Therefore, student teachers should be included in the teaching-learning experience the very first day. For example, student teachers can be asked to collect homework papers, take roll, or make their own seating chart. They should be encouraged to move around the room to answer individual questions or asked to work with small groups. The cooperating teacher should explain the reasons for using certain teaching strategies and get the student teachers involved in preparing classroom materials.

It is important to hold a miniconference at the end of the first day. Student teachers can ask questions; cooperating teachers react to the questions and observations and, again, address any areas of apprehension.

The Student Teacher-Pupil Relationship

The student teacher's first contact with the class is the cooperating teacher's introduction. This introduction should be carefully planned. In most cases, it affects the relationships of the student teacher during the entire student teaching experience. Therefore, when introducing the student teacher, the cooperating teacher should define his or her new roles, as well as the roles of the student teacher and pupils. The student teacher should be given the status of a teacher whose expertise and skills make a real contribution to classroom learning. Finally, the cooperating teacher should project an attitude of delight at having a student teacher as part of the class and give him or her the opportunity to offer a few words of greeting to the class if desired.

Intergroup Relations

Adjustment to a new role can represent a real dilemma for student teachers who are often only a few days away from the college classroom. Pupils call them teachers, university personnel still view them as students, and cooperating teachers view them as colleagues in specific instances and as students at other times. It is no wonder that student teachers often have difficulty in deciding what relationships should be established with pupils. Indeed, initially, student teachers often are concerned with survival and assume an approved stance that brings acceptance from the class. Such relationships, while appropriate when dealing with peers, are often inappropriate when interacting with pupils. Too often such actions lead to pupil rejection and general disrespect for the student teacher as a teacher.

Student teachers, with cooperating teachers' assistance, must work to establish an appropriate, productive relationship with pupils both inside and outside the classroom. Potential problems should be identified and guidelines addressed for dealing with them. The number one priority is for the student teacher to develop a positive and cooperative relationship with all classroom pupils. There will be a testing period when pupils check to find out the student teacher's parameters regarding class behavior and misbehavior—so the student teacher must be prepared! The student teacher should explore "What if" situations, try to think of all possible situations that could happen when the cooperating teacher is out of the room, and talk through such situations. However, the cooperating teacher should not tell student teachers what to do in every possible situation but rather help them develop their own decision-making skills.

Many student teachers misunderstand the nature of an appropriate student teacher-pupil relationship. They think that being liked—being "buddies" with students—will lead to respect and recognition as a classroom authority. Most experienced teachers know that trying to be a buddy to pupils will undermine respect for the student teacher. The student teacher must understand that respect takes time and is earned through professional actions.

Other student teachers attempt a "hard line" relationship with pupils. They have been told that successful teachers are firm and business-like and do not smile until Christmas. According to this advice, once authority has been established one can become more tolerant. Such advice is a myth and should be ignored. Theoretically it may be sound; but, student teachers are usually too insecure to be either convincing or authoritative in their interactions with pupils.

Student teachers must be helped to treat pupils as worthwhile individuals with ideas and opinions that are worth consideration by the class. They must show that they enjoy teaching and enjoy helping pupils; above all, they must learn to show respect for pupils as individuals. That is, student teachers must learn to respect pupils' individuality. Ethnic, racial, and sex stereotyping must be avoided. High expectations should be held for all students, but they should not be the same for all whites, all Hispanics, all blacks, all people of Irish extraction, all poor students, all males, or all females. Each group will have its bright, its lazy, its honest, its dishonest, its athletic, and its dull, but all must be taught. When student teachers agreed to enter a classroom, they agreed to accept the responsibility to teach each pupil regardless of individual motivations, abilities, personality, and parents.

Pupils often turn to their teachers for advice and guidance. Although student teachers are not the teachers of record and are new to the classroom, pupils may turn to them for advice and guidance because they are respected adults who are readily available. In short, cooperating teachers should prepare student teachers to deal with pupils' personal problems and requests. Such problems and requests vary depending on the maturity and age of the pupils, and they range in complexity from the simple to complex. For example:

- Is it okay to smoke marijuana?
- I believe a friend is selling drugs. Should I report him?
- Should I bite Mary back? She bit me.
- Should I get married?
- My parents don't understand me! Should I move out?

Most experienced teachers have dealt with similar problems. But questions like those cited are new to student teachers, so they need to be prepared. Consequently, cooperating teachers should discuss proper actions and procedures when they do occur. Some questions should be directed to qualified counselors, some should be directed to the cooperating teacher, and some the student teachers should handle themselves.

Finally, student teachers must learn to treat all students equally. Absolute fairness is important. They must give attention to all students without any hints that one student is better than another. Student teachers must learn that honesty is the best policy. Even young children quickly recognize insincerity and resent it. Genuineness (realness) in the teacher-pupil relationships is of utmost importance. Student teachers must learn that teaching and relating positively with students is much easier when they are frank and real with pupils.

Student teachers will have joyful experiences, as well as sorrowful experiences with pupils. There will be days of discouragement and days of physical, emotional, and mental weariness. Indeed, there will be days when some student teachers will be ready to give up on becoming a teacher. They simply can't understand or relate to pupils who are not interested in learning, or not interested in social studies, or not interested in literature, or not interested in science. On such days, the cooperating teacher should help the student teacher deal with the realisms of teaching.

The relationships that develop between student teachers and pupils are complex. These relationships are significant, often quite close, and sometimes intense. However, they should not be as personal or as emotional as family relationships or close friendships. Generally, the best standard by which to judge the appropriateness of student teacher-pupil relationships is the extent to which pupils are helped to learn.

Ethnic and Gender Relations

As prospective teachers, student teachers need to understand the culture of the students with whom they interact. Indeed, because the United States has become significantly more diverse in its population makeup, this need is significantly greater today then it ever has been. National surveys suggest that there will be an ever-increasing, multicultural school population into the twenty-first century and beyond. Therefore, cooperating teachers must prepare student teachers for the ethnic as well as sexual diversity they will face in the future.

Appreciation for ethnic, racial, and sexual diversity will help these prospective teachers to determine the appropriate instructional practices for a diverse student body. Cooperating teachers should help student teachers identify school cultural bias in the form of omissions, distortions, and factual errors and assist student teachers in looking for textbook negative-value judgments concerning the customs and lifestyles of any culture or group. Textbooks should also be checked to see that language, concepts, and imagery don't create distortions and stereotypes. Make sure that content shows how individuals from our diverse culture all played a role in forming our history, science, literature, and music. Finally, cooperating teachers should help student teachers work with students in the development of necessary critical thinking skills to detect and cope with bias in our society.

Students are different. They are a product of their environment and culture. Thus, helping student teachers learn about students' cultural backgrounds aids in understanding and appreciating the students' behaviors; thus, student teachers can better determine strengths and weaknesses. Indeed, a knowledge of students' cultural backgrounds often provides the key to the influences that shape their personality and interests. Although it is important that student teachers come to understand and become familiar with students' cultural background, it is also important that such

information be shared with the whole class so students grow as members of a multicultural society. Thus, the study of other cultures should be a part of the classroom instructional program. Cultural units can be developed, for instance, in such areas as art, history, science, and literature.

Student teachers must be helped to develop truly multiethnic approaches to instruction. Under such approaches, other ethnic and racial groups, such as Afro-American, Jewish American, Italian American, Mexican American, Vietnamese American, Native American, Puerto Rican American, and so on, would receive as much emphasis as the dominant Anglo-American. Obviously, the ethnic groups that should be emphasized would depend on the local clientele to be served. For example, in Oklahoma, it would make sense to emphasize The Native American and Afro-American.

As the nation approaches the twenty-first century, women are gaining greater equity. Therefore, student teachers should be helped to guard against materials that present one gender as being superior to another. Moreover, student teachers should be guided to avoid reinforcing gender stereotyping (for example, assigning jobs in the classroom according to gender).

Students and Drugs

Drugs continue to be the number one problem facing the public schools. As such, student teachers must be made aware of the problem and how to handle it. This is a difficult task because students' drug use is difficult to detect. Even when recognized, most student teachers lack the expertise to offer help. Thus, student teachers must be made aware of indicators of drug abuse, as well as district resources and drug prevention programs.

Cooperating teachers need to get student teachers involved in setting up drug prevention programs and, above all, make sure that these future teachers are well informed about drugs and their effects on students. By learning about what to look for and local prevention activities, student teachers will be better prepared to deal with the problems in their own classrooms.

Effective Professional Relationships

An important component of student teaching is developing an appropriate working relationship with fellow professionals—cooperating teachers, university supervisors, principals, district student teacher coordinators, and other school personnel. These professionals greatly influence the overall quality of the student teaching experience. Thus, it is important that cooperating teachers assist student teachers with these relationships.

Cooperating Teachers

Most likely the success and professional development of student teachers will be contingent on the relationship that the cooperating teachers establish with them. In short, the student teaching experience represents a period of adjustment for both the cooperating teacher and the student teacher. The student teacher is probably competent in content knowledge and trained in methodology, but he or she may not know how to relate to pupils and assume the role of a classroom teacher. Therefore, cooperating teachers should work to establish a relationship based on guidance, support, and personal involvement. The task is to guide student teachers to develop the skills needed to function in a new and challenging environment. The cooperating teachers should provide the periodic feedback needed to develop and refine identified classroom skills. They should talk with the student teachers about strengths as well as weaknesses. They should communicate their expectations and help student teachers develop an understanding of motivation and its relation to instructional techniques and materials. The more insights that cooperating teachers can provide about student teachers' performance the smoother the path will be for making the transition from college students to classroom teachers.

A positive relationship between cooperating teacher and student teacher is essential to a successful student teaching experience.

Initially, cooperating teachers need to work closely with student teachers in planning both short- and long-term lessons (daily and unit plans). As student teachers become experienced, they can be given more freedom in planning. However, cooperating teachers should communicate the importance and need for planning. In short, cooperating teachers need to communicate that planning results in (1) more effective teaching, (2) better sequencing and organization of a lesson, (3) better understanding of the content to be taught, (4) increased learning, and (5) better use of class time.

Plans should be thorough and detailed during the initial weeks of student teaching. Moore (1989) suggests that a daily lesson plan include the following sections:

1. **Objectives.** The specific learning intent for the day. They should be stated in performance terms.
2. **Introduction.** An activity used to begin the lesson.
3. **Content.** A brief outline of the content to be covered in the lesson.
4. **Methods and Procedure.** A listing of the developmental activities.
5. **Closure.** The lesson wrap-up activity.

6. **Resources and materials.** A listing of instructional materials needed for the lesson.
7. **Assignment.** The in-class or homework assignment to be completed for the next class period.

Student teachers should discuss lesson plans with their cooperating teachers at least 24 hours before instruction so that necessary modifications can be made. Sometimes cooperating teachers will note things that experience tells them will lead to problems, and they can make suggestions to eliminate the potential problem areas. Indeed, cooperating teachers should encourage their student teachers to submit a weekly plan for approval. This procedure helps student teachers establish better direction for goals and objectives. Whatever the requirement, make sure that student teachers always have a written, approved plan prior to instruction.

A common disappointment expressed by student teachers is that there is inadequate analysis made of their teaching performance (Pfeiffer and Dunlap 1982; Glickman and Bey 1990). Student teachers often desire specific help, so cooperating teachers should not be reluctant to give it to them. They should give student teachers encouragement by commenting on their strengths or something that was done particularly well. Also, they should help identify weaknesses and suggest specific ways that might lead to improvement.

Cooperating teachers should stay with their student teachers until they are ready to solo, and then return to observe them teaching often enough to give constructive criticism that will help student teachers grow professionally. An observation record of each day that the student teacher is observed is one means of providing this constructive criticism.

Many times student teachers have a somewhat idealist concept of teaching. Some student teachers, generally secondary, believe that all pupils are eager to learn and simply love their subject. Cooperating teachers should preserve this idealism, helping the student teacher to understand and deal with the realism of the classroom. In short, student teachers need support as well as constructive criticism. Although a student teacher may use a different teaching style, he or she can be just as effective. Suggested approaches are:

- Judge student teachers' effectiveness carefully and slowly and, only after careful analysis, offer suggestions regarding changes needed to be more effective.
- Try to avoid making demands.
- Let student teachers experiment to some degree.
- Do not be overly critical of student teachers' ideas; ask why they want to do it differently.
- Weigh the pros and cons of a student teacher's ideas against the needs of pupils.

Just because an idea or approach is new does not mean it is not a good one. Cooperating teachers should remember that they can also learn from student teachers. However, it is important to remember that cooperating teachers have the ultimate legal responsibility for the class.

Student teachers who are not enthusiastic and willing to spend time with their cooperating teachers working on problem areas may be heading for trouble. Cooperating teachers should try to determine the reasons why student teachers are not being more involved. It may be that they are employed part time or have other demands on their time. Also, student teachers who show no interest in out of classroom activities may require additional support. Student teachers should feel that they are a part of the classroom, the school, and the community. For example, cooperating teachers should invite student teachers to faculty- and school-related functions and help them become aware of school policies and procedures. Cooperating teachers should expect and demand loyalty, cooperation and honesty with regard to the school administration, other school personnel, parents, and pupils. In effect, they should help student teachers build the sense of cooperation and duty required of all professionals.

Finally, cooperating teachers should avoid competing with their student teachers. Sometimes pupils will voice preference for the student teacher's teaching over the cooperating teacher's. Such remarks should be allowed to pass without comment.

University Supervisors

Relationships between student teachers and university supervisors are also important. University supervisors have been given the responsibility for overseeing and critiquing student teachers' work in the classroom. They will generally also have the responsibility of assigning final grades.

University supervisors are there to help the cooperating teachers through the student teaching experience and make it a growth experience. To this end, they will observe student teachers and offer suggestions for improvement. Cooperating teachers should help student teachers accept and make use of these suggestions rather than look at the suggestions as personal attacks on their competence. Cooperating teachers should communicate the idea that university supervisors are not the enemy, and it's not us against them. That is, they should avoid forming the unwritten law of nonbetrayal in which everyone in the classroom cooperates to see that a good image is presented to university supervisors. Student teachers should be encouraged to ask university supervisors for suggestions on identified weaknesses or unclear points rather than to react defensively and make excuses.

University supervisors should be viewed as guides, confidants, and troubleshooters. Their knowledge of the teaching process can be of inestimable value in helping student teachers become fully functioning teachers. Therefore, university supervisors should not be overlooked as resource persons. Avoid viewing them as simply evaluators and critics.

After an observation, the university supervisor should give the student teacher written feedback. A conference should then be scheduled at a later

Written feedback is a necessary component of the supervisory process.

date with the student teacher or with the cooperating teacher and the student teacher. The university supervisor's written feedback should be analyzed independently by the student teacher and university supervisor and discussed at the scheduled conference. This discussion should be straightforward, open, and honest with an accepting atmosphere and a helping relationship.

Traditionally, university supervisors schedule weekly seminars that student teachers are required to attend. These seminars represent sharing sessions whereby student teachers can focus on classroom problems and ideas and analyze positive and negative individual teaching behaviors. Of equal importance, however, is the sense of colleagueship and support gained from these seminar sessions.

Other School Personnel

Teaching requires that teachers communicate with other professionals and school staff. Therefore, student teachers must learn to develop good relationships with other school personnel, including other faculty, administrators, counselors, secretaries, cafeteria workers, and custodial staff. From time to time, teachers must work with each of these individuals. Indeed, as most teachers know, it is especially important to be on good terms with the custodial staff. Such a relationship will often get requested supplies more quickly, a cleaner classroom, a clean chalkboard, and needed furniture.

Student teachers should be introduced to the school personnel with whom cooperating teachers come into contact. Also, cooperating teachers should communicate the individual's responsibilities and add a few comments that will serve as cues in recalling the person. After making a few such introductions, cooperating teachers should suggest that student teachers introduce themselves to other school personnel with whom they come in contact.

Informal gatherings in the teacher's lounge, in the lunchroom, or at faculty meetings provide excellent opportunities for student teachers to get acquainted with faculty members. Also, student teachers should know where the faculty congregates informally. To help develop skills for interacting with other teachers, cooperating teachers should arrange for student teachers to spend time with other teachers.

Student teachers should meet with the chief school administrator (principal). In fact, this meeting should take place when student teachers first arrive. The chief school administrator should give student teachers a brief orientation about the school, community, and school policies, encouraging them to fully participate in school activities and meetings. Many administrators also like to take student teachers on a tour of the school facility. Finally, cooperating teachers need to keep in close contact with principals and district student teacher coordinators regarding the professional development of student teachers. If problems develop, the channels need to be kept open between the administration and the cooperating teacher.

Relationship with the University Supervisor

The relationship between cooperating teachers and university supervisors will vary in formality and significance among teacher preparation programs. Frequency of observations, after-school seminars, conferencing techniques, and evaluations will also vary among programs. Unfortunately, too often cooperating teacher and university supervisor relationships are nothing more than a quick check on how things are going or a check for problems. There is no professional approach to supervision; that is, there is little support and limited university supervisor involvement.

The building of professional approaches to supervision requires a positive, working relationship among cooperating teachers, university supervisors, and student teachers. If such relationships are not forthcoming, cooperating teachers should promote them by requesting more frequent university supervisor visits, by requesting the collection of feedback data, by requesting three-way conferences for critiquing and providing feedback, and by requesting evaluation conferences.

Finally, final grades must be determined for student teachers. Although university supervisors will usually have the responsibility for giving these grades, they should be collaborative efforts. Whatever process is used to arrive at final grades, they should reflect the student teachers' competency. Therefore, since cooperating teachers have more opportunity to assess this competency, they should make sure that they are involved and communicate their opinion on student teacher final grades

Relationship with Parents

Teacher-parent conferences are an increasingly popular way of reporting pupil progress to parents. Student teachers, however, often do not have a great deal of contact with parents. Such contact is often vital. Research suggests that effective communication between teachers and parents results in better learning for pupils (Arends 1991). Many times this sharing of information can serve as encouragement and direction for the learner. Moreover, the conferences can give parents the opportunity to clarify questions and to make suggestions. Conferences also give teachers the opportunity to gather additional information about learning problems or behavior problems.

Because parent conferences can be very helpful to supplement work with pupils, student teachers need experiences in face-to-face discussions with parents. Learning techniques for soliciting the parents' cooperation is an important component to effective teaching. Therefore, if possible, student teachers should have experiences in conferring with parents.

Since teachers and parents are partners in the growth of their children, it is important that student teachers learn to establish friendly relationships with the parents. Therefore, cooperating teachers should also communicate to student teachers the importance of attending school functions—meeting of parent-teacher associations, community events, and other social situations.

Relationship with Community

Teachers are important members of the community in which they teach. They should be involved in issues that may adversely affect learning, such as censorship of books and other community problems. Thus, student teachers need experiences and training in community relations. In effect, they must learn to be ambassadors for education. That is, they should learn how to shape positive rather than negative attitudes toward education. These attitudes are important because they affect how well the community supports education.

A second factor that has an effect on community relations is awareness. Student teachers should be made aware of community businesses, industries, and recreational facilities. Awareness of general socioeconomic, racial, and ethnic balance of the community should be communicated. Student teachers should be encouraged to spend some time becoming familiar with the community and its people. They should walk or drive around the community area and observe the types of businesses, homes, and people. During the student teaching experience, they should also be encour-

aged to attend recreational activities, including concerts, ball games, and festivals.

Concerns and Problems

Conflict in school situations is a common occurrence. Thus, although the student teaching experience will be quite valuable and beneficial to all involved, problems and concerns arise because of personalities, roles and responsibilities, procedures, and philosophies.

Cooperating teachers may want to work with student teachers; yet, when the time comes they may be reluctant to turn their classes over to student teachers. Other cooperating teachers may experience jealousy as their students respond to student teachers and seek their advice and help. These teachers often give student teachers no opportunities to plan and carry out activities independently.

Occasionally, cooperating teachers favor the "sink or swim" philosophy. When student teachers arrive, these teachers may turn over their classes with comments such as, "I'll be in the teachers' lounge if you need me."

Cooperating teachers sometimes give student teachers the impression that what was learned in college was worthless and will not work in the "real world" of the classroom. This attitude puts students teachers between two opposing views—cooperating teachers' and university supervisors'.

Student teachers often have feelings of inadequacy, insecurity, and fear of failure. These feelings come from finding themselves needing to adjust to situations that may be potentially threatening. Indeed, student teachers who are required to teach in front of professionals (cooperating teachers and university supervisors) may feel inadequate, which can lead to anxiety, nervousness, depression, fear, and frustration. There is concern over success; after all, a teaching career is at stake, with student teaching being the final test as to the individual's adequacy.

Acceptance as a teacher can sometimes be a problem for student teachers. Student teachers who enter other teachers' classrooms are not always automatically accepted as teachers. Attempts for acceptance may result in student teachers taking an overly authoritarian stance or may lead to student teachers informally associating with students.

There are problems associated with student teaching. However, each problem is usually unique and demands an individualized approach with open communication. The triad (cooperating teacher, college supervisor, and student teacher) should analyze each problem logically and consistently and arrive at a solution that is most defensible. The solution arrived at should be one that is best for the pupils and that is of most benefit to the student teacher.

Beyond Student Teaching

Student teachers often need help and support in the search for teaching position. This process will generally begin during student teaching. Cooperating teachers and university supervisors can and should provide insights and assistance to student teachers in finding openings, writing application letters, writing reference letters, and developing a resume. Indeed, cooperating teachers can even assist the student teacher in developing a portfolio or videotapes for future employers.

Helping the student teacher prepare for an interview is perhaps the most vital assistance that cooperating teachers and university supervisors can provide. Such assistance can be provided by helping student teachers anticipate questions that may be asked. Help the student teacher think through some responses to questions such as: How would you handle discipline? How would you motivate students? How would you organize your classroom for reading? What are your strengths and weaknesses as a teacher? Why do you want to teach in this school district?

University supervisors should help student teachers get in touch with the university placement office and help set up a placement file. The cooperating teacher and university supervisor should also talk over with their student teachers possible sources of favorable references.

Summary

Student teaching requires interactions. Interactions with pupils, cooperating teachers, university supervisors, various school personnel, parents, and individuals in the community. Such interactions can lead to the establishment of relationships at different levels: cultural, sociological, and psychological. However, most school relationships will be at the cultural and sociological levels.

Student teachers generally fall into one of three personality types, including nonassertives, friendship-seekers, and workers. Nonassertives tend to be passive, friendship-seekers want to be liked, and workers tend to be quite effective in the classroom. However, care should be taken to avoid labeling student teachers as to certain personality types.

It is important that cooperating teachers prepare for the arrival of their student teachers. Preparation involves studying background information and planning an initial informal meeting. After meeting their student teachers informally, cooperating teachers should plan and hold professional conferences to address topics such as school procedures, the school calendar, pupils, and the community.

Cooperating teachers must work to establish good relationships with their student teachers, as well as to assist their student teachers in the development of positive working relationships with pupils, university supervisors, parents, and the community. Student teachers should be introduced to classroom pupils and other school personnel as colleagues and professionals. Potential problems and pitfalls should be identified and discussed.

Conferences are essential to a successful students teaching experience. Student teachers and cooperating teachers need to schedule formal meetings to discuss procedures and concerns, to explore new techniques, to decide on needed data, and to design instructional activities. Periodically, university supervisors should be involved in three-way conferences to provide additional data.

Cooperating teachers who can exemplify effective teaching and maintain quality supervision may find that relationships with student teachers are demanding. At times, these relationships may be difficult and a real challenge. The results, however, will be very rewarding.

Questions and Discussion Topics

1. What should cooperating teachers do to prepare for student teachers? How should the skills of the student teacher be used in the classroom? Should cooperating teachers plan an orientation to the students; to the building; to the district?

2. How should cooperating teachers introduce student teachers to the class? How should they communicate recognition of status as teachers, including their competency? Should cooperating teachers give student teachers the opportunity to speak to the class?

3. Survey cooperating teachers who have had student teachers and record the type of relationships reported. What are the survey results? What do the results suggest about the cooperating teacher experience?

4. What special conditions in the class might cause student teachers to have problems developing good relationships with students? How can cooperating teachers work to help student teachers overcome these difficulties?

5. Discuss the student teaching experience, both positive and negative. What changes can be suggested to make it a better experience?

6. How can cooperating teachers establish good working relationships with university supervisors? Are periodic conferences needed with student teachers; with university supervisors; with both student teachers and university supervisors present? How can such conferences be made beneficial?

7. Discuss concerns and problems that may arise in establishing working relationships between student teachers and cooperating teachers and between student teachers and university supervisors.

CHAPTER 3

Communication

CHAPTER KEY CONCEPTS

Body Language
Empathic Listening
Facial Language
Feedback
Gestures
Hearing
Language of Space and Motion
Language of the Voice

Language of Time
Metaverbal
Nonverbal Communication
One-Way Listening
Two-Way Listening
Verbal
Verbal Communication
Vocal

Overview

Communication is essential to the supervision process. Indeed, supervisors should be sensitive to cultivating effective communication skills if they are to establish an effective, helping relationship with student teachers.

Unfortunately, supervisors too often do most of the talking when they interact with student teachers; student teachers do most of the listening. Perhaps because of their talking, supervisors tend not to really listen to the problems that student teachers are experiencing in their daily interactions with pupils.

This chapter addresses the total communication process—talking and listening. As such, it addresses both the sending and receiving of information and messages.

Objectives

Upon completing your study of chapter 3, you should be able to:

1. Explain the importance of communication to the supervision process.
2. Diagram the model of the communication process.
3. Differentiate among the verbal, vocal, and metaverbal components of a message.
4. Name the variables associated with the verbal and vocal components of a message.
5. Explain the role that nonverbal communication holds in the communication process.
6. Provide examples of various nonverbal behaviors commonly used in the classroom.
7. Name and explain the four spatial distances.
8. Explain the importance of listening.
9. Name and define the different types of listening.

10. Name and describe variables that interfere with listening.
11. Explain the importance of feedback in the communication process.

Of all the knowledge and skills possessed by a supervisor, those concerning communication will be among the most significant and the most useful. Through communication, supervisors interact with student teachers that they guide and direct; the student teachers learn. Without effective communication, the supervision process is doomed to failure.

As a practical skill, communication consists of the ability to speak, read, and write. However, of equal importance to the communication process is the ability to listen. Most people put a great deal of emphasis on the ability to read and write with little attention put on speaking, and very little attention is given to nonverbal communication and listening. However, the most persuasive communicators do more than talk; they observe, and they listen.

This chapter focuses on the total communication act, examining verbal and nonverbal communication and the art of listening that serve important functions in the communication process.

Communication Process

Communication is the act of sending and receiving messages that are distorted by noise, have some effect, and provide some opportunity for feedback. The communication act can be viewed as including the following components:

1. Sources—receivers
2. Messages
3. Noise
4. Sending or encoding processes
5. Receiving or decoding processes
6. Feedback
7. Effects

These elements are the universals of the communication process. That is, they are present in every communication act, regardless of whether it is with pupils, colleagues, student teachers, or with oneself.

The communication process is illustrated in Figure 3.1. Supervisors must be intimately involved in this communication process as they interact with student teachers on a daily basis in developing and refining their teaching effectiveness.

As depicted in Figure 3.1, the communication process can be viewed as a five-phase process

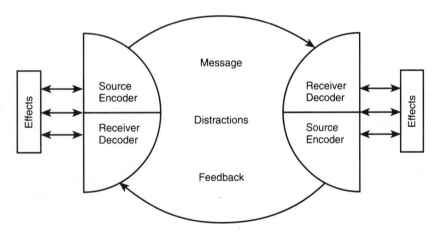

Figure 3.1 Communication process (five phases)

with each individual performing two functions: sending and receiving. First, the source encodes (composes) a desired message into a form that we hope will be understood by the receiver and transmits this message. The message can be sent by speaking, writing, gesturing, frowning, or smiling. The transmitted message is received and decoded by a receiver. It is received by listening, reading, seeing, or smelling. The receiver then becomes a source and encodes some form of reaction to the message. The receiver's reaction will generally be in some nonverbal form that will tell the sender whether the received message was understood or not. Thus, as messages are sent, the sources also receive messages in the form of feedback and must constantly decode and react to this feedback. The reaction to the feedback may be to continue with more information, to clarify the original message, or to repeat the message.

A typical supervisory interaction episode illustrates the communication model. Example: a supervisor wants to emphasize a problem area to a student teacher, so he or she encodes and sends the message, "Your pupils appeared to have trouble with your examples." The transmitted message is received and decoded by the student teacher as meaning the examples were rather poor. When the supervisor sees feedback (the student teacher nods his or her head in agreement), he or she feels that the communication has been successful and continues with the analysis of the student teacher's lesson. However, if the supervisor observes that the student teacher did not agree (no reaction), he or she might want to reemphasize the point with specific pupil reactions to some of the examples. This example shows the importance of the supervisor's attention to and use of feedback in the communication process.

Communication of any kind will have some effect or some consequence. In fact, there are three types of communication consequences: (1) the acquisition of new information or awareness (cognitive effect), (2) a change in attitudinal or emotional states (affective effect), and (3) the learning of a new skill (psychomotor effect). Most often the consequences involve all three types of effects.

Distractions often distort or interfere with the ability to communicate. The hum of an air conditioner, hall noise, the sunglasses worn by the supervisor or the student teacher, cars passing in the street, constant movement of the supervisor or student teacher, the clothes worn by the supervisor or student teacher, may all be regarded as distractions because they can interfere with the effective transmission of your messages. Distractions can also be psychological. Biases and prejudices, for example, can distort or make it more difficult to get across an accurate message. These sources of distractions must be overcome if messages are to be received and decoded accurately by the interacting participants at an observation conference.

Messages may be sent or received in verbal, vocal, physical, or situational form. Thus, supervisors must be skilled at sending messages through any one or combinations of these modes. But of equal importance is the ability to decode messages (feedback) transmitted by student teachers. This latter ability is directly related to how well one listens.

Communication is more than just talk.

Verbal Communication

Supervisors talk to communicate information to student teachers. However, nonverbal variables other than words sometimes communicate messages. Indeed, Goodall (1983, pp. 14–15) breaks spoken messages into three components: verbal, vocal, and metaverbal. The verbal component is the actual words spoken and their meanings; the vocal component includes voice firmness, modulation, tone, tempo, pitch, and loudness; while the metaverbal component is the implications or intentions of the spoken words.

Verbal Component

Words must be interpreted, which can lead to misunderstandings. Indeed, the message communicated in any interaction depends on the words, as well as the meanings and connotations attached to the words. These meanings are learned as a result of experiences and, thus, are often arbitrary. For example, a discussion of terms such as *values, stimulus variation, advanced cueing,* and *reinforcement* will have varying outcomes depending on the students teacher's past experiences. Despite the formal dictionary definitions, supervisors must make sure that their verbal discussions are related as much as possible to the experiences of the student teachers. This calls for an assessment on the part of the supervisor as to what the student teacher brings to the interacting episode (for example, intelligence, courses completed, whether they are elementary or secondary majors, and prior instructors). This information may show that the verbal aspects of your messages are outside the experience base of the student teacher.

Another misuse of words is lack of knowledge of word meanings. It is sometimes possible for a person to talk endlessly about a subject and sound quite knowledgeable when, in fact, the individual hasn't the slightest idea of the word meanings. These bluffing behaviors with words should be avoided when the supervisor interacts with student teachers. They will usually see through the supervisor's lack of knowledge, and the supervisor will lose their respect.

Hurt, Scott, and McCroskey (1978, p. 76) suggest that the following variables may also have some effects on whether a message is received and decoded accurately:

1. **Organization.** Good or well-organized verbal information tends to be understood best, as well as information presented first or last.
2. **Message sidedness.** Two-sided messages that present opposing views tend to be understood best.
3. **Language intensity.** Verbal information that deviates from a neutral position appears to be understood best.
4. **Concreteness and ambiguity.** The more concrete a message, the better. However, supervisors must take care that their messages aren't made so simple that the basic concept is lost.

Generally, such variables as those discussed earlier, and those suggested by Hurt, Scott, and McCroskey, tend to increase the attention of the listener, which is the supervisor's primary aim in conferring with student teachers. The increased attention should result in increased skill refinement.

Vocal Component

How people say words brings them to life. Changes in tones, voice loudness or strength, rate, inflection, or pitch can change the very meaning of a message. For example, messages such as "Right!" or "Maybe!" can communicate different meanings depending on the tone and modulation.

Also, the rate at which people speak impacts their message. When a supervisor speaks rapidly, he or she can convey the message to the student teacher that the topic isn't really important and should be finished as soon as possible. In contrast, when a supervisor speaks at a slower rate, he or she often communicates that the topic is important and should be carefully considered.

Voice tone, inflection, and pitch impact words. Tone and inflection communicate word seriousness or validity. For example, the seriousness of such messages as, "That lesson was great!" or "You were dynamic today!" or "That lesson needs a lot of work!" will be affected by the supervisor's tone and inflection. Moreover, Hennings (1975, p. 17) points out that "the high-pitched voice can grate on a decoder's nerves so that the listener turns off to words spoken; the very deep voice can distract from the message." Therefore, when supervisors interact with student teachers, they should guard against using tones, inflections, or a pitch that might distract from their messages.

The loudness, rate, tone, inflection, and pitch can also send emotional information. A loud voice with a fast rate and pitch can communicate excitement or enthusiasm; whereas a soft voice with a slow rate and even pitch can communicate disinterest. Also, voice variations can express joy, eagerness, anger, wonder, awe, displeasure, determination, and indecisiveness. Thus, skill in using their voices can greatly assist supervisors in directing the professional growth of student teachers. Therefore, supervisors should practice the effective use of their voices. It will pay dividends.

Supervisors should be aware of the effect that a monotone voice can have on listeners. It can cause their minds to wander and, in general, result in a loss of attention. Variety in the voice can overcome these negative effects to some extent. Indeed, supervisors can be more effective and keep student teachers attentive by varying their voice loudness, rate, tone, inflection, and pitch.

Metaverbal Component

Sometimes when people speak there is an implied or intended message that cannot be directly attributed to the meaning of the words or how they are spoken. This is referred to as the metaverbal component of a message (Goodall 1983). A supervisor may, for example, ask a student teacher to discuss the positive aspects of a lesson when actually he or she wants to discuss the student teacher's poor performance.

Metaverbal messages are often tricky to use and should be used with care. The student teacher is being asked to hear beyond the words—to be reflective. Sometimes student teachers lack the experience or ability to be reflective. With such student teachers, it is best to be open and explicit.

As supervisors interact with student teachers, all basic components of verbal communication contribute to the messages received. In other words, they are hearing what is said at three levels: what is said, how it is said, and why (implied) it is said. Therefore, supervisors should use care and match their intent with their message.

Nonverbal Communication

Communication can be nonlinguistic. That is, messages can be sent without the use of words (Galloway 1976). This form of communication is referred to as nonverbal communication. Since some researchers in the area of communication claim that over 80 percent of our communication

The unwritten word is an extremely important form of communication.

is nonverbal in nature, it is important that supervisors be proficient with its use.

Although the primary means of sending messages is with words, the way people dress, their posture, the way they look, move, use their voice, and use space also deliver a message (Eisenbery and Smith 1971). These nonverbal messages can reinforce, modify, or even contradict verbal messages as, for example, when a student teacher says with a sigh of relief, "I wish you could observe me more often." Indeed, the nonverbal part of communication can be more important than the verbal part because it expresses real feelings. Nonverbal information determines what our reaction will be in certain situations or in deciding what our future behavior will be. For example, when the student teacher says, "My lesson planning is going fine, and I enjoy doing it for you" in such a way that the supervisor suspects otherwise. Thus, actions often do speak much louder than words.

Sometimes nonverbal communication can be designed to evoke a particular response while at other times it can be accidental. In either case, it influences perceptions, attitudes, or feelings because nonverbal cues are often not taken at face value, but rather inferences are made from them to determine what to believe. Thus, nonverbal clues are the medium chosen by supervisors and student teachers to unwittingly reveal attitudes and feelings toward each other and the supervision process in general. Therefore, supervisors must be alert to their nonverbal expressions and the effect they can have on student teachers. An awareness of the effects that nonverbal communication can have is the first step toward controlling them.

Facial Language

People's faces and eyes are probably the most conspicuous parts of their bodies and, as such, people communicate much information through their facial expressions. In fact, according to Miller (1981), the face is second only to words in communicating an individual's internal feelings. Miller further suggests that facial expressions can be involuntary or voluntary, readily visible or fleeting. Whatever the type, remember that facial expressions can reinforce, modify, or contradict what one says verbally.

Most facial expressions are intentional. They are used to send a message (for example, a smile for a job well done) or to mask true feelings (for example, a stern look of displeasure). These expressions are formed by movement of such facial muscles as the mouth, eyebrows, forehead, chin, or nose. Wrinkling the forehead, for instance, can communicate deep thought, lifting the eyebrows can reveal wonder or surprise, a sneer can show anger, and a jutting chin can show firmness. Conversely, fleeting facial expressions are often unintentional and are usually quickly covered up with other expressions. For example, a supervisor may feel sudden disgust, anger, or dislike for something his or her student teacher said. The supervisor does not want to communicate this to the student teacher. Therefore, the supervisor's true feelings or emotions are quickly masked with other intended expressions.

Involuntary facial expressions often take place under some type of traumatic or delightful circumstances. They are microexpressions that flash across people's faces in situations where they are fearful, angry, happy, or surprised. When conferring with student teachers, these expressions are often fleeting and are usually covered up with other expressions as soon as possible. However, under certain circumstances a supervisor may want to retain such expressions to convey a message to the student teacher. For example, supervisors sometimes use expressions of displeasure when a student teacher has not prepared adequately for a lesson.

Supervisors commonly use voluntary facial expressions to communicate with student teachers. In fact, effective supervisors have perfected the use of facial expressions. They can convey a message with a simple look. Two common examples are the smile of approval and the frown of displeasure.

The eyes can send many kinds of messages. As Miller (1981, p. 14) notes, a person's eyes "can be shifty and evasive, conveying hate, fear, and guilt, or they can express confidence, love, and support." Moreover, eye contact can be used to open communication, prolong communication, or cut off communication entirely. Indeed, eye contact can often be used to control interaction. When a supervisor wants the student teacher to speak, he or she makes direct eye contact with the student teacher. Conversely, when a supervisor wants to continue talking, he or she refrains from making direct eye contact.

Direct eye contact—a stare—can often be used to cut off remarks or to direct behavior. A stare used in conjunction with silence can be quite effective in bringing about a change in the student teacher's behavior. In fact, since there is no need for the student teacher to become defensive, a stare with silence can sometimes be even more effective than negative verbal comments.

Body Language

The use of body movements and gestures (kinesics) in communication represents an important source of information to listeners. Indeed, gestures with the head, arms, hands, and other body parts are most pervasive communicators. Gestures may provide information, as when communicating feelings, or when the supervisor nods his or her head in agreement while the student teacher speaks; they may emphasize a point, as when an individual taps something that he or she has written; they may call for attention, as when an individual taps the table. In other words, our physical actions are constantly sending information to those who are observant and attentive.

The overuse of body movement and gestures can be detrimental to effective communications. For example, the use of too many gestures can sometimes distract from the importance of a message. In effect, the overuse of gestures can result in a listener attending to the gestures rather than the message.

Posture is another type of kinesic communication. A tense, rigid body often communicates closeness and insecurity; a relaxed body suggests strength, openness, and friendliness. The way one stands or sits can also communicate information. A body orientation toward the listener tends to suggest security and comfort in the communication interaction.

The way one dresses communicates. It is often difficult to take a speaker seriously, for example, if he or she is dressed in ill-fitting, wrinkled clothing. Conversely, we tend to pay attention to an attractively dressed speaker. Supervisors then would be well advised to dress befitting their roles as mentors.

Language of Space and Motion

The conference space arrangement can shape communication. That is, the arrangement of objects and materials, within the confines of the available space, signifies meaning.

Environment The physical makeup of the conference setting can create moods and, in doing so, affect the interaction. Indeed, the attractiveness of the setting appears to influence the happiness and energy of the interacting individuals. These findings are supported by Miller (1981, p. 24) in his summary of research related to student reactions in ugly and beautiful classrooms. He states that "subjects in the ugly room had reactions of monotony, fatigue, headache, irritability, and hostility, while subjects in the beautiful room responded favorably with feelings of comfort, pleasure, importance, and enjoyment for completing the assigned tasks." Thus, Miller's findings suggest that a well-decorated, pleasing setting is more conducive to open communications and is more effective at keeping the interaction directed toward pertinent issues.

Territoriality Territoriality is commonly observed among individuals (Worchel and Shebilske 1989). For example in a library, one may mark his or her territory with a jacket or books when he or she leaves the room. Likewise, in a classroom, when a pupil takes the assigned seat of another pupil or when a pupil takes the seat normally occupied by another pupil, the regular occupant often becomes disturbed and resentful.

Territoriality can also be observed when a supervisor and student teacher hold a conference. Too often the supervisor arranges the seating with a desk or table between the student teacher and himself or herself. This too often leads to restrictions in the interaction. Also, such restrictions can convey messages of closedness and separation. A better arrangement would be side-by-side seating at a small table so that observational materials can be reviewed together.

Proxemics Proxemics is the study of the meaning and use of space. Hall (1969) suggests that people choose a particular separation distance when interacting that depends on their feeling toward each other at the given time, the context of the conversation, and their personal goals. Conversations between intimate people, for example, usually take place within 18 inches (intimate distance). Conversations between friends usually take place 3 to 4 1/2 feet apart (personal distance). Business and social interactions usually take place with a separation of 4 to 7 feet (social distance).

Even through the generalizations about appropriate interaction distance are tentative, supervisors should recognize the value of the use of space in their interactions with student teachers. Generally, supervisors want to use the personal distance range in their interactions with student teachers. Interactions at this range communicate openness along with a friendly supportive message.

Language of Time

Time represents an effective communicator. How a supervisor decides to use observational or con-ferencing time communicates important attitudinal information. When a supervisor spends little time observing, or passes it by completely, he or she communicates that observing the teaching of the student teacher is unimportant or that he or she has little interest in doing it. Such actions can unintentionally communicate similar attitudes to student teachers.

Pauses or silence represent another use of time often used to communicate. Pausing just before or after making a specific point, for instance, often signifies that the point is important. Thus, pauses are often used to cue student teachers that an important point is going to be made or that the last point made was important enough to reflect upon.

Time can also be used to communicate a variety of emotional responses. Silence, for example, can reflect disagreement or a determination to be uncooperative. And, of course, silence is often used to show lack of interest. In fact, a supervisory conference will often result in silence when the supervisor is poorly prepared or when the supervisor fails to support his or her viewpoints.

Supervisors should and do ask many questions. However, they often find it difficult to wait a sufficient time between asking questions and receiving the student teacher's response (use wait-time). Too often supervisors expect almost instantaneous responses to their questions, and, when not forthcoming, they tend to answer the questions themselves. Supervisors must learn to increase their wait-time so that student teachers have time to reflect on different aspects of their performance.

Finally, silence and the sense of time varies with different cultures, subcultures, and regions (Devito 1985, pp. 161–162). The Apache, for example, encourage silence. For some Afro-Americans, time is only approximate. In New York, time is viewed as being sacred; being late is serious. In San Francisco, on the other hand, being late is not a serious problem. Supervisors should take a close look at their student teachers' concept of time before they react to situations that involve time. Perhaps the student teacher is running on a different clock and needs assistance in developing a more adequate time concept.

Language of the Voice

As mentioned earlier, vocal cues greatly influence a listener's perception. The adage, "It's not what you say, but how you say it that counts" is often true. A supervisors' response such as, "That was an excellent activity in today's lesson!" will convey a message different from a simple monotone, "That was an excellent activity in today's lesson." As noted earlier, when a contradiction occurs between a verbal and vocal message, the latter is usually believed.

Supervisors should watch their vocal messages. Different vocal intonations sometimes communicate different meanings than are intended. Messages can be changed by varying the loudness/softness, using high pitch/low pitch, varying the tone, or the quality of speech. Supervisors should be aware of and pay attention to the effect of their voice intonations. That is, they should learn to speak so there is congruence between their verbal and vocal messages.

Table 3.1 summarizes the definitions for verbal and nonverbal communication, as well as their application.

Listening

Hearing and listening are not the same —hearing is automatic, whereas listening is an art that must be learned. Hearing is the transmission of eardrum vibration caused by sound impulses to the brain, while listening occurs when the brain gives meaning to the transmitted impulses. Thus, listening is an active process.

Many times people hear, but they do not listen. Supervisors may hear boring student teacher lectures, for example, but not listen to them. Really listening is hard work—harder than talking. Although listening takes effort and discipline, it is a must for effective supervision.

Virtually everyone does some serious listening; however, few do it well. Basic to improving the ability to listen well is awareness of the need to improve listening skills. When the training received in reading, writing, and speaking is compared with the training received in listening, listening will be found wanting. This state of affairs is ironic when one realizes that 60 percent of communication involves listening.

To listen well, people first must learn to cut down on their talking. But cutting down on talking is only the beginning step in becoming a good listener. Listening is more than just not

Table 3.1
The Communication Components

Type	Description	Uses
Verbal Communication	Communication associated with the spoken word. Can be through verbal, vocal, or metaverbal components.	Communicate knowledge and/or ideas through verbal component. Communicate emphasis and attitudinal message with vocal component. Send implied messages through metaverbal component.
Nonverbal Communication	Nonlinguistic communication. The sending of messages without words.	Communicate desires through use of face, motion, time, voice, body, and space.

talking. Listening, as with thinking, is an intense, active process. It takes self-discipline and concentration. In fact, Barker (1971, p. 4) suggests that the active listening process has four components: hearing, attending, understanding, and remembering.

Hearing

Hearing is physiological; it is the nonselective process of sound waves striking the eardrums, which results in electrochemical impulses being transmitted to the brain. Therefore, along with the information people wish to process and understand they will have noise that masks the desired message. In fact, hearing can be affected by exposure to continuous loud tones or noise such as loud music and city noises.

Attending

Although listening starts as a physiological process, it quickly becomes a psychological one as the individual focuses on what is heard. This focusing is directly related to what is important to the individual, as well as the relevance of the message, the setting, the intensity of the message, concreteness of the message, and the duration of the message.

Listening involves focusing on the message being transmitted. In some cases, an individual may not be interested in what the speaker is saying or may not see the importance of the message, but the listener will never know unless he or she sits it out and listens. Essentially, the individual must focus attention, stop talking, stop fidgeting, and stop letting his or her mind wander. The individual must "lock in" on what the speaker is saying while blocking out everything that may interfere.

Blocking out everything around is not an easy task and, in fact, is not always desirable behavior for supervisors who often wish to note everything that is happening in an observational setting. In fact, supervisors must learn to be aware of what is going on in all areas of a classroom and to pay attention to pupil behaviors. Thus, supervisors need total awareness so they can better assist student teachers with their classroom management skills.

The way people view a speaker also affects their willingness to listen. If the speaker is described as being very intelligent or someone of importance, people tend to listen with greater intensity. This tendency also applies to speakers who are well groomed and attractive, with ideas, attitudes, and values similar to the listeners. Other factors such as size, dress, and name may also have an effect on the tendency to listen.

Listening, like talking, has a verbal and a nonverbal component. The words heard are only one aspect of listening. People can also gain information through nonverbal means, that is, through the interplay of gestures, feelings, and body movements that are constant when people interact. Thus, people sometimes believe they are sending one message (verbal), but their voice, choice of words, and gestures (nonverbal) can be sending a completely different message.

Sokolove, Sadker, and Sadker (1986, p. 232) suggest four nonverbal cues that often affect communications. These writers suggest that attentiveness can be improved by giving special attention to:

1. **Eye contact.** The eyes should focus directly on the speaker, being careful that the direct eye- to-eye contact does not make the speaker uncomfortable.
2. **Facial expressions.** Facial expressions should show that one is listening. These expressions should give feedback (positive and negative) to the speaker about whether the message is being communicated and understood.
3. **Body posture.** One should show that he or she is a relaxed listener. A relaxed listener tends to relax the speaker and stimulate him or her to say more. In fact, a listener who is relaxed and leans toward the speaker communicates interest.

4. **Physical space.** The listener should move to a position so that he or she and the speaker have comfortable separation.

Although much of the nonverbal information received is on a conscious level, people also glean information from others at the subconscious level (for example, when a supervisor knows that the student teacher isn't really interested in his or her opinion). Even though people may not be aware of it, subconscious information plays an important part in producing their impressions and helps in developing an understanding of messages being sent by a speaker. Indeed, inferences, sometimes inaccurate, regarding people are often formed on the basis of subconscious information.

Understanding

Understanding relates to the decoding of received information. In this phase, the individual must actively judge the worthiness and relevance of the information, as well as organize it (Friedman 1983, p. 5). The individual must make a judgment about the information and decide, ''Am I really interested?'' This judgment is often based on the source of the information—whether the source is reliable, a friend, or a professional. The worthiness of received information is also related to the social context. For example, the same message delivered casually as a supervisor leaves an observational session and delivered formally at a post observation conference would most likely call for different judgments.

Remembering

Remembering is the last and perhaps the most important phase of the listening process. Whether specific information is remembered or not is directly related to how it is evaluated. In other words, before an individual sends the information to long-term memory, he or she must decide that it is worth remembering. In this evaluation process, the individual is ''weighing the message against beliefs, questioning the speaker's motives, challenging the ideas presented, suspecting the validity of the message, holding the speaker's ideas up to standards of excellence, wondering what has been omitted, thinking about how the message could have been improved, and in other ways evaluating what is being said'' (Friedman 1983, p. 5). This evaluation process generally takes place with respect to the internal beliefs and values one holds. However, the individual must learn to evaluate information on its own merit, which isn't always an easy task. However, it is well worth the effort, especially to supervisors of prospective teachers.

Past experiences and internal feelings often have an effect on a supervisor's evaluation. All supervisors have emotional filters that affect how they evaluate what they hear. These filters may block words or phrases or, conversely, allow certain words or phrases to rush in and overly impress them. Feelings may at times even change what people hear, as with such words as ''AIDS,'' ''drugs,'' or ''teacher empowerment.'' Listening, like observing, can be selective to some degree.

Nichols and Stevens (1957, pp. 102–103) offer the following guidelines to reduce the effects of filters on evaluation:

1. Be self-disciplined. In effect, withhold evaluation until the total message is received.
2. Don't take all that is heard at face value. Hunt for evidence in opposition to the received information.
3. Make a realistic self-analysis of received information. Test received information against biases, values, and feelings.

Sometimes people are poor listeners because they have developed bad listening habits. These bad habits may include:

1. **Pseudolistening.** Pseudolistening is the faking of listening. Good pseudolisteners can look a person in the eye, nod and smile in agreement, and may even

occasionally answer questions. In other words, they give the appearance of attentiveness, but they are usually thinking about other things.

2. **Insulated listening.** Some people avoid listening because they do not want to deal with an issue or when it takes mental exertion to understand what is being said.

3. **Selective listening.** Selective listeners attend to a speaker's remarks only when they are interested or when the speaker's remarks are easy to understand. Of course, all of us are somewhat selective at times, for instance, when we screen out commercials (as we watch television) and background noise (as we work).

4. **Attribute listening.** Attribute listeners are interested only in the delivery and/or the physical appearance of the speaker. These individuals are often more concerned with criticizing the speaker's style of delivery or physical appearance. They associate the importance of the message with the way it is delivered or with the appearance of the speaker.

5. **Stage hogging.** Stage hoggers want to do all the talking. They are interested only in expressing their own ideas. If they allow others to speak, it is only while they catch their breath. Many supervisors, for example, want to do all the talking at supervisor-student teacher conferences. These supervisors too often give student teachers little opportunity to voice their opinions. When these supervisors do listen, they often cut off remarks. In a word, supervisors must be especially sensitive to the habit of stage hogging. Remember stage hogging isn't really conversing; essentially, it can be equated to making a speech.

6. **Defensive listening.** Defensive listeners take innocent remarks as personal attacks. Student teachers are often notorious for being defensive listeners. They often take supervisor feedback remarks about their behaviors and skills as being overly critical. Supervisors must be sensitive to their tendency and the tendency to be overly sensitive and defensive regarding the remarks about appearance, physical attributes, and teaching abilities.

Generally, an awareness of the bad habits associated with listening is enough to assist you in overcoming their effects. However, one should practice working on overcoming any bad habits to becoming a better listener.

Thinking can have an effect on listening. It is a well-established fact that most people can process information at a faster pace than it can be delivered. Therefore, when people listen, they have time to take in their environment and to think, going off on mental tangents. This extra thinking time could be better used in reflecting on and analyzing what is being said. So, when interacting with student teachers, supervisors should try to use extra thinking time to reflect on what they are saying.

Although most people want to be better listeners, they often lack the skill.

Styles of Listening

We often listen for different reasons and with different ends in mind. Indeed, listening should and does vary from situation to situation (Wolvin and Cookley 1979). Listening to a student teacher explain the procedure that would be followed in an upcoming lesson, for example, would call for a different style of listening than if a supervisor were helping the student teacher with his or her classroom management problems. Three styles of listening are one-way, two-way, and empathic.

One-way listening One-way listening takes place when an individual is not actively taking part in the exchange of information; that is, it is passive listening. The individual listens without talking and without giving nonverbal feedback to the speaker. One-way listening gives speakers the opportunity to develop their thoughts and ideas without being unduly influenced by the listeners. Common examples of one-way listening are observing a student teacher lesson or watching television.

One-way listening gives a speaker free reign, with the listener acting as a sounding board for the speaker's ideas or problems. Student teachers sometimes need such a person who will just hear them out without giving a reaction. The occasional need for a sounding board explains why some people enjoy talking to their pets.

One-way listening has limited value to supervisors. Indeed, except for the few cases we have addressed, it isn't very effective for the simple reason that a supervisor will too often misunderstand at least part of a student teacher's comments. Messages, for example, that are overly vague require that follow-up questions be asked so they will be correctly interpreted. In other cases, speakers can give wrong information, or listeners can simply get information wrong. Thus, a speaker can say four grams instead of six or a listener can transform four grams into six. On the whole, even though one-way listening has value and various uses, there are other better listening styles.

Two-way listening Two-way listening actively involves both the speaker and the listener in the exchange of information. In practice, listeners provide feedback to the speaker by reacting nonverbally or by asking for more information.

Asking for additional information when a message is unclear is a valuable tool in the supervision process. Often a supervisor must ask the student teacher to elaborate on points or vice versa. For example, a supervisor might want a student teacher to provide more details on the method to be used to teach a lesson on problem solving, or a student teacher might ask the supervisor to clarify his or her observational data-recording procedures, or a supervisor might ask a student teacher to generate more options in dealing with a classroom behavior problem.

Paraphrasing a speaker's message is another technique for providing feedback. Such rephrasing feedback might be stated in such form as, ''So you're telling me that you are having problems with this class because of one pupil.'' The thing to remember in restating the speaker's message is to paraphrase the words rather than parrot them.

Although active listening usually comes as a verbal response, it can be nonverbal in form (for example, a nod of understanding or a frown to show a lack of understanding). When the speaker is observant, nonverbal active listening techniques can be even more effective than the more common verbal techniques.

Two-way listening offers some real advantages for supervisors. First, it boosts the odds that supervisors accurately and fully understand what student teachers are telling them. In effect, active listening serves as a double-check on the accuracy of the supervisor's interpretation of student teacher statements. A second advantage of active listening is that it often stimulates student teachers to explore issues in greater depth. Lastly, the use of two-way listening can encourage student teachers to solve their own problems by giving them the opportunity to talk through the problems and receive feedback from supervisors.

Empathic listening Listening with feeling is referred to as empathic or reflective listening. It is an earnest attempt to feel what the speaker is experiencing or feeling and respond to those feelings. Only when one listens with feelings can he or she understand another's meaning fully. Empathic listening requires careful attention to the speaker's verbal and nonverbal cues so they can be put together into a statement that reflects the content as well as the associated feelings to glean the full meaning of the speaker's message.

The response portion of empathic listening attempts to avoid misinterpretation of the speaker or to clarify the message. Sokolove, Sadker, and Sadker (1986, p. 230) suggest that the listener's function in empathic listening involves holding up a mirror for the speaker's words, feelings, and behaviors. Through the process associated with empathic listening, one attempts to provide direct feedback regarding the success of a speaker's communication. This response can take the form of simple paraphrasing of the speaker's words or can be an interpretation of the speaker's message as reflected in the verbal and nonverbal behaviors. For example, a supervisor's response to the content of a message that a student teacher dislikes teaching an advanced science class might be, "I believe that you are saying that you dislike teaching this science class because you find the laboratory experiments too difficult for the pupils."

Furthermore, a supervisor's response to a student teacher statement can be related to the content component of the message or the affective component of the message. For example, a response toward the content of a message might be a statement such as "I believe that you are saying . . ." or "You appear to think . . ."; whereas to reflect the affective component of a message, he or she might respond with "I think that you are feeling . . ." or "You appear to feel . . ."

There are no quick methods for achieving empathy with student teachers, but it is important to work toward this end. Supervisors should learn to see the point of view of student teachers. For example, if a student teacher is often late with his or her lesson plans, the supervisor should try to put himself or herself in the role of the student teacher to understand reasons for the lateness. Sometimes student teacher behaviors will appear foolish and ridiculous, but the supervisor needs to look at such situations from the viewpoint of the student teacher.

In summary, skill in the various types of listening is an essential tool for effective supervision. Table 3.2 summarizes the three types of listening. The importance, to supervisors, of all three listening types cannot be overemphasized. In fact, your listening skill is directly related to your supervisory effectiveness. All supervisors should be good listeners.

Feedback

Feedback is extremely important to communication. Indeed, many communication problems arise because of failure to be attentive to feedback. Feedback may come from oneself (source) or from the listener (receiver), may be positive or negative, and may be immediate or delayed.

Table 3.2
Listening

Type	Description	Uses
One-Way	Passive listening with no interaction between speaker and listeners.	Give students the opportunity to develop thoughts or solve their own problems without external input. Give students the opportunity to just listen to auditory input.
Two-Way	Active listening with exchange between speaker and listeners.	Ask for clarification when unsure of message. Encourage students to talk through problems.
Empathic	Listening with an attempt to experience speaker's feelings.	Determine students' real feelings about various subjects.

When people communicate with another person, they also hear and communicate with themselves. That is, they receive feedback from their own messages—they hear what they say, they feel the way they move, and they see what they write. On the basis of this self-feedback, a person may correct himself or herself, restate something, or smile at what was said.

Also, when an individual speaks to another person, that person constantly returns response messages. This feedback can be in the form of a frown, a smile, a pat on the back, or a simple nod of the head, depending on how the message is viewed.

Finally, feedback may be positive or negative. Positive feedback tells the speaker that the communication is going well and should be continued. Negative feedback tells the speaker that the communication is not going well, and there is a problem. Negative feedback represents a corrective message that informs the speaker that changes are needed.

Interpersonal communication results in immediate feedback; a speaker sees a frown or a smile—the speaker hears agreement or disagreement responses immediately. However, feedback from written communication is usually delayed, for example, while awaiting the reaction to a written critique of one's performance.

Effective supervisory communication requires that the specific messages encoded and transmitted are received and accurately decoded by student teachers. This process is continual and two-way. Student teachers are continually decoding the information that supervisors are sending, and they are sending messages to the supervisors in return. These student teacher feedback messages, in general, are usually nonverbal in nature.

Student teachers are continually sending nonverbal messages of understanding or uncertainty, agreement or disagreement, likes or distaste, concern or lack of concern, attention or inattention. When supervisors receive a message, they should use this feedback to modify or clarify their original message; namely, they should respond by re-explaining, using further examples or changing their mode of exchange. Identifying and responding to student teacher feedback is a skill that supervisors should master for effective supervision.

Summary

Communication is central to the supervisory process; without the ability to communicate, student teacher growth could not take place. Communication exchanges consist of both a spoken and nonverbal message with the spoken component having a verbal, vocal, and metaverbal component. The verbal component is the actual words spoken; the vocal component is the meaning attached to the words, depending on variables such as pitch, loudness, tone, and rate; and the metaverbal component is the implied or intended message. Most supervisors are aware of the importance of verbal communication. However, information is also gained through nonverbal communication. That is, people glean information from an individual's facial language, body language, use of space and motion, use of time, and use of the voice.

Supervisors and student teachers need to develop better listening skills. Listening is a four-step process: hearing, attending, understanding, and remembering. It is impossible to learn without skill at all four of these listening steps. Many people have developed bad listening habits that should be overcome if they are to be effective at listening. Indeed, supervisors must overcome bad habits and become proficient at one-way, two-way, and empathic listening.

Sadly, when interacting with student teachers, supervisors generally do most of the talking. They have not learned to use nonverbal communication effectively, and rarely, if at all, have they learned to use feedback and to really listen to their student teachers. Since supervisors fulfill their function through the exchange of ideas, it is essential that they develop an understanding of and skill in all facets of the communication process.

Questions and Discussion Topics

1. To recognize that effective communication can be good or bad, have the class share with student teachers incidents in which communication improved a situation and incidents in which communication made a situation worse.
2. Use the bad habits described in this chapter to describe faulty listening behaviors you use daily. In what circumstances are you guilty of these habits? Around whom? In what settings? At what times?
3. Play a videotape of a student teacher conference without the picture. List information being exchanged by the teacher or the students through nonverbal communication.
4. Play the tape in #3 with only the picture. List information being exchanged by the teacher or the students through nonverbal communication.
5. Play the tape in #3 with both sound and picture. Did you notice any implied messages? If so, what were they? Give your reasons for making these conclusions.

CHAPTER 4

Observational Techniques

CHAPTER KEY CONCEPTS

Descriptive Data
Duration Measure
Flanders Interaction Analysis
Frequency Measure
Nonstructured Observation

Reproduced Data
Structured Observation
Time-Sample Measure
Valued Data
Verbatim Data

Overview

One of the most difficult problems in clinical supervision is that of obtaining accurate information on the effectiveness of the student teacher. However, trained supervisors know how to collect accurate information. Their data-gathering techniques are more than simply watching and recording what is seen. Their techniques are well-planned and structured.

The collection of accurate information requires structured data collection. A variety of systems can be used to collect structured information: narrative systems, category systems, and multiple-coding systems. The type of system to use in each observation session depends on the information needed.

Chapter 4 focuses on the collection of accurate data for decision-making in the student teaching experience.

Objectives

Upon completing your study of chapter 4, you should be able to:

1. Compare and contrast nonstructured and structured observation.
2. Differentiate among the three common types of data.
3. State two reasons why it is important to be able to differentiate among the different types of data.
4. Differentiate between objective data and subjective data.
5. Contrast frequency measure, duration measure, and time sample measure.
6. Explain the purposes of structured observation.
7. Describe procedures that a supervisor should follow in making structured observations.
8. Describe verbal and nonverbal classroom interaction observational techniques.

Professional responsibilities as a supervisor require that information be collected and analyzed to determine an accurate picture of what goes on in the classroom. To accomplish this end, data related to identified student teacher skills and behaviors must be collected. The information collected will be used to analyze the student teacher's teaching, as well as student learning, the learning environment, and student attitudes toward learning and schooling. Based on these analyses, certain conclusions will be made regarding the student teacher's effectiveness. These conclusions will then form the basis for the next phase of the supervision cycle. Therefore, the more accurate supervisors can make their observations, the more accurate their data will be and the more help supervisors can give student teachers.

Observation Types

There are basically two types of observation: nonstructured and structured. In nonstructured observation, the supervisor simply watches and takes note of the student teacher behaviors, characteristics, and personal interactions that seem significant. Nonstructured classroom observation tends to be anecdotal and subjective.

With structured observation, the supervisor typically measures the frequency, duration, magnitude, or latency of specific behaviors or events. However, since classroom interaction is complex and fast-paced, it is difficult to record every instance of some targeted occurrence. For example, it is often difficult to keep a record of the types of questions asked individual students, or the movement of the student teacher during the lesson, or the reinforcement techniques used by the student teacher, or student time on task.

One of the greatest obstacles to becoming an effective supervisor is the danger of misinterpreting what is seen. Everyone has past experiences and biases that can easily distort what is seen. An observer must be aware of these experiences, and biases must be eliminated if accurate information is to be recorded.

Types of Data

Collected data is valuable only to the extent that it can be used to improve the performance of the student teacher. Thus, the specific kind of data needed depends on what aspect of the student teacher's performance is being studied. A brief introduction to the major types of data follows.

Valued data is defined as "data that involves the judgment of an observer" (Hansen 1977, p. 351). That is, the supervisor must make a value judgment regarding the observed behavior or event. For example, having observed the number of questions asked by the student teacher, or the student teacher's use of movement or reinforcement, or the students' time on task, the supervisor makes a subjective statement regarding what was observed. Thus, following the observation, the supervisor might record, "The number of questions asked by the student teacher was appropriate." or "The student teacher used movement effectively." or "The student teacher didn't use enough reinforcement." or "The student teacher was ineffective at keeping students on task." Valued data, then, is nothing more than a subjective value judgment by the supervisor and is useful only when the supervisor's judgments can be trusted to be consistent with tested techniques for effective teaching.

Descriptive data is defined as "data that have been organized, categorized, or quantified by an observer but do not involve a value judgment" (Hansen 1977, p. 352). This type of data demands that the supervisor decide in which behavioral category (if any) an observed behavior belongs. It also means counting the number of times a specific behavior is observed. For example, a supervisor might classify student teacher questions as being divergent or convergent, or might classify student teacher reinforcement statements as positive or negative, or might label the student teacher movement as necessary or unnecessary, or might decide which student teacher statements represent encouragement—and record all such cases. Once recorded, a judgment must be made regarding the appropriateness of the observed behaviors. This judgment can be made by the university supervisor, the cooperating teacher, or the student teacher. The value of descriptive data is related to the supervisor's expertise in recognizing and categorizing specific behaviors and then evaluating their appropriateness, that is, in turning descriptive data into valued data.

Reproduced data is data that has been recorded in video, audio, or total transcript (verbatim) form and can be reproduced when desirable (Hansen 1977, p. 354). The data includes a total reproduction of the targeted environment or behaviors. In this type of data collection, the supervisor might decide to record the behaviors in the form of a list. Thus, the supervisor's record might consist of a listing (verbatim) of student teacher statements or questions or a listing or diagram of the student teacher's movement during a lesson. The data is valued only when the supervisor can be trusted to operate the equipment properly or to record the observed behaviors accurately. When data from verbatim reproductions is eventually extracted and used, it inevitably falls into one of the other two categories.

People look, but do they really see? Observing, especially in an objective way, is difficult to learn because it requires detachment and noninvolvement. People tend, too often, to include their own feelings, attitudes, and biases in what they observe. Therefore, since the ability to make objective observations is a relatively unrefined skill for many supervisors, it must be developed and practiced.

Structured Observations

Observations can, if made correctly, provide highly accurate, detailed, verifiable information not only about student teachers and students, but also about the context in which the observations are being made. However, supervisors should always keep in mind that behavior is complex and is the product of many interrelated causes. Thus, those who make observations of human behavior may be easily misled into drawing false conclusions (Cartwright & Cartwright 1974). Specific skills and techniques that help to study and analyze the teaching-learning environment in a structured and objective fashion thus become essential skills for supervisors. Trained observers not only acquire more accurate information than do casual observers, but trained observers also apply what they learn more effectively because they follow certain procedures. Although supervisors who have developed their observation skills make special efforts to be unbiased and objective, even those who are highly trained tend to be selective in what they see. That is, everyone chooses which behaviors or actions to pay attention to and which to ignore in a given situation. For example, trained clinical supervisors have learned to ignore those behaviors that are not part of the agreement formed in the preobservation conference.

Given any situation, a wide range of observations are possible. No observer can monitor everything that takes place in a classroom. A classroom environment is just too complex. For instance, if a supervisor is recording the interactions in a reading group, it would be difficult to record accurately all the behaviors occurring in the rest of the classroom. For this reason, it is best to limit the data to be gathered during a single observation session. The target group can be studied intensively, which should lead to an accurate picture of the specific behaviors being studied. Another focusing strategy is to limit the number of behaviors looked for at one time (about five or fewer in the beginning). Limiting the number of behaviors is especially important to beginning supervisors who often try to gather too much data at a single observation session.

Developing an observational plan is clearly needed if a supervisor is to make accurate recordings within an observational setting. Structured observation represents such a plan in that it provides a useful means of identifying, studying, classifying, and measuring specific interacting variables within the learning environment. Structured observation requires that supervisors

Observations should be limited to targeted behaviors.

develop specific observational skills such as the ability to:

1. Differentiate between objective and subjective data.
2. Determine the setting in which the behavior will be observed.
3. Determine when the environment will be observed.
4. Determine the method for observing and recording the targeted behaviors or events.

Individual plans may differ with respect to these elements, and this may result in totally different observations. But, although they may differ, some type of structured plan is needed to generate the kind of reliable data needed for supervision purposes.

Objectivity in Observation

Behavior can be defined as "that which is observable and overt; it has to be seen and it should be countable" (Tillman et al. 1976, p. 262). It is impossible to be completely objective in the collection of data. The very decision of what to record, what not to record, or how to categorize the information involves subjective judgments. Thus, being objective does not mean discounting feelings, attitudes, and thoughts. It simply means using them to produce data that is objective. Ob-

servers should always strive to record what is actually happening rather than what they think is happening. Observers should try to be aware of the difference between what is happening and its interpretation.

The context surrounding behavior should also be noted, for very often this information will be useful when drawing inferences and conclusions and arriving at decisions. Observers should think broadly about all behaviors in the observational setting and include in their collection of data such items as time, place, the people involved, and objects in the environment.

Good observation involves selective interpretations of behavior as well as explicit descriptions of specific, observable acts. To avoid erroneous interpretations, the distinction between observable acts (behaviors) and inferences (interpretations of behaviors) should be kept in mind. Consider the following statements:

1. The student teacher is a proficient questioner.
2. The student teacher is too rigid.
3. The student teacher is making good progress.
4. The student teacher is very creative.

None of these statements specifies overt, observable behavior. Terms such as proficient, rigid, good, and creative are open to interpretation; they are really interpretive conclusions or inferences rather than objective happenings. Objectivity requires specifying the behaviors that lead to such subjective interpretations. For example, the student teacher may be asking questions at all levels of Bloom's Taxonomy, which led the supervisor to conclude that he or she is a proficient questioner.

Observations must also be objective if they are to be of value. Compare the following statements with those cited earlier:

1. The student teacher asked ten question in the lesson, using all levels of Bloom's Taxonomy.

2. The student teacher remained behind the podium for today's entire lesson.
3. The student teacher always had at least three activities planned for each period this week.
4. The student teacher always has at least two teacher-created games ready for those students who finish their seatwork early.

Note that these observations are overt, observable behaviors that can be counted. They could lead to the inferences and conclusions stated earlier.

Even though an observer cannot always see processes or characteristics directly, he or she often can make a reasonable judgment about whether or not they exist, based on the behaviors exhibited by an individual. What the observer does, based on behavioral evidence, is make an inference regarding the presence or absence of certain characteristics and processes. This supporting evidence must be observable so that others can review it and decide whether or not they agree with the inference.

Observers should always be careful in drawing inferences and conclusions because they can never be absolutely sure that they are accurate. A major concern of observers should be to maintain constant vigilance regarding the question: What behaviors constitute ''reasonable'' support for the inferences or conclusions being made?

Even though observers can never be absolutely sure of the inferences they make, their justification increases in proportion to the observable behaviors supporting them. Observers who habitually make inferences based on little behavioral data are not carrying out the role and responsibilities of a trained supervisor. These same observers too often make unsupported recommendations.

Observation Setting

In most instances, the setting for supervisory observations is limited to the classroom or the school grounds where the student teacher is doing his or her teaching. However, a supervisor may be interested only in a limited part of classroom.

For example, the observer may want information pertaining only to a specific teaching behavior or class activity. However, even when limiting the focus of observations, observers should include environmental data that might influence the targeted behaviors.

Observation Time

The interval of time that data is to be collected is usually determined by the teaching-learning situation and the data being collected. If a student teacher's behaviors are being observed during instruction, the supervisor probably would not want to collect data during seatwork or independent study periods. However, in making general observations, the supervisor will be interested in all aspects of behavior in the environment for a specified period. For most purposes, 45 minutes appears to be an adequate period for a representative sampling of behaviors in the learning environment.

Supervisors should also keep in mind that their presence in a classroom may influence some behaviors within the observational setting. This influence, in general, usually tends to decrease over time. Therefore, supervisors would be wise to spend some time in the setting before making their observations.

Observation Arrangements

Observations made without a definite purpose or preconceived plan of operation can be both tiresome and unprofitable. Although such unplanned experiences might be interesting, even entertaining to the novice observer, over any length of time, the whole experience can become an ordeal. These unplanned observation experiences are nothing more than a ''look and see'' exercise with a ''catch what you can'' outcome. However, trained supervisors understand what is to be accomplished during each observational session. Supervisors need to know exactly what behaviors are to be observed to achieve the intended purpose of the observation, and they need to be able to see behaviors as both separate, discrete phenomena and interactive behaviors within the dynamics of the observational setting.

If a supervisor is to get to the heart of what is happening in an observational setting, he/she must give full attention to the experience. Making objective observations is often such a strenuous activity that supervisors cannot concentrate for long periods. There will be times when they will want the meanings of what is happening. Sometimes exact words, if possible, will be recorded. At other times, the voice quality, body posture, facial expressions, or gestures should be noted. Whatever data is needed, the use of structured observational techniques should greatly enhance the recording of the data.

Recording Data

Observational data should be collected in a manner that is easy to record and use. There are essentially three sampling measures that supervisors can use: frequency measures, duration measures, or time-sample measures. Frequency measurement is employed when an observer wants to determine the number of times certain actions or behaviors are exhibited in a specified time. The observer simply keeps a tally of the number of times the actions or behaviors are exhibited in the given time interval. Duration and time-sample measurements involve data that may not be discrete. That is, it may involve behaviors that continue for a length of time or that take some time to occur. Duration measurement involves either the length of time a specific action or behavior continues or the time needed for its occurrence following a given direction or a signal. The time a student teacher lectures or the time it takes for the student teacher to take the class attendance are examples of duration measurement.

Time-sample measurement is used to sample behavior at predetermined time intervals such as five minutes or fifteen minutes. The behavior can be continuous or discrete. An observer can simply check for the behavior at the end of the specified time interval. For example, in checking the movement patterns of the student teacher, the observer might want to record his or her position at five-minute intervals.

Of course, an observer would not want to use, or even desire to use, all measurement types each time an observation is made. Moreover, there is no observational system that can or should be used in all situations. The particular technique to use depends on the kind of data the observer wishes to collect. To obtain accurate data related to classroom behaviors with minimal distortion of the classroom processes being studied, careful consideration should be given to the recording procedure itself. Four quite different approaches have been used in the past. One is to make a direct recording of the behaviors, or to record indirectly, using a mechanical recorder (audio or video). A second approach is to use a checklist to record the desired data. The other two approaches require that some type of instrumentation be developed or used. In one approach, the observer uses symbols and classroom seating charts to record the data. In the other, the observer memorizes numbered categories of behaviors for later instant recall during a classroom observation.

Verbatim

Selective verbatim note-taking is the most commonly used method for gathering data. It is a word-for-word record of verbal statements in the classroom. When the novice supervisor first starts observing and recording what is seen, he or she often tries to record everything. But in the hectic, multifaceted classroom, a supervisor soon discovers that it is almost impossible to accurately observe and record so many different stimuli at one time. The novice supervisor soon finds that the observational focus must be narrowed, and specific aspects of the classroom must be targeted. For example, the focus may be on the praise and encouragement statements made by the student teacher, or the higher order questions asked by the student teacher, or the sarcastic statements made by the student teacher in response to incorrect student responses.

Selective verbatim has some advantages as a technique for classroom observation. It has a major advantage of being relatively simple to use. All the supervisor needs is a pad and pencil. Also, selective verbatim provides an objective, noninterpretive record of the student teacher's behavior. It holds up a "verbal" mirror to the student teacher, which can be analyzed whenever convenient.

Finally, there are limitations associated with using selective verbatim. The problem is with "selectivity." That is, the larger context of the classroom interaction can be lost when the focus is narrow as required in selective verbatim recording. Still another problem associated with selective verbatim is that the supervisor may select apparently trivial behaviors for recording.

Some supervisors make use of audio- and videotapes in gathering classroom data. However, in analyzing these tapes, the supervisor does not have use of the facial expressions, gestures, and eye contact that often supplement the recording of information in the classroom. Of course, this is more of a problem with audiotaping than with videotaping. However, both tapings have the advantage of giving the student teacher a great deal of information about his or her voice, speech patterns, and clarity of directions.

Checklist Records

The use of checklists as guides for gathering data, regarding student teacher competencies, is common in most teacher education programs. In most cases, these checklists are used solely to evaluate the student teachers. However, they can also be used to provide formative data. However, when used in clinical supervision, key aspects of effective instruction should be identified by the triad, and these identified components should be used to construct the desired checklists. In some cases, the checklists consist of those teaching skills that are deemed essential to effective teaching. The supervisor simply rates the student teacher on the identified skills, and the student teacher continues to work on those areas identified as being weak. In other cases, the checklist is developed and used to record the time duration of selected activities. Table 4.1 presents a typical

Table 4.1
Time in the Classroom

	Time Started	Time Stopped
Taking attendance		
Collecting lunch money		
Making assignments for homework		
Collecting homework or seatwork		
Organizing groups		
Shifting from one activity to another		
Students entering late		
Students leaving early		
School events		
Outside interruptions		

checklist for the use and organization of classroom time. It was constructed to provide instant information about events in the classroom that can affect the time-on-task of students.

Seating Chart Records

Seating charts make excellent instruments for recording observational data. Symbols can often be used to represent specific behaviors, and these symbols can be recorded on seating charts or other convenient forms. The particular system used to record data should be simple and tailor-made to the specific observation. For example, if only two behaviors are being observed, the observer might use an X for one and a Y for the other on a seating chart to record their occurrence as shown in Figure 4.1.

Another example of the use of a seating chart to keep a record of four behaviors in the classroom is shown in Figure 4.2. Six numbers have been recorded for one-half the class that was chosen to be observed in this session. Only one-half the class was observed because it is difficult to record this amount of data for an entire class. Also, the number of behaviors recorded each session should be limited so that the record doesn't become too cluttered with details. Data can be recorded for each occurrence of a behavior (frequency measure) or it can be recorded at predetermined time intervals (time-sample measurement) such as every five minutes.

Another technique that involves the use of a seating chart is observing the movement patterns of the student teacher and students. Figure 4.3 shows an example of the movement patterns of a student teacher during a thirty-minute lesson. Such patterns are important because they can

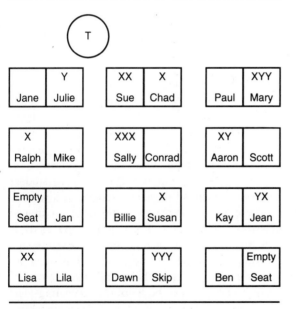

Legend:
X — Teacher asked question
Y — Student needed help

Figure 4.1 Recorded data for classroom observation (circle represents the teacher)

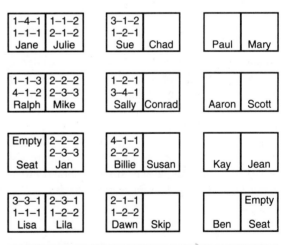

Legend:

1 — Quiet and on task
2 — Talking to other student
3 — Out of seat
4 — Talking with student teacher

Figure 4.2 Seating chart record of classroom behaviors

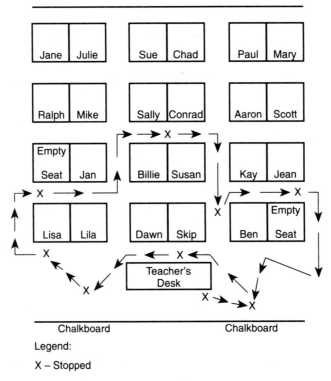

Legend:

X – Stopped

Figure 4.3 Student teacher movement record

indicate student teacher or student confidence levels, they can affect classroom management, or they can indicate student teacher preferences for certain students or areas of the classroom (Acheson and Gall, 1980).

Simplicity in the recording of data is the key to using seating charts to record data. Figure 4.4 lists other examples of symbols that should prove useful in recording data on seating charts.

Classroom Interaction

Teaching is not, as some critics and student teachers seem to think, just a matter of telling. Teaching is a dynamic enterprise with continual interactions among the participants. Therefore, if the dynamics of classroom life is the object of analysis, a useful technique is interaction analysis.

Effective teaching involves interactive communication patterns that are skillfully directed. Thus,

supervisors and student teachers should be interested in looking at and analyzing classroom interaction patterns. From such analysis, one can learn (1) whether a class is student-teacher-dominated or pupil-dominated, open or repressive, and (2) whether the teaching style is direct (student freedom to respond is minimized) or indirect (student freedom to respond is maximized).

There are a number of methods of looking at classroom interaction. These interaction analysis schemes vary from simple to complex. Even though the simpler schemes are not as useful as the more sophisticated methods, the simple interaction analysis techniques can be helpful in detecting glaring faults in the use of various teaching skills. The simplest of these methods calls for the supervisor to simply tally each instance of student teacher (S) and pupil (P) talk as, for example S S P P S S S P S S S S P P S S S S S P S S S S S S S P P P.

Label	Symbol	Definition
Male	M	The individual is male.
Female	F	The individual is female.
Student Behaviors		
Correct response	+	Student answered correctly.
Wrong response	−	Student answered incorrectly.
No response	0	Student did not answer.
Inappropriate response	=	Student made inappropriate verbal response.
Student disruptive	D	Student caused problem in class.
Teacher Behaviors		
Reinforcement	+ +	Teacher used positive reinforcement.
Criticize	− −	Teacher criticized student behavior.
Question	?	Teacher asked question.
No response	00	Teacher ignored student question/behavior.

Figure 4.4 Recording symbols SOURCE: Adapted from Good, T. L., and Brophy, J. E. (1987). *Looking in Classrooms.* New York: Harper and Row, Publishers.

Interactions are an important feature of effective teaching.

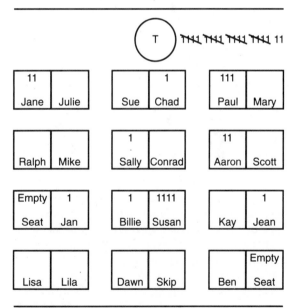

Figure 4.5 Simple form of interaction analysis (circle represents the student teacher)

Although this record shows how often the student teacher talks compared with the students, it does not reveal how long each talked.

A somewhat more detailed form of this technique is for the supervisor to sit at the back of the room and record on a form, such as that shown in Figure 4.5, the number of times each person speaks. Again, the class seating chart can be used to record this type of data.

The two techniques just described can be refined to yield more information by recording who is talking at regular intervals (for example, every three, five, or ten seconds). This variation has the advantage of providing information on which persons are interacting, how often they interact, and approximately how long each person speaks.

Another technique that makes use of the seating chart yields a somewhat more sophisticated interaction. This analysis uses a simple coding system that identifies each student the teacher speaks to and defines the nature of the interaction. The supervisor then records each interaction of the student teacher with the class or with individual students. This system provides information relative to equal access and success in the classroom. Often, shy or less able students are lost in the urgent eagerness of a few to participate. A simple example of this system is shown in Figure 4.6. Once recorded, a summary chart (Figure 4.7) should be completed independently by each triad member who analyzes the data for patterns and prepares recommendations based upon his or her analysis.

One of the most sophisticated and best-known interaction analysis techniques is the Flanders analysis system (Amidon, Casper, and Flanders 1985). This system is commonly taught to supervisors who want to view typical patterns of verbal exchange in the classroom. The Flanders Interaction Analysis System is concerned only with verbal behavior. In the Flanders system, classroom verbal interaction is divided into the ten categories listed in Figure 4.8. By memorizing and practicing the code, the supervisor needs only to write down a single number to represent a type of verbal activity. To conduct an observation and analysis, the observer records the category of action present in the classroom every three seconds or whenever a change in category occurs. Then, at the conclusion of the observation, the observer arranges the records into a ten-by-ten matrix for further analysis (Figure 4.9). A detailed analysis of the matrix reveals the dynamics of the classroom and the general classroom atmosphere. Computations carried out with the matrix data (Figure 4.9) indicate the percent of teacher talk and the percent of student talk in the

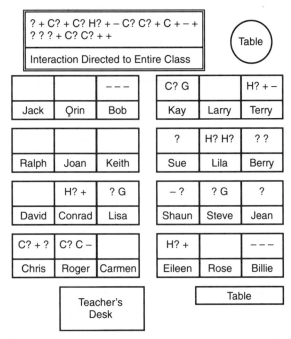

Legend:

? = Knowledge-level questions (direct questions): require a right answer, simple recall of facts.

H? = Higher cognitive questions: require students to think, apply, interpret, analyze, synthesize, create, or evaluate.

C? = Checks for understanding: require students to show that they understand the content or procedures of the lesson.

+ = Praise or acknowledgment: student's academic responses, actions, or products are praised or acknowledged.

C = Correction: student's academic responses or products are wrong, and teacher corrects them.

G = Guided correction: student's academic responses or products are wrong or incomplete, and teacher guides, probes, restates.

– = Reprimand: teacher reprimands behavior.

Figure 4.6 Interaction seating chart

classroom. Distinct and informative comparisons can be made among response comments (categories 1, 2, 3), which indicate an indirect style of teaching, and initiation remarks (categories 5, 6, 7), which reflect a direct style of teaching.

The ratio of the indirect to the direct (I/D) categories gives an indication of whether the student teacher's overall approach is indirect or

		Class	Individuals	Total
Number of students in class. ___24___

Number of students spoken to. ___15___

Where were the students spoken to sitting? ___Mainly right side___

Where were the students not spoken to sitting? ___Left side, back___

	Class	Individuals	Total
Number of direct questions asked?	4	7	11
Number of checks for understanding?	7	3	10
Number of open-ended questions?	1	5	6
Number of guides?	0	3	3
Number of praises?	9	4	13
Number of reprimands?	2	9	11

Figure 4.7 Summary of seating chart interaction observation

direct. The "asking questions" (category 4) are not labeled either direct or indirect. When this category is eliminated, a revised I/D gives insight about whether the student teacher's approach to motivation and control is direct or indirect. Additional data may be gleaned from the matrix. For example:

1. How much time does the student teacher spend lecturing? (column 5)
2. Do students resist the student teacher's influence? (cells 6–7 and 7–6)
3. Does the student teacher accept, clarify, and use student emotions? (category 1)
4. Does the student teacher use and extend student ideas? (cell 3–3)

For information on other insights that can be gained from an analysis of the interaction matrix, see the Amidon, Casper, and Flanders Training Manual (see Bibliography). The use of the Flanders Interaction Analysis System gives supervisors (1) the ability to draw conclusions about the verbal classroom climate and (2) the ability to make inferences about the communication strategies fostered in the classroom.

The time between recorded observations in the Flanders Interaction Analysis System can be modified somewhat so that more time is made available for recording notes related to observa-

tions and to allow more time for diversity in the student teacher activities. Depending on the time desired for note taking and the total time of the observation session, the time between recorded observations can be set between 10 and 30 seconds. The Flanders System is a complex technique to use. Therefore, some supervisors use a simplified version of it. In this version, the observer records the interaction going on in the classroom on a form, such as shown in Figure 4.10, but does not arrange the tallies in a matrix. This simplified version does not give as clear a view of the classroom as does the application of the complete system.

The Flanders Interaction Analysis System gives an excellent overview of the verbal interaction in the classroom, which should reveal some important insights into the student teacher's teaching. In addition, the Flanders System is quite useful in making student teachers aware of the tendency for teachers to dominate classroom discussions and interactions. However, to get an even better picture of the classroom climate, an analysis of the nonverbal classroom interactions can be conducted.

For the student teacher to have an accurate picture of the total interaction pattern requires an awareness of the nonverbal communication that is often continual in the classroom. An awareness of

TEACHER TALK	**INDIRECT INFLUENCE**	1. *Accepts Feeling: Accepting and clarifying the feeling tone of students in a nonthreatening manner. Feelings may be positive or negative. Predicting or recalling feelings is included.
		2. *Praises or Encourages: Praising or encouraging student action or behavior. Jokes that release tension, but not at the expense of another individual; nodding head, or saying "um hm?" or "go on" are included.
		3. *Accepts or Uses Ideas: Clarifying, building, or developing ideas suggested by a student. As more of the teacher's own ideas come into play, shift to Category 5.
		4. *Asks Questions: Asking a question about content or procedure with the intent that a student answer.
	DIRECT INFLUENCE	5. *Lectures: Giving facts or opinions about content or procedures; expressing the teacher's own ideas, asking rhetorical questions.
		6. *Gives Directions: Giving directions, commands, or orders with which a student is expected to comply.
		7. *Criticizes or Justifies Authority: Making statements intended to change student behavior from unacceptable to acceptable pattern; bawling out someone; stating why the teacher is doing what he/she is doing; extreme self-reference.
STUDENT TALK		8. *Responds: Talk by students in response to teacher. Teacher initiates the contact or solicits student statement.
		9. *Initiates: Talk by students, which they initiate. If "calling on" student is only to indicate who may talk next, observer must decide whether student wanted to talk. If so, use this category.
		10. *Silence or Confusion: Pauses, short periods of silence, and periods of confusion in which communication cannot be understood by the observer.

* There is NO scale implied by these numbers. Each number is classificatory; it designates a particular kind of communication event. To write these numbers down during observation is to enumerate—not to judge a position on a scale.

Figure 4.8 Summary of categories for Flanders interaction analysis SOURCE: Amidon, E. J., Flanders, N. A., and Casper, I. G. (1985). *The Role of the Teacher in the Classroom*, 3rd ed. St. Paul, Minn.: Paul S. Amidon & Associates, Inc., p. 8. Used by permission.

the messages being sent by the student teacher helps him or her better understand what the students' silent messages mean. The student teacher should be aware that students have learned to be adept at reading the nonverbal messages of their teachers. Therefore, it is important that the student teacher learn to send appropriate nonverbal messages.

An instrument, adapted form the work of Flanders, for recording nonverbal behaviors has been

Second

	1	2	3	4	5	6	7	8	9	10	
1	1				1				1		
2		4	1					2			
3		1	6	1				2			
4			1	14				5			
5	1				48			6			
6						1		4			
7							4		1		
8		2	2	5	6	4		11			
9	1						1		9	1	
10									1	2	Matrix Total
TOTAL	3	7	10	20	55	5	5	30	12	3	150
%	2	4.5	6.5	13.5	36.5	3.5	3.5	20	8	2	

First

Teacher Talk
Columns 1–7 = 105
105 ÷ 150 = 70%

Indirect (1–4) ÷ Direct (5–7) = I/D Ratio
$$40 \div 65 = \frac{40}{65} = .61$$

Student Talk
Columns 8–9 = 42
42 ÷ 150 = 28%

Indirect (1–3) ÷ Direct (6–7) = Revised I/D Ratio
$$20 \div 10 = \frac{20}{10} = 2.0$$

Figure 4.9 Flanders interaction matrix analysis SOURCE: Amidon, E. J., Flanders, N. A., and Casper, I. G. (1985). *The Role of the Teacher in the Classroom,* 3rd ed. St. Paul, Minn.: Paul S. Amidon & Associates, Inc., p. 22. Used by permission.

Category	Tallies
1. Accepts feelings	
2. Praises or encourages	
3. Accepts or uses ideas of students	
4. Asks questions	
5. Lectures	
6. Gives directions	
7. Criticizes	
8. Student response	
9. Student initiation	
10. Silence or confusion	

Figure 4.10 Simplified version of Flanders form

developed by Love and Roderick (1971). The Love-Roderick Scale is presented in Table 4.2. Notice that some of the categories are the same as those in the Flanders Interaction Analysis System. This scale can be completed by the supervisor, identifying items that need to be improved.

Summary

Supervisors are required to make judgments and decisions regarding the skills and progress of their student teachers. The validity of these judgments and decisions depends to a large extent on the ability to collect accurate data and to reach valid conclusions based on the data. Therefore, skill at being an observer and making valid observations are an essential skill for supervisors.

There are basically three types of data: valued data, descriptive data, and reproduced data. The best type of data to collect depends on the situation and the intended use of the information.

Structured observation offers techniques for improving the supervisor's ability to make valid observations. The use of structured observation depends on the following subskills: (1) the ability to collect the type of data best suited for the purpose of the observation, (2) the ability to differentiate between behaviors and inferences, and (3) the ability to plan for the observational experience with respect to the setting and the time.

There are four different approaches that can be used to gather information on the actions and behaviors of student teachers. First, supervisors can make a verbatim record of the exact interactions in the classroom. Second, a checklist can be used to record the desired information. Third, symbols and a seating chart can be used to record desired information. Finally, verbal and nonverbal interaction patterns of classroom behaviors and actions can be collected and analyzed.

Attention to the observation techniques covered in this chapter should make one a better supervisor. As a result, the supervisor will be of greater assistance to the student teacher working in his or her classroom.

Questions and Discussion Topics

1. Which information-gathering technique would be the most beneficial for use with a student teacher who wanted to improve his or her teaching effectiveness; communication skills; human relations skills?
2. Develop a checklist that can be used to gather information on the teaching effectiveness of a student teacher.
3. Develop a seating chart and symbols that could be used to gather specific information related to the student teacher and student behaviors in the classroom.
4. What are some strengths and weaknesses of the Flanders Interaction Analysis System?; the Love-Roderick Scale?

Table 4.2
Love-Roderick Scale of Nonverbal Analysis

To record observational data, circle the appropriate words in the right column that describe the student teacher's nonverbal behavior in the classroom during a ten-minute period.

1. *Accepts student behavior	Smiles, affirmatively nods head, pats on the back, places hand on shoulder or head
2. *Displays student ideas	Places index finger and thumb together, claps, raises eyebrows and smiles, nods head affirmatively and smiles
3. Displays student ideas	Writes comments on board, puts students' work on bulletin board, holds up papers, secures nonverbal student demonstration
4. Shows interest in student behavior	Establishes and maintains eye contact
5. Moves to facilitate student-to-student interaction	Physically moves into position of group member, physically moves away from the group
6. *Gives directions to students	Points with hand, raises hand, reinforces numerical aspects by showing the number of fingers, extends arms forward and beckons with hand, points to students for answers
7. Shows authority toward students	Frowns, stares, raises eyebrows, taps foot, throws book on desk, shakes head, walks or looks toward deviant, walks or looks away from deviant
8. Focuses students' attention on important points	Uses pointer, walks toward person or object, taps on something, thrusts head forward, employs nonverbal movement to give emphasis to a verbal statement
9. Demonstrates/illustrates	Performs a physical skill, manipulates materials/media, illustrates verbal statement with nonverbal action
10. Ignores or rejects a student's behavior	Lacks nonverbal response when one is ordinarily expected

*The names of these categories are the same as those in the Flanders Interaction Analysis System

SOURCE: Love, A. M., and Roderick, J. A. (1971, October). Teacher nonverbal communication: The development and field testing of an awareness unit. *Theory Into Practice,* 295–296. Used by permission.

CHAPTER 5

Legality and Ethics

CHAPTER KEY CONCEPTS

Defamation
Due Process
Ethics
Expulsion

Libel
Slander
Suspension
Tort Liability

Overview

The legal responsibilities of teachers, associated with teaching, have generally been well defined by the statutes of most states. However, the legal status of student teachers in many states is still unclear.

Student teachers are professionals and, as such, should act appropriately. They should use school law as a guide to develop a professional code of behavior and adhere to it.

This chapter focuses on the legal aspects of the classroom. The selection of cooperating teachers is examined, as well as the legal status of student teachers and pupils. Without a knowledge of the rights of student teachers and pupils, supervisors are ill-equipped to protect and guide the professional development of the student teachers with whom they work.

Objectives

Upon completing your study of chapter 5, you should be able to:

1. Discuss the current state of regulations related to being selected and serving as a cooperating teacher and the status of incentives associated with this function.
2. Explain the legal status of student teachers as outlined in the statutes of various states.
3. Define tort liability and explain its application to student teachers.
4. Discuss policies related to using student teachers as substitute teachers.
5. Define libel and slander and explain how cooperating teachers and student teachers can protect themselves from potential libel and slander charges.
6. Outline the steps that cooperating teachers should follow to protect themselves from professional liability.
7. Discuss the rights of pupils related to freedom of expression, suspension and expulsion, search and seizure, and appearance.
8. Discuss the importance and content of a code of ethics to the student teaching process.
9. Outline a possible code of ethics for student teachers.

What legal requirements do states have for serving as a cooperating teacher? What is the legal status of student teachers? Can student teachers be used as substitute teachers? Because we live in a legalistic society, such legal questions related to student teaching are important to those individuals involved in the experience.

Legal Requirements of Cooperating Teachers

The most important member of the student teaching team is the cooperating teacher (Guyton 1989). Indeed, student teachers often contend that during student teaching they learn the most from their cooperating teachers. It is the cooperating teacher who is present every day to give the student teacher feedback on how well he or she is doing as a teacher. Because cooperating teachers are so important to the success of the student teaching process, it is important that quality teachers be selected to serve this important function. To be effective, this quality selection process should be mandated by state education departments. The teachers should be compensated to some extent; however, this is often not the case.

Selection of Cooperating Teachers

States have issued varying regulations regarding the selection of cooperating teachers. Indeed, most states have few requirements for being named a cooperating teacher or generally leave the selection process to training institutions (Guyton 1989). Some states, however, do have teaching experience requirements, while others also require some form of supervisory training.

Haberman and Harris (1982) found that twenty-four out of fifty states have no mandated requirements, sixteen out of twenty-six states required two or three years of teaching experience, three states required a masters degree, and nine states required a supervision course. However, these mandated requirements have been modified somewhat in recent years. For example, some states now require that cooperating teachers hold a supervisory certificate or be given inservice supervisory training before being assigned a student teacher.

State departments of education have not addressed sufficiently the issue of quality in cooperating teacher selection. When training is provided, it most often is some form of orientation to the institution's programs, and the most prevalent means for providing this orientation is through written materials; that is, they are mailed a student teacher handbook.

Compensation for Cooperating Teachers

It is not uncommon for teacher training institutions to offer incentives to either school districts or cooperating teachers for working with their student teachers. In fact, seven states have mandated such incentives. These incentives usually take the form of monetary compensation or graduate course tuition fee waivers. The monetary compensation generally ranges from 25 to 1,000 dollars; while the tuition fee waivers vary from less than 100 to several 100 dollars depending on whether the institution is public or private. Generally, teachers who receive tuition fee waivers are given the option of using them or selling them for whatever they can get.

Legal Status of Student Teachers

Student teachers often hold an ambiguous legal status within the classroom. In fact, there is much variance in the treatment of this subject among states. Some states have legal provisions for student teachers; three examples are North Dakota, Indiana, and North Carolina. The North Dakota statutes (1987) read:

> A student teacher is one who teaches in a regular classroom situation as part of the requirements in professional education.

The Indiana statutes (1969) are more explicit and stipulate that:

"Student Teacher" shall mean a college student enrolled at the College assigned by it to teach in the School Corporation, as part of his preparation for entering the teaching profession.

North Carolina statutes (1990) provide a definition of student teacher, as well as how the student teacher will be assigned. The statutes read:

A "student teacher" is any student enrolled in an institution of higher education approved by the State Board of Education for the preparation of teachers who is jointly assigned by that institution and a local board of education to student teach under the direction and supervision of a regularly employed certified teacher.

Several states make student teachers the legal recipients of the same rights and liabilities as certified and contracted teachers. For example, the Montana statutes (1987) state:

A student teacher, while serving such nonsalaried internship under the supervision of a certificated teacher, shall be accorded the same protection of the laws as that accorded a certificated teacher and shall, while acting as such student teacher, comply with all rules of the governing board of the district or public institution and the applicable provisions of 20-4-301 relating to the duties of teachers.

Similarly, the Florida statutes (1988) give student teachers the same rights as certified teachers but put a stipulation on them. The Florida statutes state:

A student who is enrolled in an institution of higher education approved by the state board for teacher training and who is jointly assigned by such institution of higher education and a school board to perform practice teaching under the direction of a regularly employed and certificated teacher shall be accorded the same protection of the laws as that accorded the certificated teacher while serving such supervised internship, except for the right to bargain collectively with employees of the school board.

Finally, Kansas and Rhode Island (Henry and Beasley 1982) require that student teachers apply for and be issued a student teaching certificate prior to student teaching.

It remains that the only stipulation in most states is that student teaching be completed in the presence of a regular, qualified teacher. Clearly, statutes related to student teaching are needed in these states. Even though many states have not formally provided statutes related to the legislation of student teaching, the fact that these states require student teaching for initial teaching certification legalizes student teaching to some extent. Those personnel involved in student teaching should seek information about the legal status of student teachers in their state.

Discipline Policies

Another area of concern and importance to student teachers will be state, district, and school discipline policies. Therefore, the cooperating teacher should advise his or her student teacher of these policies. Since many state statutes now forbid the use of corporal punishment, the cooperating teacher should be sure to discuss with the student teacher the corporal punishment policy that is in effect at the school. In fact, it is recommended that student teachers be advised to avoid using any form of corporal punishment.

Student teachers must know their legal rights related to discipline. Such policies often reflect the organization and the procedures that are integrated into the classroom.

Professionalism

Regardless of the legal status that states give student teachers, they should learn to view themselves as professionals. As such, cooperating teachers should model the desirable attributes of a professional and provide student teachers with an understanding of what it means to be a professional. Thus, cooperating teachers should model appropriate dress, grooming, and behaviors.

Cooperating teachers should also model continued professional growth. This means that cooperating teachers should show student teachers methods for keeping up to date with teaching as a profession. In other words, they should make sure that student teachers become aware of district professional growth opportunities, refresher courses available at local universities or colleges, and research opportunities.

Cooperating teachers should try to inform student teachers about the various educational professional organizations. Professionalism calls for involvement in bringing improvement to the profession. Many teachers are able to influence the profession through involvement in professional organizations and are often inspired through such memberships.

Tort Liability

Tort liability can be defined as, "a civil (as distinguished from criminal) wrong arising out of a breach of duty that is imposed by law and not by contract" (Valente 1987). Tort law then applies to individuals who are negligent or at fault in the execution of their legal duty. Torts result from negligence and may be required to pay money damages to an injured party. Specific tort laws on negligence exist in most states.

Since tort liability states that individuals are responsible for their negligent acts, teachers are responsible for their actions in relation to their pupils. Thus, student teachers who can be viewed as enjoying the same rights as certified teachers are responsible for their actions toward the pupils with whom they are working. In effect, the fact that an individual is a student teacher does not absolve him or her from responsibility for her or her actions. Indeed, this responsibility is shown in the Kansas State Board of Education regulation (Henry and Beasley 1982) that states:

> Student teachers, while in the performance of their duties and responsibilities as student teachers, shall be legally liable for their own acts and conduct, and shall be afforded protection under the law, to the same extent as their cooperating teachers and other officers and employees of the school district.

Although the probability of a student teacher being sued is slim, state statutes make provisions for some protection. Essentially, student teachers are protected in some states by statutes that grant them the same protection as regularly certified teachers or that which is afforded to school district employees.

Teacher liability often extends beyond the classroom.

Accidents

Accidents are apt to happen during the usual events of the classroom. When such accidents or injuries occur and result in a suit, the court generally considers whether the person in charge exercised reasonable care and acted sensibly. Therefore, the cooperating teacher should be alert to conditions or actions that might lead to accidental injury in the classroom. For example, he or she should be alert to the student teacher who, for various reasons, has a tendency to leave the classroom unsupervised. Such conditions and actions should be discussed with the student teacher and corrective measures taken. This does not mean trying to curtail all activities that may result in injury or a law suit. It does mean, however, that the student teacher should extend the same degree of care for pupils that a reasonable and prudent person would show in similar circumstances.

Again, it is suggested that the cooperating teacher check the state liability policies related to student teachers and the liability insurance that is often available to student teachers. Many student professional societies (such as student education associations) carry liability insurance with membership.

Defamation

Torts of libel and slander are known as defamation (McCarthy and Cambron-McCabe 1987). Defamation is defined as the publication of false information that injures a person's reputation in society. Libel is written defamation, and slander is spoken defamation. Generally, there have been few defamation cases involving students. Most defamation cases in the schools involve teachers who challenge the evaluations placed in their personnel files or statements made by parents to school officials. Although the risk of defamation is always present, it is not a frequent basis of litigation in the schools.

Substitute Teaching

The question of using student teachers as substitute teachers (paid or unpaid) has gone unanswered by most states. However, a few states do give a definitive answer to the question. For example, Kansas statutes (Henry and Beasley 1982) read:

> Persons may not act as student teachers in the state of Kansas without valid student teaching certificates. Certificated student teachers are prohibited from serving as regular or substitute teachers in Kansas schools while performing student teaching.

Still other states stipulate the number of days that a student teacher can be used as a substitute. Nebraska statutes, for instance, state that a student teacher can be used as a substitute for two days, while Indiana statutes limit the number of days to one only.

Many institutions have regulations that discourage or forbid the use of student teachers as substitute teachers. Indeed, these institutions require that an authorized substitute be assigned to any classroom when the regularly assigned cooperating teacher is absent.

The diversity of the regulations regarding the use of student teachers as substitute teachers is often complex and unclear. It may even vary within a state due to the regulations of different universities or due to policy differences among school districts. If cooperating teachers are uncertain about what policies exist in their district, they should seek clarification before any consideration is given to using a student teacher as a substitute.

Law and Unacceptable Evaluation

Occasionally, a student teacher must be given a poor grade or must be removed from the classroom because of unacceptable conduct or performance. In such cases, cooperating teachers should take the correct legal steps to avoid professional liability. In short, they must protect themselves from libel and make sure that the student teacher is given due process.

As noted earlier, libel can be defined as a false or intentional written statement or graphic that puts a person's reputation up to disgrace, ridicule, or contempt. When a negative performance evaluation must be written about a student teacher, the cooperating teacher must take care that he or she protects himself or herself from potential libel charges. Helm (1982) offers five suggestions for minimizing the chance of charges of libel:

1. Write statements of fact rather than opinion, and write objective rather than subjective descriptions of the student teacher's behavior.
2. Limit the information recorded to that which is relevant to or affects the student teacher's performance in the classroom.

3. Avoid public disclosures about the student teacher's deficiencies.
4. Avoid any verbal or nonverbal suggestions of malice or intent of harm.
5. Limit the likelihood of bad faith or ill will charges by communicating a concern both for the student teacher's welfare and the school's welfare.

To avoid personal liability, professionals must follow due process procedures when dealing with unsatisfactory student teacher performance. Basically, this is a four-step process. First, the behaviors associated with the problems should be well-documented with frequent observations and follow-up conferences that address needed changes. Second, a *written* objective description of the problems and statements of expected changes should be provided for the student teacher, the principal, and the university supervisor. These notifications should be provided by the middle of the student teaching experience and should outline exactly what is to be done to improve the classroom performance. The third step is to collect additional data relative to the problem areas. Frequent observations with adequate follow-up conference discussions should be completed. The collected data should be carefully analyzed and discussed. Finally, if the required improvements are not forthcoming, the appropriate grade should be submitted. In extreme cases where the student teacher's actions are detrimental to the pupils, he or she should be removed from the classroom.

Student teachers removed from the classroom should have the opportunity to appeal the decision. For example, the student teacher could present his or her case to a special appeals committee consisting of university and public school personnel.

The key to due process is documentation. Written documentation with open dialogue related to all issues should be presented to all involved parties.

Rights of Students

Student teachers, like all classroom teachers, must deal with the legal rights of pupils. Without a knowledge of these rights, the student teacher will be ill-equipped to be a fully functioning teacher.

Freedom of Expression

Pupils, as well as teachers, do not forfeit their rights when they enter the school building (Strahan and Turner 1987, p. 220). In short, they retain their rights to freedom of speech or expression. For example, the pupils' publication of a school paper enjoys constitutional protection as long as it does not pose the threat of school disruption, is not libelous, and is not judged vulgar or obscene.

Suspension and Expulsion

A suspension is often defined as a temporary exclusion, ten days or fewer, whereas an expulsion refers to exclusion from school for ten days or more. Expulsions can be for as long as a semester or a school year. Generally, the court has ruled that pupils have the legal right to an education that cannot be taken away without due process. As a result, every state has outlined the procedure that a school must follow in the suspension and expulsion of pupils. However, since expulsion is more severe, it requires a more extensive due process procedure. O'Reilly and Green (1983) suggest the following criteria when expulsion is being considered:

1. Notice of charges be given to pupil,
2. Pupil be granted right to counsel,
3. Pupil be granted the right of a hearing before an impartial tribunal,
4. Pupil has the right to avoid self-incrimination,
5. Evidence must be presented against the pupil,
6. Accused has the right to cross-examine any witnesses,

7. Witnesses must testify,
8. Accused has the burden of proof,
9. Record of the hearing must be kept, and
10. Pupil has the right to appeal. (pp. 148–150)

Search and Seizure

The key to search and seizure is reasonable cause (McCarthy and Cambron-McCabe 1987; Strahan and Turner 1987). If you can show that there was reasonable cause for a search (body search or locker search), a search is not considered illegal. For example, if you see someone exchanging drugs, and/or other students report that the individual sells drugs, this would likely be considered reasonable cause for a locker search. However, strip searches are considered to be unconstitutional, and rightly so.

A locker search can be justified under certain conditions.

Appearance

The issue that has generated the most controversy, and the most court cases, in recent years has been dress codes and hair styles. Generally, the courts' reaction to these issues has been mixed. On the one hand, they have upheld the rights of schools to have dress codes as long as they are reasonable and clear, and pupils are aware of the regulations. Conversely, when challenged, the rulings have suggested that schools may not control what pupils wear unless it is immodest and disruptive. Rulings on hair styles have varied from location to location, and they tend to grant freedom of choice regarding hair styles.

Professional Ethics

Ethics is the realm of value that relates to good and bad. Ethics deals with the criteria of conduct in our lives and motivation of conduct. Student teaching is a time during which student teachers should further refine their ethics and develop their professional integrity. To this end, it is necessary that student teachers, cooperating teachers, and university supervisors accept certain ethical tenets. Student teachers, in fulfilling the expectations of their roles, should adhere to the following ethical tenets:

1. Student teachers should recognize that cooperating teachers hold the final responsibilities for the classroom instruction.
2. Student teachers should act as professional practitioners and keep confidential all information concerning the schools and the pupils.
3. Student teachers should be available at the appointed time for conferences.
4. Student teachers should serve as physical, mental, intellectual, moral, and ethical examples to pupils.
5. Student teachers should deal sympathetically with pupils without prejudice or partiality.
6. Student teachers should recognize their duties, responsibilities, and privileges.
7. Student teachers should respect the professional rights and personal dignity of cooperating teachers and other staff members, university supervisors, and student observers in the classroom situation.
8. Student teachers show pride in and consider themselves members of the profession.

9. Student teachers as learners should keep up to date on professional matters and current affairs.

Cooperating teachers also have ethical considerations that they should follow in guiding and working with student teachers in the classrooms. These ethical considerations include:

1. Cooperating teachers should give student teachers the necessary help and guidance to promote maximum growth.
2. Cooperating teachers should give student teachers the opportunity to make suggestions and contributions to the welfare of the class.
3. Cooperating teachers should give student teachers the opportunity to teach.
4. Cooperating teachers should share their ideas and materials with student teachers.
5. Cooperating teachers should provide time for conferences and planning.

Finally, university supervisors, in fulfilling the expectations of the role, should adhere to the following:

1. University supervisors should recognize that student teachers are self-fulfilling individuals with ideas, talents, interests, and goals of their own.
2. University supervisors should realize that the welfare and instruction of the pupils takes precedence over student teachers in classrooms.
3. University supervisors should always respect the judgment of cooperating teachers in matters affecting the instructional program of pupils.
4. University supervisors should refrain from criticism of any kind that reflects on cooperating teachers and administrators; and supervisors should not permit such criticism from student teachers.
5. University supervisors should refrain from criticizing the school, its program, and its administration policies.

Student teachers should develop their own code of ethics. According to Lanier and Cusick (1985, p. 711), an oath is needed so that education students can express their feelings of dedication and professionalism. This code should entail a series of reciprocal responsibilities (pupils and student teachers) and expectations. Roles and responsibilities must be assumed, expectations established, and guidelines set for meaningful and mutually beneficial experiences. Basic to such ethical practices are openness, honesty, mutual respect, and understanding. In other words, student teachers should conduct themselves as professionals at all times.

Lanier and Cusick (1985, p. 711) suggest that a code of ethics should include four elements, including: (1) a dedication to the profession of education and to the ideals of the profession, (2) a dedication to students, (3) a belief in democratic principles, and (4) a belief in equal opportunity for political, social, and economic equality and that education leads to that opportunity. An oath with these elements would help education students better understand and internalize the value of the career that they have undertaken.

Student teachers should live by a personal code of ethics. Such a code can be developed by the student teacher or can be adopted from existing codes such as the American Federation of Teachers (AFT) Code of Ethics presented in Figure 5.1 or the code of the National Education Association (NRA) presented in Figure 5.2. No matter what their personal code of ethics or beliefs may be, all professional educators should adhere to and are liable to the AFT and NEA Code of Ethics.

Summary

School laws and state regulations are established and enforced to protect the rights of all individuals who are involved in the education process. Cooperating teachers, student teachers, pupils, and parents are guaranteed the right to practice

I. TEACHER–STUDENT COMMITMENT

1. The teacher works to develop each student's potential as a worthy and effective citizen.
2. The teacher works objectively to stimulate the spirit of inquiry, the acquisition of knowledge and understanding, and the thoughtful formulation of worthy goals in each of his students for their advancement.
3. The teacher works to develop and provide sound and progressively better educational opportunities for all students.

II. TEACHER–PUBLIC COMMITMENT

1. The teacher believes that patriotism in its highest form requires dedication to the principles of our democratic heritage.
2. The teacher shares with all other citizens the responsibility for the develoment of sound public policy and assumes full political and citizenship responsibilities.
3. The teacher has the privilege and the responsibility to enhance the public image of his school in order to create a positive community atmosphere which will be beneficial to education.

III. TEACHER–PROFESSION COMMITMENT

1. The teacher believes that the quality of his service in the education profession directly influences the nation and its citizens.
2. The teacher exerts every effort to raise professional standards, to improve a climate in which the exercise of professional judgment is encouraged, and to achieve conditions which attract persons worthy of the trust to careers in education.
3. The teacher urges active participation and support in professional organizations and their programs.

IV. TEACHER–DISTRICT COMMITMENT

1. The teacher strives to do the job for which he was hired to do, with honesty and to the best of his
2. ability.
The teacher pledges to communicate this code, along with a positive attitude toward it, to all
3. teachers.
The teacher disacourages the breaching of this code and requests that all charges be presented in writing to the Union Executive Board for their deliberation and judgment.

Figure 5.1 Code of ethics of the American Federation of Teachers, AFL-CIO (Adopted February 10, 1971) SOURCE: American Federation of Teachers, AFL-CIO. Reprinted by permission.

and promote the education of pupils in a safe and acceptable environment.

Cooperating teachers must give student teachers guidance about their legal status. That is, they must have a working knowledge of professional liability and their right to due process.

Cooperating teachers must sometimes give poor evaluations or remove a student teacher from the classroom. In such cases, it is important to follow the correct procedures and avoid professional liability. Moreover, it is important to follow due process procedures in cases of unacceptable performance.

Pupils, like teachers, have rights. Within certain limits, they have freedom of expression, the right to due process in cases of suspension and expulsion, freedom from search and seizure without cause, and freedom of dress and hair style.

Student teachers need to internalize a code of ethics that entails a set of responsibilities for both pupils and themselves. Ethics practices such as openness, honesty, mutual respect, and understanding should be an integral part of a student teacher's code of ethics.

Questions and Discussion Topics

1. Obtain a copy of state school statutes. What do these documents say about teacher responsibilities; teacher rights; student rights? Do the statutes address the legal status of student teachers?
2. Obtain a copy of a local school district's teacher and student handbooks. Do these handbooks address the rights and responsibilities of teachers of pupils?
3. Should schools have a pupil dress code and a teacher dress code? Should schools have hair style regulations for pupils and teachers? Discuss the pros and cons of these issues.
4. Ask a lawyer to comment on the legal dimensions of teaching and the rights of teachers and pupils. Invite a lawyer to class to discuss these issues.

Preamble

The educator, believing in the worth and dignity of each human being, recognizes the supreme importance of the pursuit of truth, devotion to excellence, and the nurture of democratic principles. Essential to these goals is the protection of freedom to learn and to teach and the guarantee of equal educational opportunity for all. The educator accepts the responsibility to adhere to the highest ethical standards.

The educator recognizes the magnitude of the responsibility inherent in the teaching process. The desire for the respect and confidence of one's colleagues, of students, of parents, and of the members of the community provides the incentive to attain and maintain the highest possible degree of ethical conduct. The Code of Ethics of the Education Profession indicates the aspiration of all educators and provides standards by which to judge conduct.

The remedies specified by the NEA and/or its affiliates for the violation of any provision of this Code shall be exclusive, and no such provision shall be enforceable in any form other than one specifically designated by the NEA or its affiliates.

Principle I — Commitment to the Student

The educator strives to help each student realize his or her potential as a worthy and effective member of society. The educator, therefore, works to stimulate the spirit of inquiry, the acquisition of knowledge and understanding, and the thoughtful formulation of worthy goals.

In fulfillment of the obligation to the student, the educator:

1. Shall not unreasonably restrain the student from independent action in the pursuit of learning.
2. Shall not unreasonably deny the student access to varying points of view.
3. Shall not deliberately suppress or distort subject matter relevant to the student's progress.
4. Shall make reasonable effort to protect the student from conditions harmful to learning or to health and safety.
5. Shall not intentionally expose the student to embarrassment or disparagement.
6. Shall not on the basis of race, color, creed, sex, national origin, marital status, political or religious beliefs, family, social or cultural background, or sexual orientation, unfairly:
   a. Exclude any student from participation in any program.
   b. Deny benefits to any student.
   c. Grant any advantage to any student.
7. Shall not use professional relationships with students for private advantage.
8. Shall not disclose information about students obtained in the course of professional service, unless disclosure serves a compelling professional purpose or is required by law.

Figure 5.2 Code of ethics of the education profession SOURCE: Code of Ethics of the Education Profession, National Education Association, 1975. Reprinted by permission.

Principle II — Commitment to the Profession

The education profession is vested by the public with a trust and responsibility requiring the highest ideals of professional service.

In the belief that the quality of the services of the education profession directly influences the nation and its citizens, the educator shall exert every effort to raise professional standards, to promote a climate that encourages the exercise of professional judgment, to achieve conditions that attract persons worthy of the trust to careers in education, and to assist in preventing the practice of the profession by unqualified persons.

In fulfillment of the obligation to the profession, the educator:

1. Shall not in an application for a professional position deliberately make a false statement or fail to disclose a material fact related to competency and qualifications.
2. Shall not misrepresent his or her professional qualifications.
3. Shall not assist entry into the profession of a person known to be unqualified in respect to character, education, or other relevant attributes.
4. Shall not knowingly make a false statement concerning the qualifications of a candidate for a professional position.
5. Shall not assist a noneducator in the unauthorized practice of teaching.
6. Shall not disclose information about colleagues obtained in the course of professional service unless disclosure serves a compelling professional purpose or is required by law.
7. Shall not knowingly make false or malicious statements about a colleague.
8. Shall not accept any gratuity, gift, or favor that might impair or appear to influence professional decisions or actions.

Figure 5.2—*Continued* Code of ethics of the education profession SOURCE: Code of Ethics of the Education Profession, National Education Association, 1975. Reprinted by permission.

PART 2

THE SUPERVISION PROCESS

Supervision is one of the most critical aspects of the preparation process for preservice teachers. Supervision that focuses on the instructional activities within the classroom enables the student teacher to integrate years of college preparation into successful applications of instructional practices that will result in improved learning opportunities for students.

The initial chapter of Part 2, chapter 6, focuses on the models of supervision, with primary emphasis on the rationale and undergirding framework of Clinical Supervision. Further applications of this model reflect its philosophical commitment to the use of classroom-derived data as a basis for conferencing and improvement of the instructional process.

In addition, chapter 6 presents brief descriptions of other supervisory models that may be integrated with clinical supervision in a preservice teacher education program. These descriptions, along with identified weaknesses of each model, offer salient characteristics of each supervisory model and provide guidance for those planning to implement the model.

Supervision requires different expectations, roles, and activities for each member of the triad. Chapter 7 focuses on the university personnel, while chapters 8 and 9 address the roles and responsibilities of public school personnel and student teachers, respectively.

Evaluation of student teachers is a nebulous area. Chapter 10 provides guidelines for evaluation, along with criteria that distinguish between formative and summative evaluation. Guidelines for the use of each type of evaluation are included with suggestions for involving the student teacher, through self-analysis, in the evaluation process.

CHAPTER 6

Models of Supervision

CHAPTER KEY CONCEPTS

Accountable Supervision
Artistic Supervision
Clinical Supervision
Developmental Supervision
Instructional Supervision

Limits of Clinical Supervision
Scientific Supervision
Self-Assessment Supervision
Training Program

Overview

The determining factor in the initial success of any prospective teacher is the type and quality of supervision provided during the student teaching experience. Unfortunately, the relationship between the student teacher and those responsible for supervision—the public school teacher and the university personnel—can be adversarial and provides only summative evaluation.

This chapter provides guidelines for focusing on the involvement of the student teacher in the improvement of instruction. This involvement requires a different type of supervision from what is normally provided for student teachers. Through a type of supervision that encourages the active involvement of the student teacher in examining the instructional activities within the classroom, increased student learning is more likely to result.

Objectives

Upon completing your study of chapter 6, you should be able to:

1. Describe the attitude of most student teachers toward supervision and provide a rationale for this attitude.
2. Describe the underlying assumptions of clinical supervision.
3. Describe supervisory requirements for successful implementation of clinical supervision.
4. Describe the sequence necessary for clinical supervision by identifying the five steps of the clinical supervision model.
5. Describe briefly each of the five steps in the clinical supervision model.
6. Describe pitfalls and limitations of the clinical supervision model.
7. Describe other models of supervision, how they relate to clinical supervision, and how the principles of clinical supervision can be incorporated into each model.

Student teaching is the first opportunity for a prospective teacher to begin to move into a collaborative relationship with others in the teaching profession. To achieve this relationship, it is essential that there be a cooperative supervisory effort among the student teacher, the university supervisor, and the public school teacher.

Supervisory Skills

Student teaching represents an introduction to the concept of supervision. However, many student teachers do not like to be supervised. Indeed, this dislike of supervision often starts with the student teaching experience and follows most teachers throughout their careers. Wiles (1967) found that only 1.5 percent of 2,500 teachers perceive the supervisor as a source of new ideas. The results of this study were parallel to one by Cogan (1973) who found that many teachers view supervision as an active psychological threat. Other research found that supervision is an organizational ritual that does not play an important part in the professional lives of the teacher (Blumberg 1984). Krajewski (1976) found that most supervisors lack the necessary skills to adequately analyze teacher behavior in the classroom. Supervisors of student teachers as all supervisors, should develop and master a repertoire of supervisory skills. That is, they should develop the skills to link the needs of students, school systems, and student teachers. Proper development of such linkage helps the student teacher develop and maintain a positive attitude toward supervision.

Supervisors should possess certain skills that are critical for successful supervision. In fact, Katz (1974), identified the three essential supervisory domains as technical, human, and conceptual (how the supervisory process fits into the overall framework of the organization). Moreover, Franco (1985) identified six critical supervisory skills as giving feedback, planning, problem solving, assigning and monitoring work, setting standards, and handling performance problems.

Unless a person possesses these skills, success as a supervisor will be limited.

The development of effective supervisory skills requires an examination and analysis of supervisory actions that enable the supervisor to be a viable force in the improvement of instruction. Blumberg and Amidon (1965) found that supervisors who emphasize indirect behaviors tend to receive more positive ratings from those being supervised. Indirect communication is an example of one component of clinical supervision that would be viewed more positively by student teachers. In a supporting study by Shinn (1976), the supervision technique of teachers was compared with the actual supervisory techniques used. While all of the techniques of supervision were rated as worthwhile by the teachers, indirect supervisory activities such as, "Listens more than talks," "Acknowledges my comments," and "Gives praise and encouragement," were rated higher than direct communication. These indirect behaviors, which are an integral part of the clinical supervision process, provide a positive view of supervision that is not available with any method except clinical supervision. Thus, clinical supervision contains the type of supervisory activities that teachers find most effective.

A study by Martin (1975) showed that public school teachers who were trained in clinical supervision techniques viewed their own supervision (by a building administrator) as more positive and informative than those public school teachers who had no specialized preparation in clinical supervision. Martin's study also suggests that clinical supervision removes the mystique from supervision and enables the supervision process to become a useful process that aids in improving instruction within the classroom. Supervision should enable educational institutions to merge the needs of student teachers, public school teachers, students in the public school classroom, higher education institutions, and the public school systems. In doing so, it should allow the analysis of classroom instruction so that appropriate recommendations can be provided regarding the improvement of instruction. Such feedback enables student teachers to reach their potential and still meet the needs of others. The supervisory model most likely to help this occur is the Clinical Supervision Model.

Clinical Supervision

Clinical supervision, which focuses on the improvement of the student teacher's classroom instruction through the collection of records of what the student teacher and students do in the classroom during the teaching-learning process (Cogan 1973), is a term that is viewed with skepticism by many involved in teacher education programs. This suspicion is caused by the use of the word "clinical," which conjures images of some type of medical model, either physical or psychological, especially one in which the subjects are not exhibiting desirable behavior. Kilbourn (1982) described this situation by stating that there is some degree of confusion as to what clinical supervision entails, and the term itself brings to mind ambiguous and not always pleasant activities. In a supervisory context, the term "clinical" refers to the place where the supervision occurs—the classroom. Clinical supervision, developed by Cogan (1973), focuses on the point of application of pedagogical skills—the public school classroom. This face-to-face interaction within the classroom examines the actual behavior of the student teacher and students as events occur rather than examining this interaction from a distance.

Furthermore, Goldhammer (1969) advocates that clinical supervision should center on data from first-hand observation of actual teaching events. Supervision should focus on direct face-to-face interaction between the supervisor and the student teacher as teaching behaviors and activities are analyzed for the purpose of instructional improvement. This basic concept of clinical supervision is supported by Cogan (1973) who referred to this type of supervision as a profes-

The focus of supervision should be on classroom activities.

sional colleagueship that takes place between the supervisor and the student teacher.

Underlying Assumptions

Clinical Supervision is founded on some assumptions that provide the basis for all clinical supervision activities:

1. Student teachers are capable of analyzing their own teaching and providing input into ways to improve their teaching. For this to be most effective, student teachers should examine situations, behaviors, practices, effectiveness, and accomplishments. This process is called reflection (Valverde 1982) and is the foundation of reflective teaching. By asking, "What am I doing and why?" the student teacher establishes the practice of self-monitoring in a constructive and deliberate manner.

2. Teachers are the agents of change in the instructional process in the public schools. If there is to be real improvement in the teacher's intellectual and behavioral skills, this change must occur at the site of instruction. Curricular changes that occur outside the classroom, such as curriculum revision projects, are less effective than changes that focus on the instruction by

the classroom teacher. To implement this change, it is necessary to empower student teachers with a sense of destiny control that allows them to develop skills necessary for growth in the future.

3. Clinical supervision emphasizes student teacher growth instead of student teacher defects. Clinical supervision assumes that student teachers possess the drive and personal resources to solve their problems. The role of the supervisor is to help the student teacher identify and clarify problems, receive data from the supervisors, and use the skills of the supervisors to develop solutions.

4. Student teaching is the apex of a student's professional education career. The practical application of the knowledge base is essential to completing professional education and for later success as a teacher. Failure to provide closure and complete the professional education cycle destroys the sequential concept of moving from introductory field experiences through student teaching. Student teaching provides the capstone of the application of the knowledge base that undergirds a professional education program. Figure 6.1 contains a theoretical model of the knowledge base essential for professional education.

5. Supervisors must be present to observe. They cannot provide assistance without acknowledging the events that are occurring within the classroom. This presence of university supervisors and cooperating teachers is essential for the prospective teacher to achieve maximum growth as a student teacher.

6. The supervisors should provide feedback to guide and improve the instructional strategies of the student teacher. One primary purpose of evaluation is to provide feedback to guide future instructional endeavors. The supervisors should assume

the primary role of providing formative evaluation (to offer improvement) rather than summative evaluation (to make decisions or recommendations regarding grades and employment). However, all supervisors should accept the dual role requirement of many supervisory positions.

7. Clinical supervision of student teachers can improve instruction by using analyses of classroom teaching/learning through systematic interpretation of data. This requires the focus to be observational evidence rather than unsubstantiated evidence. This systematic, databased observation and interpretation of data is the basis of all interpretive judgments regarding instructional performance.

8. The relationship of the public schools and higher education can be enhanced through the use of a clinical supervision model. Historically, public schools have focused on the practical aspects of teaching; higher education has focused on the theoretical aspects of teaching. The use of clinical supervision can encourage collaboration through equal treatment of the supervisory and responsibility roles of public school teachers and higher education personnel. This collaboration can help alter the ambivalent view of supervision—it's a good idea but not for me—that is held by many public school teachers.

9. Clinical supervision, a student-teacher-centered process of verbal interaction based on the analysis of instruction, can bring about desired changes in student teacher behavior. The manipulation of instructional variables by applying principles of behavioral science in a social environment allows supervisors to assess forces, give weight to various events, and make applied practical professional judgments.

10. The structure of clinical supervision forces it to be ethical, unbiased, and sensitive. An effective evaluation system (Stufflebeam

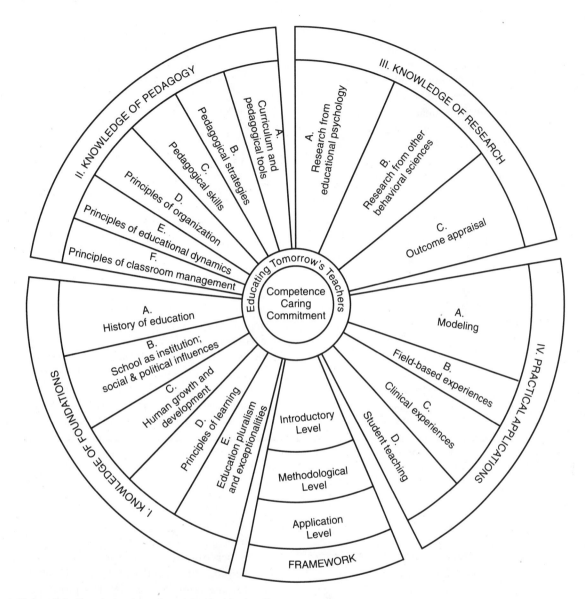

Figure 6.1 Knowledge base for professional education

1988) has bias control to prevent the information-gathering process from becoming distorted, which corrupts decisions, actions, and recommendations. This is because of the necessary phases of the clinical supervision process that allow student teachers to become aware of the system as well as to review data used in interpreting their performance. The training process that supervisors must undergo to become effective at clinical supervision provides added objectivity to the supervision process.

11. Clinical supervision, because of its feedback to student teachers as one of its

processes, encourages them to become more independent and less in need of guided practice. The joint responsibility of the university faculty member and the public school teacher is gradually lessened and replaced with greater responsibility assumed by the student teacher. Progress is measured in terms of how much support a student teacher needs to become proficient in solving a particular problem. Clinical supervision does not suddenly remove the support but encourages the student to become progressively more independent. This clinical supervision approach helps student teachers think more clearly and more creatively about the world and achieve a level of self-analysis and self-sufficiency that more clearly defines specific roles for all. A visual representation of this process is indicated in Figure 6.2

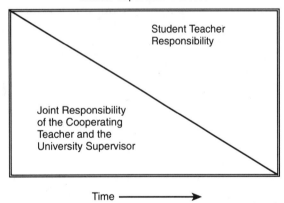

Clinical Supervision Process

Student Teacher Responsibility

Joint Responsibility of the Cooperating Teacher and the University Supervisor

Time ⟶

Figure 6.2 Increased student teacher responsibility model

Clinical Supervision Cycle

Clinical supervision is supervision that focuses on improvement in student teaching performance by analyzing teaching through a series of five sequential steps. These five steps are illustrated in Figure 6.3.

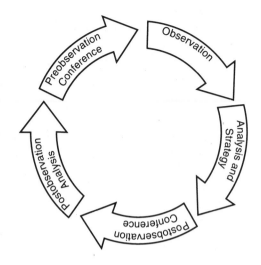

Figure 6.3 Clinical supervision cycle

The clinical model, which is founded on open communication among the university supervisor, the cooperating teacher, and the student teacher, reflects the concerns of student teachers. The model is based on the student teacher being provided with a service that focuses on the quality of instruction. This concern, expressed by modifying student teacher behavior through the use of classroom data, helps the student teacher engage in reflective teaching through self-analysis. Weller (1977) identified the following elements of clinical supervision:

1. Student teachers should learn specific intellectual and behavioral skills to improve instruction.
2. Supervisors should take responsibility for helping student teachers to develop skills for analyzing the instructional process, based on systematic data.
3. Supervisors should emphasize what and how the student teacher teaches: to improve instruction—not to change the student teacher's personality.
4. Planning and analysis should center on making and testing instructional hypotheses based on observational evidence.

5. Conferences should deal with a few instructional issues that are important, relevant to the student teacher, and amenable to change.
6. The feedback conference should concentrate on constructive analysis and the reinforcement of successful patterns rather than on the condemnation of unsuccessful patterns.
7. Feedback should be based on observational evidence, rather than on unsubstantiated value judgments.
8. The cycle of planning, observation, and analysis should be continual and cumulative.
9. Supervision is a dynamic process of give-and-take in which supervisors and student teachers are colleagues in search of mutual educational understanding.
10. The supervisory process is centered primarily on the analysis of instruction.
11. Individual student teachers have both the freedom and the responsibility to initiate issues, analyze and improve their own teaching style, and develop personal teaching styles.
12. Supervision can be perceived, analyzed, and improved in much the same manner as teaching can.
13. Supervisors have both the freedom and the responsibility to analyze and evaluate their own supervision in a manner similar to teachers' analysis and evaluation of their instruction.

The clinical supervision cycle requires the full use of five interdependent steps to ensure that student teachers achieve at their full potential. Failure to adequately develop the skills necessary at any one level breaks the chain of continuity and lessens the impact of clinical supervision and the positive effect it has on the student teacher. However, some clinical supervision supporters find that most failures to reach the full potential are due to a lack of preparation skills on the part of the university personnel and public school teachers.

Each step in the clinical supervision process and supporting information explain additional skills needed in a specific step in the clinical supervision cycle.

Preobservation conference The most controversial part of clinical supervision is the preobservation conference. Hunter (1980) maintains that a preobservation conference is too time-consuming and creates both supervisor and teacher bias; these conferences fail in their primary function, which is the building of rapport between those supervising and student teachers. Conversely, Lordon (1986) maintains that the preobservation conference is a key ingredient in orienting supervisors to the variabilities in student teachers' assignments. That is, by asking questions about pupils and clarifying the roles of those supervising, the preobservation conference establishes a common frame of reference for the planning of the observation. A basic requisite to successfully implementing clinical supervision is to establish or reestablish rapport between the student teacher and those supervising. Once this rapport has been established, they can cooperatively identify the specific categories of student teacher or student behavior that are to provide the structure of the observation. Because the results of the observations will be categorized according to what is collaboratively agreed upon, serious consideration should be given to these categories.

Student teachers often have concerns about the specific categories that should be observed. Supervisors, based on experiences as teachers and any personal knowledge of the student teacher, are usually able to provide input into specific categories. Although these categories may be determined by implementing the knowledge base through the instructional model, some typical categories might be sequencing, motivation, active student participation, evaluation techniques, and learning modalities. Care should be taken in assuming supervisory roles. Some supervisors develop a personal interest in the success of the student teacher and try to increase the likelihood that the student teacher will have success. Indeed, at times this desire for success can be so intense that there is the tendency to provide too much structure. The student teacher interprets this structure as increased requirements and becomes overwhelmed by the process and, therefore, becomes dysfunctional.

Effective supervision requires a cooperative endeavor of all involved.

Another common focus of the preobservation session is the examination of the lesson plans to be implemented during the observation. An understanding of the student teacher's lesson plan, so that the student teacher can implement it according to his/her references or so the supervisors can modify according to their reference, provides a common base for dialogue in planning. Any changes requested by the supervisors must be consistent with the student teacher's constructural framework if the improvement of instruction is to be successful. The student teacher should provide the supervisors with information about the decisions that led to the development of the lesson to be observed. This should include the student teacher's rationale for planning the lesson format and subsequent activities. The student teacher should go over the plans step-by-step and explain the rationale for including each activity. Many student teacher ideas that occur without any type of advance planning will not be successful. In other words, successful teaching doesn't "just happen." Indeed, Moore (1989) suggests that effective teachers often appear not to plan, but they very probably have indeed—formally or informally—carefully planned lessons. Problems, either in knowledge or discipline, are usually based on a lack of explicit understanding of the relationship among components of a successful lesson. Discussion of specific topics such as objectives, teaching strategies, specific learner characteristics that may impede the lesson, and the method of evaluation to be used to measure the objectives can provide information regarding what observational data needs to be collected. Moreover, such discussion may result in alternate approaches being selected for use in the instructional sequence.

One area of lesson planning that deserves critical examination by the supervisors and the student teacher is the questioning to be used in the lesson. Through the process of discussing the exact wording of questions, a supervisor can help a student avoid the pitfall of having an entire lesson struggle because the opening of the lesson failed to achieve a highly developed response from the pupils. Rather than place the student teacher in the potentially difficult position of choosing between a meaningless question that can be answered in one word and a highly complex question that may not be answered, together they can formulate a questioning strategy to enhance the lesson. This lessens the danger of imposing requirements that are too stringent for the student teacher, while maintaining acceptable pedagogical practices.

Other preobservation conference topics for discussion include the method of data collection (audio, video, or script), what is to be done with the collected data, tasks for the supervisor and the student teacher, and what research on the instructional process the student teacher plans to employ in the lesson. The inclusion of research implications allows the student teacher to move from theory to practice by implementing knowledge-based research from areas such as reinforcement theories, success rates of students, time-on-task, positive feedback to students, classroom logistics, or a myriad of other specific strategies that the student teacher should apply. As a closing activity in the preobservation conference, the supervisor and student teacher should develop understandings about the procedures in the rest of the clinical observation cycle. That is, they should discuss the activities and procedures carried out in the remaining four steps.

Skill analysis Management theory, including supervision, has two distinctly opposite belief systems regarding techniques for obtaining optimum output from subordinates. These two theories, X and Y, are in opposition to each other and demand opposite actions from a supervisor (McGregor 1960). Theory X is based on traditional management ideas. The three assumptions of theory X are:

1. The average human being has an inherent dislike of work and will avoid it if possible.
2. Because of the human dislike of work, most people must be coerced, directed, and threatened with punishment to get them to put forth adequate effort toward the achievement of organizational objectives.
3. The average human being prefers to be directed, wishes to avoid responsibility, has relatively little ambition, and wants security above all.

Theory Y is based on assumptions derived from research in the behavioral sciences. Its six assumptions are:

1. The expenditure of physical and mental effort in work is as natural as play or rest.
2. External controls and the threat of punishment are not the only means for bringing about effort toward organizational objectives. Human beings will exercise

self-direction and self-control in the service of objectives to which they are committed.
3. Commitment to objectives is a function of the rewards associated with their achievement.
4. The average human being learns, under proper conditions, not only to accept but also to seek responsibility.
5. The capacity to exercise a relatively high degree of imagination, ingenuity, and creativity in the solution of organizational problems is widely, not narrowly, distributed in the population.
6. Under the conditions of modern industrial life, the intellectual potentialities of the average human being are only partially utilized.

A comparison of these styles of supervision yields these conclusions:

1. Theory X, a carrot-and-stick theory, is based on external rewards and punishment. Theory Y is based on ownership and active participation in the supervision process through intrinsic motivation.
2. Theory X discourages participatory management and creativity, while theory Y encourages collaboration in the supervisory processes and encourages creativity.
3. Theory X does not concern itself with morale, while theory Y yields a greater sense of satisfaction.
4. Theory X is based on the premise that people being supervised react negatively, while theory Y states that people react positively when the supervisory style is responsive to their needs and concerns.

Supporting research by Likert (1967) has shown that higher production can be achieved by managers who adopt theory Y beliefs. This research can be applied to supervisory activities in the public school as well as to industry.

Supervisors often have differing philosophies regarding the supervision of student teachers. Most of these philosophical models are eclectic rather than pure models. The most critical characteristic of a supervisor engaged in clinical supervision is the supervisor's view of the role of supervision. At one end of the supervisory continuum is a supervisor who is a "performance-oriented" supervisor. This person is concerned only with behavioral change and accountability and is interested in what changes can be brought about in the behavior of the student teacher. Conversely, at the other end of the continuum is the "relationship-oriented" supervisor who believes that the basis for all changes in the behavior of another is a positive working relationship. Such a supervisor, even though sometimes unable to bring about change in the performance of the student teacher, often feels that a positive working relationship will have been worth the effort of working with the student teacher. Indeed, many supervisors feel that a positive relationship enhances the likelihood of future change in the behavior of the student teacher.

An integral component in the supervisory process is student teacher evaluation. However, evaluation often presents a threat to a positive working relationship. Nevertheless, if evaluation is conducted with sensitivity, it can represent a positive component to the working relationship. In fact, Stufflebeam (1988) suggests that when evaluation is conducted in a professional, considerate, and courteous manner so that the student teacher's self-esteem, motivation, professional reputation, performance, and attitude toward personnel evaluation are enhanced, the positive working relationship is not damaged. Thus, with the necessary positive relationships established, the supervisors can move more toward the "performance-orientation" mode of supervision to bring about instructional changes in the student teacher.

It is the responsibility of the supervisors to establish an attitude of trust between the student teacher and themselves. The supervisors can convey this attitude by indicating that they consider the best interest of the student teacher and the students (the improvement of instruction) as the hallmark of the supervisory process. Once the student teacher becomes aware of the supervisors as valuable resources, the competence of the supervisors, along with an attitude of mutual respect for the dignity and worth of the individual, enables a trustful relationship to emerge. One technique for improving the likelihood that the attitude of trust emerges quickly and efficiently is described by Rogers (1977) who transferred the characteristics of his successful "client-centered" approach to counseling into a dichotomy of actions that those in authority can use to establish a warm, positive relationship. This dichotomy, shown in Figure 6.4, emphasizes that for successful relationships, based on the premise of clinical supervision, a supervisor should use actions from the influence and impact category instead of from the power and control category.

Observation This second stage focuses on observation of classroom interaction as a function of the instructional process. The purpose of observation is to provide an objective record to mirror what the student teacher actually said and did during the instructional process. This is accomplished by the supervisors acting as an extra pair of eyes to increase the information being gathered. By placing supervisors in the actual instructional setting, they are able to gather data, codify it in a manner that allows easy retrieval, and later discuss the data with student teachers. Such data allows the supervisors and student teacher to accurately discuss the actions of the students and the student teacher and the impact that these actions had on the lesson.

Many of the decisions facing supervisors should have been made during the preobservation conference. That is, an agreement regarding time, location, and equipment should have been reached. The specific neutral role of the observer—not to interact not interfere in the classroom activities—has been defined. Also, any specific requests by the student teacher, such as help in dealing with specific group or individual behaviors, should have been delineated. This identification of a specific focus should help supervisors guide their

Influence and Impact	Power and Control
Giving autonomy to persons and groups	Making decisions
Freeing people to "do their own thing"	Giving orders
Expressing own ideas and feelings as one aspect of the group data	Directing subordinates' behavior
Facilitating learning	Keeping own ideas and feelings "close to the vest"
Stimulating independence in thought and action	Exercising authority over people and organizations
Accepting the "unacceptable" innovative creations that emerge	Dominating when necessary
Delegating, giving full responsibility	Teaching, instructing, and advising
Encouraging and relying on self-evaluation	Evaluating others
Finding rewards in the development and achievement of others	Giving rewards; being rewarded by own achievements

Figure 6.4 Two extremes of leadership

attention to agreed-upon areas for relevant data gathering.

Observational methods A detailed discussion of observational techniques was presented in chapter 4. Therefore, the focus of this section is on specific data-collection techniques. Most observational data is gathered by one of three means: videotaping, audiotaping or scripting. Videotaping is a method of gathering accurate data that can be replayed, stopped at critical times, and stored for reference to exact behaviors that might occur in the instructional situation.

Unfortunately, there are several disadvantages to videotaping. Many excellent supervisors do not have the skills needed to place and arrange videotaping equipment so that it can be used to maximum advantage. This process is also cumbersome

and can be distracting to students. The moving of equipment can interrupt the instructional process and create a false environment. The cost of providing a sufficient equipment inventory for all supervisors to have available videotaping equipment may exceed the budgetary constraints of many institutions. To be effective, an evaluation system should have practical procedures that produce needed information while minimizing disruption and cost (Stufflebeam 1988). Videotaping does not meet this criterion.

Audiotaping is another effective method for obtaining information about what occurs in an instructional activity. The tape can be listened to repeatedly to check for voice nuances such as tone, volume, and quality. Audiotaping is very objective because it records everything said and does not make selective judgments. Modern electronics make such equipment almost unseen by most students. Unfortunately, only about 80 percent of what goes on in an instructional activity can be extracted from an audiotape. This leaves many of the critical nonverbal clues unavailable for later examination.

The most useful method of obtaining a record of what happened in a classroom is the act of scripting or writing down the key words that are spoken by the student teacher and students. This technique can also be used to make a written record of supporting or inconsistent actions during a lesson. Scripting can be done easily with inexpensive materials—a pencil and a notepad. This information can be analyzed and organized at a later time. However, scripting is a psychomotor skill that requires many boring hours of practice to become proficient.

Supervisors should develop a list of possible abbreviations that can be used in scripting. As supervisors develop the scripting technique, they can develop the ability to scan the room while scripting, which provides additional information and enhances the scripting process. It is best if the focus is on an overview of the entire teaching/learning process. If supervisors choose to select some narrow focus, the focus area must have had a significant part in the success or failure of the lesson.

Pitfalls A major problem in accurate observational techniques is being able to focus on the overall interaction without ignoring or focusing on a minor part of the instructional process. Too often an incident, or series of incidents, develops into a crucial part of the lesson because these events are unusual or different. Supervisors must be certain that a specific event or specific events had a significant part in a lesson before they limit observational data to a narrow focus. The value of isolated events must be weighed without losing sight of the goal of collecting data about the entire lesson. Also, events that are in accordance with supervisors' belief systems may have a tendency to emerge as positive pivotal points in a lesson. Conversely, events that are not in agreement with supervisors' belief systems may be viewed as negative pivotal points in a lesson.

Another area of great concern regarding the observational stage of clinical supervision is the need to remain objective. The role of the supervisor is that of gathering data without interfering in the instructional process. While there are some student teacher actions that are always detrimental to a lesson, most of the actions of the student teacher should be taken into context by examining what role a particular action or lack of action has on the entire lesson and the learning process. Only when information obtained from the student teacher's lesson has been reflectively examined can a true analysis be made. This also requires that the data collection contain no judgmental statements but rather only objective data that is reflective of what occurred. This precludes any type of intermingling a memory of what occurred with a transcript of the lesson. These memories, when combined with perceptual biases may cause certain events to be seen in sharp focus, while other events may be obscured, magnified, or reduced (Cogan 1973). It is the supervisors' responsibility to be aware of and avoid personal characteristics that interfere with the objective gathering of data.

The supervisors must assume a role of an inert object when entering the classroom to gather data. This means that there should be no communication of any type regarding the events within the classroom. Any opinion of these events should be formed only after a careful analysis of the data. This requires a careful effort not to engage in any type of interaction with the students in the classroom. Students will want to make idle chatter or comments about what the supervisor is doing and why it is important that the supervisor visit the classroom. While chatter with students may provide some additional information, such as whether directions were understood, the supervisor must remember that the supervisory role requires a pleasant and agreeable person who is nonjudgmental in action and in no way enters into any of the interaction within the classroom. To do otherwise would contaminate the data.

Analysis and strategy Once the supervisor has finished the observation, the easiest parts of clinical supervision have been completed. The careful preparation leading to the preobservation conference and the observation will be rewarded through careful analysis of classroom data. This third step in the process requires supervisors to use all their pedagogical skills, teaching experiences, and intellectual prowess to correctly analyze classroom data and develop appropriate strategies that will lead to an improvement in the instructional process. If the supervisor has approached supervision with the concept of shared control, which requires the supervisor to focus on processes and the student teacher to focus on intentions, procedures, and the effect on students, the analysis will be more fruitful and less threatening. Failure to focus shared control is a failure to estimate the emotional significance of supervisory behavior and how it affects the student teacher. A supposition to analysis of student teacher behavior is that the collected data represents a microcosm of a consistent series of behavior patterns of the student teacher (Spaulding 1982). This allows the selection of specific student teacher behaviors because these consistent behavior patterns are usually repeated regularly and are an integral part of the student teacher's interactions with the students.

Once the supervisor has observed the student teacher and collected a script containing copious notes, an audiotape, or a videotape, the analysis should begin. The first step for the supervisor is to take the observational data, go through it and label the cause and effect situations that have been recorded. The supervisor labels decisions and actions made by the student teacher and the probable effect on the students. These decisions or actions are divided into the categories that were agreed upon in the preobservation conference. Figure 6.5 offers a framework for this activity. The number of spaces under the headings of questioning, classroom management, and lesson characteristics can be expanded as needed.

It is the responsibility of the supervisor to adhere to the categories and not to destroy the trustful relationship by suddenly announcing a change in categories because of observed behavior.

This sequence of the data analysis depends on the developmental level or capabilities of the student teacher as well as other environmental factors. Some supervisors prefer to begin by focusing on strengths to increase trust and improve the relationship before discussing weaknesses. Other supervisors prefer to begin by focusing on weaknesses to avoid anticipatory anxiety and end the conference on a positive note. Others may prefer to focus on special interest areas such as the student teacher's feelings about supervision or an overall view of the student teaching experience. Like many complex problems, there is no best way that works all the time. However, many recommend that a four-step-structure sequence be followed in preparing for and conferencing with student teachers.

In the first step, the supervisor analyzes the data for examples of strength patterns. These strength patterns can be identified by writing positive comments in the margin of a script or providing a written supplement to an audio- or videotape. It is important that the desirable characteristics of the lesson be clearly identified.

The second step is to have the student teacher identify strength patterns in an independent self-analysis of the observational data. The student teacher should try to identify specific instructional acts that resulted in the desired outcomes. This requires reflectivity on the part of the student teacher and should focus on which actions would be repeated if the lesson were to be taught again.

The third step is to have the student teacher, in an independent self-analysis of the observational data, identify needed growth patterns. This requires that the student teacher identify which instructional activities would be changed, how they would be changed, and a rationale for the

Decision/Action	Effect upon Students
Questioning	
Classroom Management	
Lesson Characteristics	

Figure 6.5 Cause and effect situations

changes. One technique that may work very well for the student teacher is to determine the cause-effect relationship between student teacher actions and student learning. The student teacher may say, ''My failure to provide sufficient wait-time during questioning may have caused brief student responses. Therefore, I need to increase the wait-time to increase the likelihood for more elaborate and longer student responses.''

The fourth step is for the supervisor to analyze the observational data to determine where growth patterns are needed. The supervisor should provide data to support recommendations; thus, providing supporting analytical information that is a critical area in the process of clinical supervision. Records should provide specific details of events that occurred or did not occur and how these events impacted the lesson. Often, student teach-

ers are not at a sufficient developmental level to enable them to do reflective thinking, that is, thinking about the thinking that went into a lesson.

Postobservation conference The purpose of the fourth step—the postobservation conference—is to provide feedback and guidance to improve instruction, reward the appropriate student teacher behavior, provide authentication of student teacher instructional patterns, provide techniques for self-improvement, and provide an incentive for professional self-analysis. This conference, which must be expertly managed, has goals that have been determined by other stages and relationships. Even the location of the conference can have serious emotional overtones to a student teacher (see chapter 3). The locational variables, including time and length of the conference, should have been determined before the observation. Changing any arrangement, such as a change in location to ensure more privacy, has potentially frightening implications to the student teacher. Moreover, the supervisor, if there is the possibility of incidental contact with the student teacher, should avoid communicating any type of evaluation (either positive or negative) to the student teacher before the conference.

To provide sufficient documentation for the successful completion of the postconference analysis, many educators recommend that the postconference be audiotaped. The supervisor should start the postconference with an explanation that this portion of the clinical supervision process is being taped to expedite the postconference analysis. The focus should be on an examination of the collected data and how that data mirrored the activity within the classroom. The postconference should follow the suggested outline in the analysis and strategy step. As the supervisor and the student teacher go over the four steps outlined in the analysis and strategy section of clinical supervision, there can be a list of possible alternatives to consider in the preparation of the next lesson. This allows the supervisor to provide support for suggestions that might improve the lesson as well as being the preconference for the next observation. The combining of a postobservation conference and a preconference is one of the greatest strengths of clinical supervision. This combination allows all preobservation conferences after the first one to be based on mutually accepted factual information.

The role of the supervisors should be to provide a ''balance'' in the growth of the student teachers. Supervisors should take care to neither destroy nor inflate the ego of the student teachers. Some student teachers may interpret all comments as criticisms; others may ignore all suggestions that could lead to improvement. This predisposition on the part of student teachers may require that supervisors be very specific in discussions. One of the most useful phrases is to ask student teachers to repeat the meaning of what

was said. This provides valuable information for the postconference analysis as well as provides clarity to the communication process.

Postobservation analysis The fifth and last step, postobservation analysis, focuses on the supervisor's role, which requires that the supervisor fully commit to the principles of clinical supervision. Just as input from outside sources can be a valuable resource in improving the teaching in the classroom, outside input can be used to improve supervision in the clinical supervision process. Using input from the student teacher and from self-analysis requires that the supervisor remove himself or herself from the role and objectively listen to the postconference recording to try to identify some relevant information. Some specific issues that should be addressed by the supervisor include a lack of congruence between time frameworks, depersonalization of the student teacher, absence of closure, predominant ''supervisor talk'' in the postobservation conference, a serious discrepancy in professional values, and supervisory behavior that parallels what the student teacher shouldn't do (such as egocentricism or absolute authority). In case of ambiguities or uncertainties, the supervisor may want to request an examination by another supervisor to determine the effectiveness of the supervisory role.

The supervisor must compare what was planned with what actually happened in the clinical supervision process. To provide objectivity to this process, the supervisor should analyze the tape to determine who selected each topic, who provided the data, who analyzed the data, and who designed the alternatives. To facilitate this approach, supervisors can design a postobservation analysis instrument, such as the one shown in Figure 6.6. This instrument should not be designed to provide limits to postconference analysis but rather to provide a sample so that the supervisors might develop their own objective data sheet to aid in the development of a satisfactory analysis sheet. Other specific supervisory analysis forms for the university supervisor and the cooperating teacher are included in the chapters 7 and 8. First, the supervisors independently rank the ability of the student teacher to analyze. Then they analyze the verbal communication by placing tally marks in the column for the student teacher, the cooperating teacher, or the university supervisor. This analysis should help determine the verbal communication and perhaps provide the supervisors with information that remained hidden when they listened to the tape. Such objective data is the hallmark of clinical supervision and provides opportunities for the supervisors to determine whether their supervisory behavior was consistent with their planned supervisory behavior. The sample Postobservation Analysis Sheet shown in Figure 6.6 can be used for that purpose.

Limitations of clinical supervision Clinical supervision has been espoused by teacher educators since the early 1960s. Unfortunately, the implementation of clinical supervision as a practical model for the supervision of student teachers has failed to materialize. The primary reason is that many universities view the cost of supervision of

Ability of Student Teacher to Self-Analyze

Low			Moderate		High

Topic	ST	CT	US	Comments
Selection of topic for discussion				
Objective data presented				
Analysis of data				
Alternatives				

List sequence of conference topics:
1. _____
2. _____
3. _____
4. _____
5. _____
6. _____
7. _____
8. _____

Figure 6.6 Supervisors' postobservation analysis of verbal analysis

student teachers as a limiting factor when they set priorities for the functions of the university. Supervision is often relegated to graduate assistants who provide no continuity and whose primary thrust is to complete a degree and to obtain a tenure-track faculty position at another university. This unimportance is reinforced by the assigning of supervisory duties to new faculty and faculty without graduate faculty status. This unimportance is further reinforced by the recognition given for publications and/or research. The supervision of student teachers, which is much more difficult and could be a more viable discriminator for promotion and tenure, is viewed as a less than satisfactory activity for university faculty. Universities are also unwilling to provide sufficient time for travel and related supervisory activities. Some universities are unwilling to develop an appropriate load formula that equates supervision with other faculty duties.

Many public schools are maintenance-oriented. Rather than encouraging professional growth of teachers for the future of the profession, many public schools are interested only in the maintenance of the same system. This ideology is not consistent with the goals of clinical supervision, and many public school personnel are unwilling to participate in a student teaching program with the potential for growth and its accompanying discomforts. Faced with a school system or a group of school systems unwilling to risk for the benefit of its students, many universities are willing to adopt a conventional student teaching supervisory system in which the public school dictates the university's supervisory practices.

Most university supervisors of student teachers are hired for expertise in a specific area and given supervisory duties as an afterthought. These faculty often have no formal instruction in supervision but rather try to survive in a world of supervision without sufficient academic supervisory preparation. If a university were to adopt a clinical supervision model, it would require university supervisors to receive extensive preparation in clinical supervision. Without extensive, special-ized preparation in clinical supervision, the process is doomed to failure. Most universities are unwilling to commit the necessary resources and unwilling to impose additional preparation requirements on faculty who supervise student teachers when the university imposes no additional requirements upon faculty not involved in supervision.

Harris (1976) proposed that the limitations of clinical supervision can be identified as belonging to one of three broad categories. The first limitation is the settings in which the model is deployed. Often the bureaucratic and/or social constraints of the public schools do not lend themselves to the implementation of a clinical supervision program for student teachers. The organizational structure is such that there is insufficient time for conferencing and observation to successfully implement the model.

A subsequent limitation is the personal limitations, which are reflected in the fact that not every student teacher or supervisor is motivated enough to make the intense time and energy commitment required of clinical supervision. The student teacher may not be willing to "pay the price" for a successful clinical supervision experience. Supervisors may not possess the creativity nor have the patience to be nondirective enough to allow the student teacher input into directing the clinical supervision process.

The third limitation is that clinical supervision assumes too narrow a scope of events affecting the quality of life in the public schools. While the behavior of student teachers in the classroom may be an integral part of this quality of life, the undertone of the implementation of clinical supervision has a great effect on the public schools. If student teachers perceive that clinical supervision will be used in punitive processes, the entire clinical supervision sequence will be perceived as negative.

To successfully implement a clinical supervision program, a university must make a commitment to improving the instructional process in the public school classroom by providing the necessary resources to implement a clinical supervision program for its student teachers. This may require extensive preparation of public school personnel in techniques of clinical supervision and may result in student teachers being restricted to public schools that are committed to improving the instructional process in the public schools.

Instructional Supervision Training Program

Based on the clinical supervision model, Boyan and Copeland (1978) developed an eight-step sequential model that focuses on classroom instructional practices: The Instructional Supervision Training Program (ISTP). The responsibility for successful use of the ISTP model rests with the student teacher who must initiate, alter, or eliminate specific instructional behaviors based on the objective data collected by the supervisor. This makes the modification of instructional techniques the primary responsibility of the student teacher who must correctly respond to the question, ''Based on this observational data, what went wrong today and how would you change it?'' The supervisor is available to provide observational data to help the student develop specific instructional strategies to answer the question. The four stages and eight steps, as modified for student teachers, are outlined as follows:

Stage I. Preobservation conference
Step 1. **Behaviorally define the problem**—this focuses upon an area of instructional concern
Step 2. **Establish base rate**—base rate of frequency of the behavior
Step 3. **Select observation instrument**—selection or creation of method of data collection
Stage II. Observation
Step 4. **Classroom observation**—data collection using the observation instrument

Stage III. Analysis and strategy
Step 5. **Analyze the data**—data is put in visual form so teacher can easily understand it
Step 6. **Examine behavioral data**—supervisor determines which behaviors to change and which to leave alone
Stage IV. Postobservation conference
Step 7. **Provide feedback**—observational data is presented in visual form
Step 8. **Strategies**—supervisor and student teacher work cooperatively to determine specific instructional strategies to correct the identified instructional problems

This approach works best with student teachers who are critical thinkers and capable of analyzing their own thinking that preceded specific instructional acts. ISTP, like clinical supervision, provides opportunities for the student teacher to perceive supervision as a supportive effort instead of a threatening effort.

Developmental Supervision

Developmental supervision is an approach to supervision based on the assumption that student teachers are adults; just as elementary teachers must have expertise in child psychology, supervisors must have expertise in adult developmental psychology. Supervisors would criticize a student teacher who expected all students within a classroom to be at the same developmental level. Yet supervisors may expect all student teachers to be at the same stage of growth and development. The role of the supervisor in the developmental supervision approach is to foster thinking skills in student teachers to help them diagnose classroom instruction and use their higher level thinking skills (Glickman 1985). If the aim of education is human development, then supervisors must match their assistance to the student teachers' conceptual level. The ultimate goal of this process would be for the student teachers to begin to take charge of their own improvement.

The three primary styles of developmental supervision are directive, collaborative, and nondirective. Associated with each style of supervision are supervisory behaviors ranging from clarifying, presenting, demonstrating, directing, standardizing, and reinforcing (through listening, presenting, problem solving, and negotiating) to listening, clarifying, encouraging, and presenting (Glickman 1981). There are two types of student teacher variables that are related to instruction and have significance in the development supervision process: the amount of commitment of the student teacher and the abstract thinking level of the student teacher.

Student teachers who have been unable to expend time and energy to move from a concern about self to a concern for others need directive types of supervisory behaviors. Also, student teachers who have a low level of abstract thinking need equally directive supervisory behaviors. Supervisors should provide simple, clear statements with advance organizers. Student teachers who are low-level abstract thinkers need frequent support and reinforcement, as well as much more frequent supervision. Conversely, those student teachers who have a high commitment and are high-level abstract thinkers need more nondirective and/or collaborative supervisory behaviors.

Developmental supervision is a process that encourages supervisors to analyze the developmental level of student teachers and to develop supervisory behaviors based on this development. One benefit of this process is that supervision will be less threatening and much more suited to the needs of each individual student teacher. Student teachers who need specific, direct support will not be thwarted by a lot of "fuzziness," and student teachers who function at high levels of abstract thinking and commitment will not suffer from useless supervisor interference.

Scientific Supervision

Advocates (Russell and Hunter 1980) of the scientific supervision approach insist that the most efficient way to improve the public school is through the improvement of the activity of teaching. This improvement is accomplished by categorizing the extent to which a classroom teacher engages in each of nine specific activities. These activities are:

1. **Diagnosis:** Identifying general objectives and assessing pupils' present attainment of them.
2. **Specific objectives:** Selecting, on the basis of the diagnosis, specific objectives for the daily lesson.
3. **Anticipatory set:** Focusing attention, reviewing previous learning, and developing readiness for what is to come.
4. **Perceived purpose:** Clarifying an objective for the pupils, explaining its importance, and relating it to previous learning.
5. **Learning opportunities:** Choosing learning opportunities that will help learners achieve objectives.
6. **Modeling:** Providing both a verbal and a visual example of what is to be learned.
7. **Check for understanding:** Assessing the extent to which pupils are achieving objectives.
8. **Guided practice:** Guiding pupils' practice of learning and checking to see that they can perform successfully.
9. **Independent practice:** Giving pupils the opportunity to practice the new skill on their own.

Scientific supervision, which may be called prescriptive supervision (Goldsberry 1988), has been received with great popularity because it establishes a "right way" to do things and there are no hidden agendas. However, this approach has received criticism from those who feel that the model does not go beyond the boundaries of observable student-student teacher interaction (Fenstermacher 1978; Peterson 1979). Furthermore, Calfee (1981), maintains that the model has no theoretical foundation, focuses on actions more than thought, and proposes, in advance, how a student teacher should conduct a classroom. If student teaching were as easy as some maintain the scientific supervision approach proposes, all research regarding thinking as a component of teaching would have to be discarded.

Accountable Supervision

An accountable supervision model is a holdover from the "accountability movement." This approach does not focus on teachers' instructional activities but rather gets its direction from the apparent student outcomes. McNeil (1971) suggests the following steps in accountable supervision:

1. The supervisors help the student teacher determine which learning objectives will be emphasized during a given lesson.
2. The student teacher and supervisor agree on how student learning will be assessed.
3. The supervisors visit the student teacher's classroom for the primary purpose of observing and determining whether or not the pupils have achieved the intended objectives.
4. The overall assessment of the student teacher's activity is made exclusively in light of whether or not students achieved stated objectives, not on whether or not there was quality instruction.

This approach takes a narrow view of the learning process by assuming that all that is important in a classroom can be objectively measured. Other situational variables such as resources, numbers and quality of students, environmental constraints, and a myriad of other variables are ignored with the focus on the measurable student outcomes. However, advocates of this approach suggest that the emphasis is where it should be—on what students learn. If the goal of the student teacher is student learning and student learning occurs, then the student teacher is meeting the goal, and learning is occurring.

Artistic Supervision

In direct contrast to the accountable supervision model, which assumes everything important is measurable, the artistic supervision model is a holistic approach to supervision that relies on the sensitivity perceptivity, and knowledge of the supervisor as a way of appreciating the significant subtleties occurring in the classroom (Eisner 1982). Teaching is defined as an art that changes according to a variety of conditions that do not always fit into preconceived, lock-step, models of how teachers must teach. Glatthorn (1984) recognizes certain limitations associated with the artistic supervision model and suggests that, at best, it can function only as a supplement to the scientific and accountable approaches and can be used only with selected student teachers, in selected environments, who are supervised by excellent supervisors.

Self-Assessment Supervision

Self-assessment supervision requires that student teachers learn to analyze their own classroom behavior. Supervisors become involved only as objective observers to collect data. However, only those student teachers who are developmentally ready can be expected to possess the self-analysis skills for examining all of their instructional delivery systems and effectively be involved in self-assessment supervision. Bailey (1981) viewed supervision as a process in which the student teacher uses a series of sequential feedback strategies for the purpose of instructional improvement. For student teachers to evaluate their own performance so they will be more aware of strengths and weaknesses associated with their classroom instruction, the supervisor should provide structure in the form of characteristics of effective instruction. Thus, the student teacher can have some type of criteria to use for comparison. The steps to providing this structure are:

1. **Self-assessment**—Provide diagnostic tools and inventories
2. **Self-awareness**—How accurate are the findings?
3. **Others' awareness**—Supervisor and students' feedback
4. **Accurate assessment**—Judge all input for accuracy
5. **Recommendations**—What should be changed?
6. **Implementation**—Put changes into practice
7. **Reassess**—Continue the process

During the initial two steps of the process, the student teacher, under the guidance of the supervisor, begins to examine the quality of instructional performance. It is best to use carefully developed inventories that are based on behaviors associated with effective instruction. Many universities, school districts, and states have some type of guidelines for effective instruction. These inventories should be specific enough to encourage teachers to make critical decisions regarding their instructional effectiveness.

The third step involves feedback from other sources. These sources may be the supervisor, the student, or some type of assessment tool used by the district. Video- or audiotaping can provide valuable information on which to build a profile of the student teacher's instructional performance.

Step four is critical in self-assessment. The student teacher must guard against rationalizing or explaining away ineffective classroom behaviors. This requires the student teacher to make a commitment to change and to the value of the supervision process. The student teacher must accept that if there is an inconsistency between the student teacher's own rating and the feedback from other sources, the student teacher must consider a change in behavior to help bridge the gap between self-perception and the perception of others.

Steps five, six, and seven complete the process and start the cycle again. As part of accepting discrepancies between self and others, the student teacher must initiate change in behavior, implement the change, and begin the self-assessment process again.

To successfully implement self-assessment supervision, a university must identify criteria of effective teaching and link that information with the self-assessment of the student teacher and the formative data that can be supplied by the supervisors. The basic philosophy of self-assessment supervision is objective perceptions and analyses of the instructional self in comparison with known principles of effective instruction. Self-assessment supervision has as its product the goal of all supervision—student teachers being able to identify their own effective teaching.

Summary

Supervision is a necessary process for the improvement of instruction in the public schools. Too often this process has been used against teachers rather than to support them and to provide assistance in improving their instructional techniques. To counteract this negative view of supervision, the clinical supervision model proposes that student teachers be introduced to the formative evaluative approach of clinical supervision. The five-step clinical supervision model provides the structure for student teacher involvement in the supervision process. The characteristics of the clinical supervision model, which is based upon trust between the student teacher and the supervisor, require individualized, close, and supportive supervision to provide the structure for changing the student teacher's attitude toward supervision. However, the clinical supervision model requires a serious commitment of time and resources; it requires a change in supervisory attitudes of student teachers, public school personnel, and university personnel.

The instructional supervision training program is an expanded model of clinical supervision in which the supervisor assists the student teacher in resolving instructional problems. The role of the supervisor is to objectively collect data to enable the student teacher to become aware of problems and to determine a course of action.

Developmental supervision assumes that student teachers are at various levels of developmental growth and the role of the supervisor is to identify the level of growth and to prepare appropriate supervisory actions. The supervisor selects from one of the supervisory styles (directive, collaborative, and nondirective) and combines that with an appropriate level of commitment and level of abstract thinking.

Scientific supervision focuses on specific lists of teacher activities that are associated with effective teachers. The role of the supervisor is to assist the student teacher in following the prescribed steps in teaching. In contrast, artistic supervision, which views teaching as an art, focuses on the role of the supervisor in recognizing the nuances that exist in every teaching situation. This avoids the concept of a consistent approach to teaching that is universally appropriate. Self-assessment supervision helps teachers become aware of their own instructional performance by comparing self-assessment checklists with data collected from others.

The focus in this chapter has been on different approaches or models of supervision. The clinical supervision model provides the structure for changing the student teachers' view of supervision as well as preparing them for a lifetime of self-improvement of instruction through reflective teaching. Whereas supervision has been from superordinate to subordinate, clinical supervision provides the structure for the student teacher to reflect on teaching and use this reflection in the supervisory process. The process of supervision is expensive in time and human resources. Only through commitment to this extensive and expensive process can universities improve the quality of instruction in the public schools.

Questions and Discussion Topics

1. What are the advantages and disadvantages of clinical supervision? What do you perceive as the strengths and weaknesses?

2. Which step do you consider the most pivotal in the clinical supervision process? Why? Which step requires the least amount of time? Which step requires the most time? Which step is the most threatening to the supervisor? Which step is the most threatening to the student teacher? Explain why you have chosen each one.

3. List the strongest characteristic of clinical supervision. What do you perceive as the most problematic limitation of clinical supervision?

4. Which type of supervision would you prefer to use as a supervisor? Which type would you prefer to use as a student teacher? Why did you choose the specific type? Would the type of school make a difference?

CHAPTER 7

Applications for University Personnel

CHAPTER KEY CONCEPTS

Analysis and Strategy
Observation
Postobservation Analysis

Postobservation Conference
Preobservation Conference
Relationships

Overview

The role of the university person, often referred to as the university supervisor, is the pivotal role in clinical supervision. An inept, untrained, or uncaring university supervisor can refuse to allow the type of relationship to develop that is necessary for clinical supervision. The university supervisor should be willing to agree that clinical supervision is a cooperative effort; one that is most effective when all members of the team share mutual respect and appreciate one another for what each person can contribute to the team. If the university supervisor maintains that his or her role is to "be in charge" of the procedures and processes relating to the supervision of the student teacher, the strengths of clinical supervision will be usurped by authoritarian supervisory techniques. Therefore, the university supervisor should be willing to break the traditional mold of supervisors. A successful university supervisor should not only work with the cooperating teacher, but also must be willing to "take chances" and provide the student teacher with

the opportunity for growth through reflective teaching and self-assessment.

Although each member of the supervisory triad has an equally important role, this chapter focuses on the university supervisor's role, which is essential if the clinical supervision process is to work toward achieving its goal—the improvement of instruction.

Objectives

Upon completing your study of chapter 7, you should be able to:

1. Describe the traditional role of the university supervisor.
2. Describe the role of the university supervisor in clinical supervision.
3. Describe the impediments to the successful implementation of the university supervisor in clinical supervision.

4. Describe specific activities for the university supervisor during each stage of the clinical supervision cycle.
5. Describe how the university supervisor's expectations differ between the typical student supervision and the clinical supervision of student teachers.

Supervision is a team effort. The success of the clinical supervision model takes productive interaction among the university supervisor, cooperating teacher, and student teacher in all five steps of the clinical supervision cycle.

Relationships

Implementation of the clinical supervision model requires the establishment of an environment and interactions conducive to certain types of relationships. These relationships are: (1) collegial relationships, (2) mutual respect for strengths and weaknesses, (3) empathetic, rational relationships, and (4) avoidance of ascendent or descendent relationships.

Collegial Relationships

The primary relationship is that of a colleague. The university supervisor should develop a new sensitivity to working in group processes where there is more of an equality among the members of the triad.

University supervisors who are authoritarian and are very knowledgeable about pedagogy may have difficulty adjusting to this new type of relationship. Often, university supervisors try to manipulate the student teacher through the use of such positive actions as incorporating an empathetic quality into each action or beginning each verbal response to the student teacher with a positive prefix. While these actions may appear to promote the relationship between the university supervisor and the student teacher, these actions may be conscious or unconscious actions of the university supervisor to take technical control of the relationship. Rather than trying to use

types of positive reinforcement to manipulate the student teacher, the university supervisor should enter into the relationship as a joint venture, with all parties engaged in mutual problem solving and equally committed to the process of involvement in a mutually advantageous relationship.

Mutual Respect for Strengths and Weaknesses

Another type of relationship that should be developed is one of mutual respect for strengths and weaknesses. The colleagueship of clinical supervision does not suppose an equal competence among members of the triad but rather an interaction of unequal competencies. The university supervisor should not assume that expertise in observation, techniques of data collection, analysis of teaching techniques, a vast reservoir of instructional strategies, and knowledge of the clinical supervision cycle is superior to a student teacher's knowledge of individual differences of students or the knowledge of antecedents of today's problems.

The university supervisor should also make certain that the cooperating teacher, with expertise in the school bureaucratic system, knowledge of home situations that may provide additional information regarding behavior situations, and a thorough understanding of the curriculum of the school, is treated as an equal part of the triad. It is this merging of heterogeneous competencies that provides the democratic structure of clinical supervision and allows each member of the triad to gain competencies from the interactions with others.

Empathetic, Rational Relationships

The university supervisor should assume an empathetic, rational relationship. This relationship begins to flourish when the university supervisor assumes the role of team leader and starts the clinical cycle. To assume a truly empathetic relationship, the university supervisor should clearly communicate an understanding of the anxieties of the student teacher. The attitudes and values of the university supervisor, which provide the foundation for accepting and dealing with the anxieties of the student teacher, must be accepted as a precondition for a truly empathetic relationship. Once the empathetic role is expressed to other members of the triad, the proper environment is established for the communication of verbal and nonverbal expressions of support and encouragement.

Ascendent or Descendent Relationships

The university supervisor must not let an ascendent or descendent role develop in the triad. There are several other types of relationships that inhibit the effectiveness of the role of the university supervisor. The student teacher may try to establish a helper-helpee relationship that causes him or her to relinquish autonomy. A superior-subordinate relationship is equally destructive because the student teacher is not able to develop autonomy, becomes docile and less creative, and does not develop an individual style of teaching in a superior-subordinate relationship. A counselor-counselee relationship inhibits the student teacher from being reflective and providing any type of input into possible solutions to instructional problems. Rather, the student teacher dumps problems at the feet of the university supervisor and cooperating teacher and expects external solutions. A relationship wherein the university supervisor or cooperating teacher becomes a rater must also be avoided. If the rater relationship is perceived, the product of clinical supervision is a grade, a recommendation, or some other type of summative evaluation instead of improvement in instructional methodology of the student teacher.

Preobservation Conference

The preobservation conference is the foundation of the entire clinical supervision cycle. The university supervisor, as the liaison between the university and the public schools, is the informal leader and should be the most knowledgeable and

effective member of the clinical supervision team. This requires a thorough knowledge of clinical supervision.

Expectations

The supervisor should expect that decisions regarding alternative teaching behaviors identified in preobservation conferences must be based on observable data obtained from the classroom teaching observations. This data, which must be objectively obtained from actual classroom observations of agreed-upon teaching situations, provides the structural framework upon which all instructional recommendations will be based. This requires the university supervisor to use specific, concise behaviors of the students or the student teacher as the source of data. No longer are vague phrases and generalities acceptable for use in a conference with a student teacher. The university supervisor should be willing to restrict suggestions to the instructional practices dictated by the analysis of this observational data.

The supervisor should expect that one characteristic of new teaching behaviors is that the initial success of the new teaching behaviors may not appear to be as successful as previously learned teaching behaviors. This requires the university supervisor to be patient and to provide support to tolerate the lack of initial success in newly implemented instructional practices. Expecting newly implemented instructional strategies to have the same success levels of previously learned instructional strategies leads to frustration on the part of the student teacher and a hesitancy to try new teaching techniques.

Roles

The university supervisor performs a multiplicity of roles in the clinical supervision process. These roles should be fulfilled to the maximum if clinical supervision is to function as it is designed. One of the primary roles of the university supervisor is to provide the practitioner with service (feedback) regarding the quality of student teaching practices. This means that the university supervisor should avoid a summative evaluation role but rather should establish a formative evaluation role. Formative evaluation provides feedback about performance throughout the student teaching experience. It also can be useful in identifying and enhancing desirable behaviors and skills as well as identifying weaknesses or absences of skills and prescribing resources to strengthen these skills.

The importance of feedback from the university supervisor is essential to student teacher development through the self-analysis of teaching. There is evidence (Seidentop 1976) that systematic analysis of student teacher behaviors, when accompanied by feedback of a formative nature, can make significant contributions to changing student teacher behavior. This feedback should be precise and related to the objectives of the lessons. This requires the university supervisor to establish parameters limiting feedback to a formative nature by clearly defining his or her role. Although bureaucracies, at either the university or public school level, may require the product of formative evaluation to be a forecast of a summative nature, the university supervisor should be cognizant of the essential nature of formative evaluation in the successful use of the clinical supervision process.

Although university supervisors may not have the traditional role, the clinical supervision role of university supervisors remains paramount in the triad. Friebus (1977) found that the importance of university supervisors is most frequently at the top, although occasionally their importance is exceeded by the cooperating teacher. This coincides with a study by Zimpher (1980) who found that the university supervisor provides a necessary zest to the triad through delineation of expectations that might otherwise be ignored. If a teacher-education program is to be accredited by external accreditation, such as the National Council for Accreditation of Teacher Education (NCATE), the knowledge base must be the thread of commonality that unites all parts of the teacher-education program. The university supervisor provides the path through which this knowledge base can be communicated through the student teaching experience. Public school input into this knowledge base, especially as it relates to the world of practice, can successfully be transmitted back to the university through the university supervisor as well as through the follow-up of graduates. The university supervisor is also an important connection between the public school and the university. This perspective allows the university supervisor to assume an "outside role" and maintain membership in the triad.

Other roles may require that the university supervisor become a colleague and view the clinical supervision process as one of collaboration where the university supervisor provides skillful service, demonstrates ethical conduct, and uses reliable observational information (Garman 1982). The skillful service role of the university supervisor is to use prolonged and specialized intellectual training and service to provide inquiry and theorizing regarding the instruction being practiced and studied. The role of ethical conduct requires the university supervisor to become part of classroom life and to use discretion and judgment in supervisory actions through consistent standards of behavior. These actions instill confidence in the student teacher and enable the university

University supervisor should become a member of a functioning triad.

supervisor to develop useful knowledge about events under study. The reliable observational information role refers to the degree to which the same events, observed by other colleagues, would be recognized or described in the same way. To fulfill the reliability role, the university supervisor may be required to develop new attitudes and skills and to improve interpersonal relationships.

The university supervisor should have an understanding of the events occurring within the classroom. This means an understanding that is not superficial—a deeper understanding of behaviors within the classroom and some of the possible underlying causes of these behaviors. This mastery of the total pedagogical process requires extensive experience in instructional strategies as well as a compassionate attitude toward the expectations, role, and responsibility of the student teacher. These personal relations skills require a sensitivity toward the attitudes and feelings of others who may require a type and depth of sensitivity not usually found in university supervisors.

One of the best ways for a university supervisor to demonstrate sensitivity toward the attitudes and feelings of others is to develop good listening skills (see chapter 3). This requires more than reacting or responding to what the student teacher says. Valuing what the student teacher says is an excellent way to demonstrate sensitivity. By responding to comments without adding or detracting from the comments of the student teacher, the university supervisor indicates that there is value in everything the student teacher says. An open mind to the intent of the student teacher also indicates sensitivity, as well as seeking to identify what is not being said by student teachers who may be somewhat evasive or tentative in conversation. However, nothing communicates sensitivity like restraint.

University supervisors should develop techniques that share rather than tell. Often student teachers are intimidated and accept whatever a university supervisor says as the truth because of the relative position of the two or because of a previous relationship at the university. Indicating

a willingness to listen to alternative opinions often indicates a sensitivity to the needs of the student teacher.

Activities

The activities associated with the preobservation conference are designed to establish agreement between the supervisor and the student teacher. Although there is no formal signing of a contract, the university supervisor should think that the agreement reached is as binding as a contract. Initial activities should relate to establishing rapport between the university supervisor and the student teacher. This requires the university supervisor to possess a knowledge of clinical supervision theory. This theory must rest on the importance of active participation by the student teacher in the clinical supervision process. Only through a thorough understanding of the clinical supervision can the university supervisor function with a positive view of the role of student teaching.

Anxiety-abatement activities are a vital function during the preobservation conference. The student teacher has been removed from the security of the university environment, where effective functioning was much more clearly defined and where the student teacher was successful. Now, within a somewhat alien environment, the student teacher is not to do as told but rather is to be an active participant in a complex, seemingly unfamiliar process.

An essential ingredient for the university supervisor is to be able to relieve the anxiety of the student teacher. Moreover, the university supervisor should be competent in assessing instructional strategies and be effective in communicating this assessment to the student teacher in such a manner that the student teacher's self-concept is raised rather than lowered.

Once the essential rapport is established, the preobservation conference begins to examine the observation itself. As indicated in Figure 7.1, the first item to discuss is the logistics of the observation.

Name of student teacher _____

Name of cooperating teacher _____

Name of university supervisor _____

Date of conference _____ Date of observation _____

Time of observation _____ Subject _____

Goals and/or objectives of this lesson _____

_____

_____

_____

During this lesson, please focus on _____

_____

_____

_____

Special situations, comments, or concerns _____

_____

_____

_____

_____

Figure 7.1 Preobservation conference agreement

The preobservation agreement should include a discussion of location, where the university supervisor is to sit, the time for the observation, whether the university supervisor should leave without any comment, and any other type of logistics essential to accomplishing the functions of clinical supervision without disrupting the instructional process in the classroom. To assist in the functioning of the initial observation, some teachers suggest that a written copy of the observation agreement be given to the student teacher. This is to ensure that all parties know the specific situations to preclude any misunderstanding of situational variables relating to the observation.

Another discussion item should be the lesson plans and their implementation. There should be

an agreement on the objectives of the lesson and the relationship that exists between any specific objective and the broader general objectives. Those involved should discuss expected activities and changes that might possibly occur as a result of the flow of classroom interaction. As for all lesson plans, they should discuss the relationship of the assessment with the objectives.

The university supervisor and the student teacher should reach agreement about the special situations that exist within that specific classroom as well as what the university supervisor should be observing. The university supervisor should allow the student teacher to be in charge of most of the preobservation conference. Often, a university supervisor allows an overactive imagination to become the focus of the lesson. This happens when the university supervisor, with good intentions, identifies a potential problem that is unseen by the student teacher. A possible conversation might be as follows:

Student teacher: I have prepared a list of possible student/student teacher interactions that might occur as a part of this lesson.

University supervisor: I have never seen a list of all possible interactions. Perhaps you had better let me examine this list and delete some of the interactions. That way you have a much more concise list, know what interactions you want, be more in control, and have lessons with a smoother flow.

This type of discussion forces the university supervisor and the student teacher into helper-helpee roles. The student teacher slowly becomes dependent on the university supervisor; the student teacher assumes less and less responsibility for the instructional activities to be used in the classroom. Meanwhile, the university supervisor communicates that ''I decide what the limits are and how lessons are to be implemented.'' This results in a lowered self-concept for the student teacher and an increased dependency of the student teacher on the university supervisor, while removing the responsibility of instruction from the triad and placing it on the university supervisor.

University supervisors should concentrate on listening instead of talking. Talk from the university supervisor should be either a paraphrase of what the student teacher said or based on what the teacher is saying. This indicates that the university supervisor is really listening instead of just merely repeating what the student teacher said. Paraphrasing or building on what the student teacher says is a way of clarifying what was said without putting the student teacher on the defensive by saying, ''What exactly do you mean by that?'' Supporting questions provide an opportunity for reinforcing desirable behaviors and strengthening areas of weakness without destroying the confidence of the student teacher.

If is impossible to anticipate all possible conversations or activities in a preobservation conference. Therefore, the following guidelines could be used by university supervisors during a preobservation conference with a student teacher:

1. **Student teacher self-confidence.** The primary activity during a preobservation conference, especially the initial one, is the establishment of a sufficient level of self-confidence in the student teacher to help ensure the success of the lesson. Therefore, comments should be supportive rather than the type that could cause the student teacher to develop questions about his or her knowledge of the instructional process and about individual limitations.

2. **Clear communications.** Special emphasis should be given to clear, concise communication (see chapter 3). All phraseology should be in terms clearly understood by the student teacher. Educational jargon that may be within the expertise of the university supervisor may be unfamiliar or may be misunderstood by the student teacher. Most student teachers will be hesitant to ask for definitions of terminology used by the university supervisor. This makes the essentials of clear communication a function of the university supervisor who should use terms easily understood by the student teacher.

3. **Indirect guidance.** The shift from the typical university supervisor high-direct style of preconferencing to the clinical supervision low-direct style of preconferencing results in greater conference productivity. The university supervisor's emphasis should be on asking questions, listening, and reflecting back to the student teacher's ideas and feelings. Blumberg and Amidon (1965) found that teachers solicited more information from supervisors who accepted and used their ideas. Occasionally, individual characteristics of the student teacher such as

compliance, submissiveness, obedience, or pleasure in being told what to do may require the university supervisor to be direct. However, if student teachers are to be reflective and become responsible for their own actions, they need opportunities to make decisions regarding the direction a class or instructional sequence takes. This requires opportunities to make decisions regarding these directions and a university supervisor with the sensitivity to know the difference between guidance and manipulation.

4. **Processes and products.** In establishing the agreement with the student teacher, the university supervisor may inadvertently establish a process that is counter-productive to the product of the instruction. If a university supervisor treats a student teacher as though he or she cannot be totally trusted to make the types of decisions necessary for a successful lesson, the student teacher will never develop sufficient selfconfidence to do an accurate self-analysis of his or her own classroom teaching behavior. Most likely the student teacher will not make the types of decisions necessary for a successful lesson. Therefore, the university supervisor should be very deliberate in the conduct of the preobservation conference and develop the type of atmosphere conducive to mutual trust and decision making on the part of the student teacher.

5. **Early success.** The success of the initial lesson is essential to the clinical supervision process. Anything that would induce anxiety in the student teacher should be avoided in the first conference. This includes requests by the university supervisor that could cause the possibility of lower initial success, regardless of the long-term advantages of these idea. Teaching techniques that might be less effective but would offer initial success should be implemented in the first lesson to be observed by the university supervisor. This helps facilitate the establishment of an initial success in clinical supervision and helps relieve excessive anxiety.

The preobservation conference is intended mainly to provide a mental and procedural framework for clinical supervision. Its functions should be to re-establish the university supervisor-student teacher relationship, provide opportunity for rehearsal of the plan for instruction, make any necessary revisions, and establish a contract for the observational process. Once these functions are confirmed, the supervision progresses to the observation stage.

Observation

The purpose of the observation is to provide a link between the promises made in the preobservation conference and the promises to be kept in the postobservation conference. Using the agreed-upon facts of the preobservation conference, the university supervisor seeks to find if there are answers to the questions or situations developed in the preobservation conference. This "contract" provides the direction to the observation by guiding the university supervisor toward where or what should be the focus of observation. This direction prevents the university supervisor from suffering from "observation overload" because of the multitude of events occurring within the classroom during the instructional process. The university supervisor must maintain an objective mental set and focus on the behaviors and indicators agreed on in the preobservation conference, thus, ensuring the maximum opportunities for clinical supervision to succeed.

Expectations

The university supervisor should enter the student teacher's classroom with a positive mental attitude, expecting to improve the instructional practices of the student teacher. This means that the university supervisor should be prepared and willing to provide the type of feedback that will form the superstructure of future student teacher improvements. This occurs only after the observations have been completed and the data analyzed to determine the relationship between the actions of the student teacher and the actions of the students. These cause-effect relationships, called temporal relationships, (Garman, Glickman, Hunter, and Haggerson 1987), are student teacher actions and resultant student behaviors that describe trends in teaching or the flow of the lesson.

A university supervisor must be cognizant of biases and ''perceptual blinders'' (Good and Brophy 1984) that prevent the observation of what is happening in the classroom. These biases may be caused by past experiences, attitudes, prejudices, or a universal list of likes and dislikes that the university supervisor feels is applicable to all teaching situations. The university supervisor should avoid the tendency to want a ''supervisor clone'' or be swayed by certain behaviors. An example would be the tendency to perceive that highly verbal student teachers are more effective than less verbal student teachers who may spend more time listening to their students. These personal biases must be recognized and avoided if the university supervisor is to effectively focus on the collection of data. Otherwise, the data analysis task becomes intermingled with the objective collection of data, and the clear, distinct, separate functions of the clinical supervision cycle become less distinct. Any hypotheses should be formulated only after the data has been collected.

University supervisors can expect, especially during the initial observation, student teacher anxiety. This means that the change in the behavior of the student teacher will be directly proportional to the anxiety level of the student teacher. The resultant action will be a change in behavior, and the student teacher with an excessive lack of ease will cause an alteration in the behavior patterns of the students. The relationship between anxiety and performance is curvilinear. A certain amount of anxiety is needed to increase perform-ance, but as anxiety increases, performance, especially on complex tasks such as teaching, declines. This anxiety interferes with the student teacher's ability to assess and assist the students. The university supervisor must expect this and be prepared to help the student teacher develop the necessary self-confidence to demonstrate the technical skills required of effective student teachers.

Roles

The roles assumed by the university supervisor during the observation are consistent with the ideals of clinical supervision. The most fundamental role of the university supervisor is that of a facilitator to institute the concept of student teacher supervision as a cooperative endeavor. This makes the role of university supervisor one of ''coaching'' rather than one of ''telling.'' Although a coach may ultimately be in charge of a game plan, there is two-way conversation between the coach and the players. A coach might not consider telling a player what to do without player input. Instead, the advice given by the coach is based on a game plan and the actions and reactions of the other team compared with what was expected. The role of the university supervisor is similar. In cooperation with the student teacher, the university supervisor assumes the role of another set of eyes and focuses on what they agreed on in the preobservation conference. This extra set of eyes can provide additional recommendations based on what is observed during the instructional process.

The university supervisor must establish the role of democratic supervision. Through democratic supervision, the student teacher can achieve maximum professional efficiency. This requires increasing the emphasis placed on the exchange of ideas and human interaction. Gwynn (1961) identified three major emphasis areas: supervision as guidance, supervision as curriculum development, and supervision as group processes. These emphases focus on the human relations aspects of supervision, and the role of university supervisor

University personnel should assume a nonauthorative manner when supervising.

changes from an inspector and manipulator of data to one who develops theoretical constructs in working with groups and individuals (Lucio 1962). As a result of the human relations role in supervision, the student teacher assumes greater individual responsibility, has more intrinsic motivation, strives for greater individual growth, has higher morale, and more efficiently implements the ideas from the university supervisor.

Another role for the university supervisor is to establish the type of interpersonal relationships that enable the student teacher and the university supervisor to give and receive in a mutually satisfactory way. In a study with teachers, Blumberg (1984) found that both supervisors and teachers reported that interpersonal transactions with each other are the cause of most problems in supervision. In applying this possible problem to the clinical supervision of student teachers, the university supervisor should develop the sensitivity to determine when such a problem exists, assuming the type of role that allows the student teacher to interact in a variety of situations without feeling threatened. This is a very difficult task that requires a supervisor of extreme sensitivity to be willing to examine the situation and determine what type of adjustments in supervisory behavior must be made. Then the university

supervisor can assume the proper role essential for this open interchange with the student teacher.

The role of the university supervisor is to continually establish an attitude of trust among the members of the triad. This means that the university supervisor is to observe and focus on what was agreed to during the preobservation conference. This may require ignoring certain behaviors of students and the student teacher. This is especially true during the initial observation. As the relationship between the university supervisor and the student teacher matures, the student teacher may feel enough at ease to suggest that the university supervisor should include relevant data, other than data specified in the preobservation conference, which may have an effect upon the instructional processes. If this does occur, the university supervisor should exercise extreme caution not to allow this relevant data to become detrimental by being the primary focus during the postconference analysis. If the student teacher never suggests the inclusion of additional data, the university supervisor should avoid mentioning it and adhere to the original agreement.

The university supervisor should focus on student behavior. Good and Brophy (1984) have indicated that the key to looking into classrooms is the observation of student behavior. By focusing on student behavior, a university supervisor will be less likely to involve a personal or professional preconceived bias regarding student teacher behavior. Once student behavior is identified, the focus can shift to the student teacher's actions or lack of actions that caused the student behavior. This focus on student data as a result of student teacher behavior strengthens the linkage between student behavior and student teacher instructional actions.

Activities

The use of observation to collect relevant objective data is the heart of the clinical supervision process. During the preobservation conference, an agreement was reached that provided the focus for analysis of instructional techniques.

It is assumed that one main priority of the student teacher was data collected in accordance with the objectives of the student teaching program of the university. A teacher education unit will have a knowledge base that provides a structure for the unit's teacher education program. During the preobservation conference, the student teacher surely selected the objectives that are part of the knowledge base of the unit's teacher education program. The role of data collection, including any checksheet type of activities based on the knowledge base in student teacher evaluation, is discussed in chapter 9. The university supervisor should be prepared to integrate this type of data collection into the other data suggested by the student teacher.

If there was agreement regarding the role of lesson plans in the observation, the first item should be an analysis of the lesson plans. Figure 7.2 provides an example of a form that can be used in lesson plan analysis.

There are two ways in which lesson plan analysis can be a part of the data collection process. One approach is to examine the lesson plans prior to the implementation of the lesson. This causes a focus on the structure and design of the lesson plans without any regard about whether or not these plans could be implemented as part of the instructional process. This would require the student teacher to give very extensive plans to the university supervisor during the preobservation conference or with sufficient lead time for the university supervisor to analyze the plans. Another approach would be for the university supervisor (1) to examine the lesson plans very briefly before the start of the lesson and (2) to analyze the lesson plans following the observation, making this analysis part of the data analysis. This is the approach suggested by Figure 7.2. Whichever approach is used by the university supervisor, lesson plan analysis should not be attempted during the instructional process when the university supervisor is supposed to be collecting data. It is impossible to analyze lesson plans and objectively collect data about classroom activities.

There is a variety of techniques available for collecting observational data. Acheson and Gall (1980) suggest data based on such data as time-on-task, verbal flow, movement patterns, and various types of checklists or timelines. One specific suggestion is the use of selective verbatim that focuses on specific student behavior or specific student teacher behavior. The university supervisor uses selective verbatim in making a written record of exactly what is said. There should be no paraphrasing or interpretation. However, this does not mean that the university supervisor writes everything that is said. During the preobservation conference, the university supervisor and the student teacher select certain verbal behaviors to be recorded verbatim. To be effective, the university supervisor must write word-for-word what is said while the selected topics are discussed. If the university supervisor uses audio- or videorecording, this can be done after the class session rather than as the instruction progresses.

Selective verbatim provides a transcript to the student teacher that focuses on what he or she said to the students and what the students said to the student teacher and to other students. This procedure sensitizes the student teacher to the importance of the verbal processes in classroom interaction. Also, the university supervisor and the student teacher can concentrate on selected verbal events. Changing behavior is complicated; it may require extensive efforts on the part of the student teacher. Limiting the focus through selective verbatim keeps the student teacher from becoming overwhelmed by all the changes that might be needed if there were no selection of specific student teacher actions and resulting student actions. The verbal mirror provided by selective verbatim allows an objective interpretation of what occurred in the classroom without extensive audiovisual equipment, which alters the environment within the classroom.

Student teacher _____

University supervisor _____

Date _____ Time of lesson _____ Location _____

Are lesson plans part of the data analysis? _____ Yes _____ No

Lesson plan analysis: Answer *yes* or *no* for each statement and prepare a brief narrative that supports the answer.

Characteristics	Y or N	Short Narrative
Preparation: The student teacher had sufficient knowledge of the skill being presented.		
Objectives: The student teacher communicated the objectives of the lesson to the students.		
Stresses sequences: The student teacher demonstrated how the topic was related to topics that have been taught or will be taught.		
Relates objective: The student teacher related the subject topic to the students' experiences.		
Explains directions: The student teacher gave directions that were clearly stated and related to the learning objectives.		
Involves all learners: The student teacher used signaled responses, questioning techniques, and/or guided practices to involve all learners.		
Explains content: The student teacher taught the objectives through a variety of methods.		
Models: The student teacher demonstrated the desired skills.		
Monitors: The student teacher checked to determine if students were properly progressing toward stated objectives.		
Adjusts based on monitoring: The student teacher changed instruction, based on the results of monitoring.		
Guides practice: The student teacher required all students to practice newly learned skills under direct supervision.		
Provides independent practice: The student teacher required students to practice newly learned skills without supervision.		
Establishes closure: The student teacher summarized and fit into content what has been taught.		

Figure 7.2 Lesson plan analysis

Just as selective verbatim has strengths, it also has weaknesses. One of the primary concerns is that the student teacher knows what the university supervisor is seeking and creates an artificial environment by focusing on a specific behavior. Ideally, these desirable behaviors will become internalized and part of the student teacher's normal instructional style or strategies. Another weakness includes the possibility that selective verbatim may cause a focus on such a minute part of the total instructional process that the overall essence of the instructional techniques of the student teacher may be misinterpreted. This is especially true if the behaviors selected are trivial and not an integral part of the instructional process.

Some selective verbatim areas that might have been selected by the triad are questioning, teacher feedback, classroom management techniques, student time-on-task, reinforcement techniques, or many other components of a well-taught lesson. Teachers probably spend as much time using questioning as an instructional activity, such as to stimulate thinking, as they spend in any specific instructional strategy. Teacher questions, student response to questions, and teacher response to student questions may very well constitute the primary instruction within a classroom. Therefore, a brief example of selective verbatim using questioning might be as follows:

Teacher: (Two minutes of talk.)
Teacher: Who discovered America?
Class: (In unison) Columbus!!
Teacher: Very good. *****Who can tell me the name of Columbus' three ships? Susan?
Susan: Nina, Pinta, and Santa Maria.
Teacher: Very good Susan. *** Patty, when did Columbus sail to the New World?
Patty: 1942, I mean 1492!
Teacher: Very good, Patty. ********** In your own words, tell me why you think sailing and navigation developed during the time of Columbus, Fred?
Fred: There was a desire of many people to make money through trading. Since there were

no trains or highways, the best way to move goods, especially items that must be imported, was with the use of ships. There was no other source of power for ships except the wind.
Teacher: Very good, Fred. ******* Why did Columbus come to the New World, Mary?
Mary: I don't know.
Teacher: What do you mean you don't know? Haven't you been paying attention to what went on in class?
Mary: (Silence)
Teacher: Very well, you may just sit there. Please answer the question, Trisha.
Trisha: Please repeat the question.
Teacher: Please listen when I ask the question! Don't you think I have better things to do than repeat the question? Tyrone, do you have any idea what the answer to the question is?
Tyrone: He was seeking spices.
Teacher: Very good, Tyrone. It is nice to have *someone* pay attention. ********* Robert, where did Columbus land, where did he think he landed, and what name did he give the inhabitants? In other words, why did he do what he did and what words are still in our culture from the time of Columbus? It is the name of a race of people and we still use the terms for people from two different continents?
Robert: He landed in the Caribbean, but he thought he was in the East Indies so he named the inhabitants, Indians.
Teacher: George, what would you suppose the people of Columbus' day gave him as a nickname?
George: The Great Explorer?
Teacher: Let's try to analyze what he did and see if we can put together a good name for him. Where did Columbus do his most famous work?
Sam: In the New World.
Teacher: On what type of terrain did he do his most famous work?
Mary: He did it at sea or in the ocean?
Teacher: Very good. What official title does a person have who has great command of the sea?

Several students: Captain!

Teacher: What rank is held by a person who tells a captain what to do?

Gary: (Waving his hand wildly) I know!! I know!! Admiral!

Teacher: Let's put these together, and you will find out that he was called "Admiral of the Ocean". (Writes on chalkboard) Now, tell us, George, of the explorers Columbus, Magellan, and Vespucci, which do you think was most influential in establishing the new world and why?

George: I think Amerigo Vespucci was because he knew what he had discovered and that is why we are called America instead of Magellan or Columbus.

   Ten seconds of teacher talk for each

This example of selective verbatim, most likely with lines indicating some type of activity unrelated to the questions, would go on for several pages. Although Hunter (Garman, et al., 1987) thinks that the observation should be limited to fifteen to twenty minutes, the duration of the observation is a function of how long it takes the university supervisor to obtain sufficient data to provide a true picture of the instructional activities within the classroom. Many university supervisors prefer to be in the classroom during the entire lesson to get a glimpse of how the selective verbatim is a part of the entire lesson.

Analysis and Strategy

This step in the clinical supervision process consists of two separate, yet intertwined, supervisory actions. The university supervisor should integrate these steps into a comprehensive action plan designed to improve the instructional activities of the student teacher.

Expectations

A university supervisor should develop an unbiased view of classroom events, since the first part is to analytically examine the objective observational data. This is analyzed according to specific guidelines. Then, specific instructional strategies are designed to help modify and improve the classroom instructional actions of the student teacher. The analysis should be done as soon as possible while the university supervisor is able to recall selected events that may not be part of the selective verbatim but may provide some background information to what occurred in the classroom. The university supervisor should review the preobservation agreement regarding the focus of the observation. If there is data that is unrelated to the agreement, the university supervisor should disregard this data. However, relevant data, which may appear to be focusing on an area unrelated to the agreement, may be included. An example of this type of data relatedness may be found in the selective verbatim discussed earlier. It would be permissible to discuss ancillary teaching concepts not specifically on questioning, if this concept could be supported from the data analysis and is integral to the success of the concerns of the student teacher. The university supervisor could be expected to examine the use of verbal reinforcement in questioning. While the concept of verbal reinforcement is not part of the agreement, it is an essential part of questioning, and the analysis could focus on how verbal reinforcement is used in this questioning session. Other variables that might be included are amount of teaching time spent questioning, pace of teacher talk, and voice characteristics of the teacher, which may inhibit or influence the questioning process. However, this is not an opportunity for the university supervisor to include anything desired under the guise that "everything a student teacher does is interrelated and, therefore, I can talk about anything I wish." Such actions will quickly destroy the relationship of the triad members and be detrimental to the clinical supervision process.

Roles

The university supervisor should assume the role of providing an external criteria check to the student teacher. The student teacher has provided, through the preobservation conference, a list of concerns and suggested areas where external validation of teaching techniques is needed. This external validation must be more than a pass or fail type of validation, but rather must be an observation-based critique and list of possible techniques to improve the effectiveness of instruction. This requires the university supervisor to ignore predispositions about what should occur within the classroom and analyze in terms of what has been agreed upon as being areas essential to the improvement of the student teacher's instructional techniques. The university supervisor should provide this information to the student teacher in a format that encourages reflection and self-analysis.

Once this data analysis has been completed, the role of university supervisor moves to that of a trusted colleague. This requires the development of strategies that provide sufficient reinforcement for existing student teacher actions and also encourage change toward specific pedagogical techniques. The university supervisor becomes a "trusted wise person" whose wisdom, knowledge, and expertise are respected and valued by the student teacher. If the collegiality has been developed and nourished, the student teacher is more likely to appreciate and be receptive to ideas, techniques, and strategies from external sources, being self-confident enough to describe strengths, weaknesses, and improvement techniques in an open forum.

The university supervisor analyzes and interprets the collected data to determine whether the agreed-upon teaching behaviors were compatible with the intent. This requires an examination of the congruence and compatibility between indicators of performance and indicators of consequence. An examination of the congruency of the student teacher's behavior, especially in terms of the relationship between student teacher behavior and desired student behavior or outcomes, is the overall responsibility of the university supervisor. The university supervisor should be aware that these inferences are tentative and are based on the ob-

jective analysis of data. The university supervisor should define the desirable instructional strategies of the student teacher, refine those instructional strategies that need modification, and help the student teacher by providing an atmosphere where the student teacher can develop new strategies to improve student learning within the classroom.

The university supervisor should focus on student teacher patterns that represent student teacher behavior significantly related to pupils' learning. These student teacher behaviors, and resulting student behaviors, should be clearly demonstrated by the data. If, for example, as a result of a student teacher interrupting the instruction to correct a student, the data indicates that the student teacher must provide more directions to get students back on task, then the university supervisor has data-supported behavior that should be modified. However, the university supervisor should take extreme care in discussing hypothesis-based behavior with the student teacher. Hypothesis-based behaviors are not as easy to support as data-based behaviors. An example of this would be a university supervisor who believed that positive reinforcement should always be used to encourage student involvement in the lesson. While there is some research to support this position, there is also research to support the concept that positive reinforcement is not always desirable (Brophy 1979). Therefore, a university supervisor should be very cautious in establishing recommendations on hypothesis-based behaviors but rather should focus on data-based behaviors. Much more tenuous than hypothesis-based behaviors are those that are founded on hunches or intuition. This type of university supervisor action should certainly be avoided because it destroys the parameters established in the preobservation conference and moves the emphasis to unknown territory.

Activities

The university supervisor should analyze the student teachers' actions, the pupil's actions, both singly and as they interact, and the performance and the results of all of these. Although a cooperating teacher might have a different set of questions to analyze and discuss in the postobservation conference, all members of the triad will analyze the same selective verbatim to provide structure to aspects of the role of each member of the triad. An analysis by a university supervisor is presented in this chapter and other analyses in the appropriate chapters.

Questioning may be categorized as narrow or broad. Narrow questions may require only factual recall or single-word answers. It is essential that student teachers know how to use each type of question and the function of each. The analysis of the questioning techniques focuses on the use of convergent and divergent questions and the use of mental operations questions. Convergent questions, with their focus on the "right answer," are often used at the beginning of a lesson and are essential to focusing on specific selected information necessary for later discussion and growth. Divergent questions are questions that allow the students to expand, their thinking process; the questions do not have a correct answer but may often raise other questions to stimulate further growth and inquiry. Traditionally, convergent questions are used at the beginning of a lesson and may, in selected areas that require the solving of a mathematical problem or reaching a scientific conclusion, be used at the end of a lesson. Divergent questions are used to allow the students the opportunity to do inquiry and think freely about a topic.

Another type of question classification scheme categorizes the mental operations required by the questions. This scheme, which combines Bloom's Taxonomy and Guilford's Structure of the Intellect (Moore 1989), classifies questions into one of four question categories: factual, empirical, productive, and evaluative. Table 7.1 shows these categories of questions.

Factual questions merely test the student's memory. These may be simple recall or recognition of something as being correct. This is the narrowest of all and requires the least involvement in the mental processes. Empirical questions require that the student analyze or integrate what is remembered into a single predictable answer. Although the answer may require thinking, the result is a single, logical, concise answer. Productive questions do not have a single correct answer. Like all open-ended questions, it is difficult to predict what the answer will be. Students must think creatively and produce something that is most likely unique. The simple recall of information provides the foundation, not the end result, of a productive question. Evaluative questions require that the students make judgments or value something. These questions usually require some type of validation statement, including the criteria used for the judgment. Although these may be for either the affective or cognitive domain, both types of questioning can be used in analyzing students' evaluation skills. Figure 7.3 classifies the questions from the selective verbatim as either convergent or divergent as well as the mental operations required in answering the questions.

Table 7.1
Categories of Questions

Mental Operations Questions	Bloom's Taxonomy	Guilford's Structure of the Intellect
Factual	Knowledge/Comprehension	Cognitive/Memory
Empirical	Application/Analysis	Convergent Thinking
Productive	Synthesis	Divergent Thinking
Evaluative	Evaluation	Evaluative Thinking

Source: Moore, K. D. *Classroom teaching skills: A primer.* New York: McGraw Hill. Used with permission.

Script Tape of Student Teacher Questioning	Convergent or Divergent	Mental Operations
Teacher: (2 minutes of talk.)		
Teacher: Who discovered America?	Convergent	Factual
Class: (In unison) Columbus!!		
Teacher: Very good. *****Who can tell me the name of Columbus' three ships? Susan?	Convergent	Factual
Susan: Nina, Pinta, and Santa Maria.		
Teacher: Very good, Susan. *** Patty, when did Columbus sail to the New World?	Convergent	Factual
Patty: 1942, I mean 1492!		
Teacher: Very good, Patty. **********In your own words, tell me why you think sailing and navigation developed during the time of Columbus, Fred?	Divergent	Empirical
Fred: There was a desire of many people to make money through trading. Since there were no trains or highways, the best way to move goods, especially items that must be imported, was with the use of ships. There was no other source of power for ships except the wind.		
Teacher: Very good, Fred. *******Why did Columbus come to the New World, Mary?	Convergent	Factual
Mary: I don't know.		
Teacher: What do you mean you don't know? Haven't you been paying attention to what went on in class?		
Mary: (Silence)		

Figure 7.3 Selective verbatim and analysis

Another technique is to identify the location and frequency of the students selected to answer questions. Using a schematic of the room and the selective verbatim used in classifying the level of questioning, the university supervisor uses a tally to represent a student who was asked a question (Figure 7.4). This allows the student teacher to

Script Tape of Student Teacher Questioning	Convergent or Divergent	Mental Operations
Teacher: Very well, you may just sit there. Please answer the question, Trisha.		
Trisha: Please repeat the question.		
Teacher: Please listen when I ask the question! Don't you think I have better things to do than repeat the question? Tyrone, do you have any idea what the answer to the question is?		
Tyrone: He was seeking spices.		
Teacher: Very good, Tyrone. It is nice to have someone pay attention. *********Robert, where did Columbus land, where did he think he landed, and what name did he give the inhabitants? In other words, why did he do what he did and what words are still in our culture from the time of Columbus? It is the name of a race of people and we still use the terms for people from two different continents?	Convergent	Factual
	Convergent	Empirical
Robert: He landed in the Caribbean, but he thought he was in the East Indies so he named the inhabitants, Indians.		
Teacher: George, what would you suppose the people of Columbus' day gave him as a nickname?	Divergent	Productive
George: The Great Explorer?		
Teacher: Let's try to analyze what he did and see if we can put together a good name for him. Where did Columbus do his most famous work?	Convergent	Empirical
Sam: In the New World.		

Figure 7.3—*Continued*

Script Tape of Student Teacher Questioning	Convergent or Divergent	Mental Operations
Teacher: On what type of terrain did he do his most famous work?	Convergent	Factual
Mary: He did it at sea or in the ocean?		
Teacher: Very good. What official title does a person have who has great command of the sea?	Convergent	Empirical
Several Students: Captain!		
Teacher: What rank is held by a person who tells a captain what to do?	Convergent	Factual
Gary: (Waving his hand wildly) I know!! I know!! Admiral!		
Teacher: Let's put these together and you will find out that he was called the "Admiral of the Ocean". (Writes on chalkboard)		
Now, tell us, George, of the explorers Columbus, Magellan, and Vespucci, which do you think was most influential in establishing the new world and why?	Divergent	Evaluative
George: I think Amerigo Vespucci was because he knew what he had discovered and that is why we are called America instead of Magellan or Columbus.		

*10 seconds of student teacher talk for each *

Figure 7.3—Continued

clearly identify the location and frequency of students selected to answer questions.

The question analysis chart and the student selection chart represents two examples of the type of data analysis the university supervisor can use to assist student teachers as they begin their practice in the classroom. This example is limited to a small analysis, using the questioning selective verbatim presented earlier in this text. Once the university supervisor has completed the data analysis, the university supervisor can begin to develop a strategy for the postobservation conference with the student teacher and the cooperating teacher.

In developing the strategy for the postobservation conference, it is essential that the university supervisor remember that the processes of the postobservation conference are as important as the product. Incidental learning, which will affect the triad and influence the future of clinical supervision, will occur, and the university supervisor should plan all strategy toward ensuring the success of repeated applications of the clinical

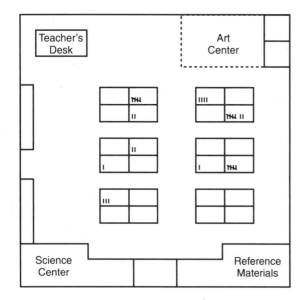

Figure 7.4 Student selection chart

supervision cycle. The university supervisor should try to keep in focus that the student teacher may tend to move toward seeking direction from the supervisor instead of depending on reflective self-assessment. Student teachers have become successful by doing what is required of them rather than by engaging in inquiry and reflection about their own behavior. Therefore, the primary function of the strategy session is to encourage the student teacher to initiate self-assessment that will strengthen the clinical supervision cycle and develop the type of lifelong self-assessment necessary for a prospective teacher to continually evaluate and modify instruction within the classroom.

A second concern is the question of quantity. One of the purposes in selective verbatim is to limit the amount of information that will be discussed in the postobservation conference. Discussing a full analysis of the data, even if it is within the confines of the agreement, can easily use so much time that the discussion focuses on past student teacher behaviors instead of cooperatively working with the student teacher toward

improving future instruction. Another concern is that discussion of all the data, instead of providing clarity regarding the supervision process so the student teacher can move toward self-assessment, the student teacher becomes overwhelmed by the amount of input into the teaching process. He or she may be unable to assimilate the information into existing teaching strategies. This causes clinical supervision to become a negative process because it wastes time and provides no useful information to the student teacher.

Another strategy concern is how the university supervisor presents the data to the student teacher. The university supervisor may present the data along with suggestions or may present the data and expect the student teacher to provide an analysis. Preferably, the university supervisor has provided the student teacher with the data without analysis, and the student teacher is preparing an analysis and strategy to present at the postobservation conference. Therefore, it is recommended that the university supervisor have a copy of just the data, to put on the table for discussion, as well as an analysis that can be used for reference during the discussion. The university supervisor should exercise restraint and share only the data with the student teacher. This allows the student teacher the opportunity to present his or her own data analysis and encourages collaboration with the university supervisor.

The university supervisor should plan the postobservation conference. This means that there should be an agenda, but part of this agenda should be a flexibility in treating issues raised by either the cooperating teacher or the student teacher. There must be an attitude of encouraging the other members of the triad to bring issues and direction to the postobservation conference. The agenda of the university supervisor should be used to keep the postobservation conference from stagnating or digressing to trivial, unimportant, or unsolvable issues. The university supervisor should be prepared to do whatever is necessary to instill a feeling of success with other members of the triad. Unless this is an integral part of the university supervisor's agenda, the success of clinical supervision could be seriously impaired.

Postobservation Conference

Each step in the clinical supervision cycle becomes dependent on the previous step or steps. If the postobservation conference is less than successful, the previous three stages were probably less than successful. It is important to recognize that the time, energy, and careful planning expended in the first three stages will come to fruition during the postobservation conference. The feedback through the formative evaluation process will provide credence to the teaching activities of the student teacher and ultimately lead to student teacher self-analysis and establish the basis for professional improvement throughout the career of the student teacher. In the initial postobservation conference, there probably will be predominant university supervisor talk and direction. The university supervisor should try to maintain an attitude that encourages the student teacher to become more in charge of the direction of the entire clinical supervision cycle. To facilitate the development of actions that reflect this attitude, the university supervisor should audiotape this postobservation conference to assist in the postobservation analysis.

Expectations

The university supervisor should anticipate that the discussion with the student teacher and the cooperating teacher will provide strategies for improving the performance of the student teacher in an instructional setting. If there is unsuccessful completion of the goals of clinical supervision, the university supervisor must assume that ineffective communication resulting in a nonfunctioning triad or goal displacement has occurred. The university supervisor is expected to remediate this situation and establish the proper type of atmosphere for successful implementation of the clinical supervision model. This may be a difficult process because no two conferences are the same, even if the same people are involved in each conference.

The university supervisor should expect some reluctance on the part of the student teacher, especially during the initial postobservation conference. The influence of time, experiences, situational variables, the developmental level of the student teacher, and emotional undercurrents such as defense mechanisms can impede the expectations of a smooth conference wherein everyone functions independently and cooperatively without any hesitation or ambivalence. Everything the university supervisor expects to happen is just a guess with no certainty of any specific action or lack of action. Therefore, the university supervisor must draw upon a lifetime of experiences to keep the postobservation conference functioning and progressing toward its goal.

Roles

The university supervisor should assume the role of a facilitator in the postobservation conference. This means that the university supervisor should assume the role of keeping the conference in the right direction without usurping the role of other members of the triad. The university supervisor should use a facilitative role to examine what happened in contrast with what was intended to happen, and provide nondirective and collaborative leadership to the triad in seeking ways to understand how pedagogical decisions affect the nature and quality of instruction and learning. Mosher and Purpel (1972) indicate that the role of the university supervisor is to use evidence from observation as an occasion to "teach" alternative and assumedly more pedagogically effective strategies. The word *teach* is used in a more Socratic way wherein the student teacher discovers the answers to his or her own questions. The university supervisor should make all efforts to avoid becoming an authority figure who is explaining everything to the student teacher, but at the same time should assume the role of helping the student teacher make more functional use of his or her own resources and, therefore, perform more effectively within the classroom.

Another role of the university supervisor is that of providing the necessary support system for the student teacher to grow into a reflective, self-directing professional. Growth can be painful and threatening, especially in an environment where others have a more clearly defined base of power than that of the student teacher. Therefore, the university supervisor must provide psychological reinforcement, praise specific excellent teaching behaviors, and reward successful elements of the instructional process. This encourages self-growth of the student teacher by providing a wider view than the student teacher can obtain from a single perspective. In providing this support system, the university supervisor must be sensitive in providing praise. Undeserved praise, or praise that is excessive or exaggerated, weakens the credibility of the university supervisor and is detrimental to the clinical supervision process.

The university supervisor has the responsibility for maintaining the integrity of the postobservation conference. Holland (1989) maintains that there are three components of a supervisory conference: the perceived purpose, the relationship that exists between the university supervisor and the student teacher in the specific situation, and how information and data about the student teacher's performance are used in the conference. Unfortunately, many postobservation conferences are somewhat similar to the recurring patterns described by Garman (1982) as a conference that is like a religious confessional in which the supervisor officiates, the teacher confesses his or her transgressions, the supervisor suggests ways to repent, the teacher agrees to recant, the supervisor assists in penance, teacher makes act of contrition, the supervisor gives absolution, and both go away feeling better. Conferences with student teachers organized according to this style of supervisor/ teacher activity destroy the integrity and the function of clinical supervision by absolving the student teacher of any responsibility for determining the effectiveness of instructional behavior

and placing this responsibility on the university supervisor. The university supervisor should avoid this type of situation by having established the procedures for the postobservation conference and adhering to these procedures.

This procedure requires specialized conference preparation on the part of the university supervisor. This specialized preparation begins with the greeting to others when the conference begins. After discussing the role of confidentiality and explaining the function of the audiorecorder, the university supervisor's remarks should stimulate spontaneous behavior on the part of the student teacher. These remarks should not be hostile and demeaning to the student teacher, but rather the remarks should build rapport and continue to improve the established relationship. A common error of university supervisors is to develop behavior that is routinized and, despite expressing claims of different behavior in different situations with different individuals, using these consistent behavior patterns with each student teacher in all conferences. This lack of variation in introductory comments during conferences may cause student teachers to view themselves as an unimportant part of a bureaucracy and may be detrimental to the clinical supervision process.

The university supervisor must constantly work at establishing and improving the morale of the student teacher within the limits and structure of clinical supervision. The control of the postobservation conference should not become an issue. It is the responsibility of the university supervisor, who has control to keep or share, to become vulnerable by deferring to the student teacher whenever possible. This means that the university supervisor should anticipate the needs of the student teacher and encourage the student teacher to assume a major share of responsibility for analyzing teaching behavior and planning for its improvement. This genuine participation of the student teacher occurs only if the university supervisor allows it. It is the university supervisor's responsibility to do whatever is necessary to make the relationship pleasant and beneficial for all members of the triad.

Activities

The activities of the postobservation conference have been determined by the series of events leading to this activity. The first activity should be a review of the preobservation conference agreement (Figure 7.1) to provide structure to the entire postobservation conference. The university supervisor then presents the data to the student teacher and the cooperating teacher. This presentation is designed to reconstruct the lesson through the use of data obtained during the observation. All discussions, recommendations, reinforcement, and suggestions should arise from and be supported by the data. This quest for the meaning of what happened in the classroom should focus on pattern analysis rather than isolated events. The triad reviews the objectives of the lesson, discusses the analysis of the lesson plan, using the criteria in Figure 7.2, discusses the data, and begins to analyze the data for possible instructional implications. While it is the primary responsibility of the student teacher to suggest a plan of action, the university supervisor should focus activities toward ensuring that the plan is practical and deals with the causes of an issue rather than with the symptoms. This requires each member of the triad to provide expertise regarding pedagogy, previous learning experience within the classroom, environmental situations, and other variables that combine to help explain student behavior as a function of student teacher behavior.

These activities must identify consistent patterns of behavior that have a major impact on the learning environment within the classroom. Examination of trivial student teacher actions or trivial student actions that are isolated or unimportant are a waste of time and may cause the focus to become tangent to where the instructional problems are located. Once the consistent behavior patterns are identified, the university su-

pervisor and the student teacher can try to identify a relationship between the objectives of the lesson and these behavior patterns. This relationship (positive in nature) is a list of behaviors the student will want to repeat.

It is at this point that the human relations skills of the university supervisor must emerge. The student teacher should have analyzed his or her own teaching behavior patterns that were inconsistent with the objectives of the lesson and the resultant effect of these activities on the students and the instructional process. During this sensitive time, the university supervisor should clearly convey the fact that any dissatisfaction is with the instructional activities and not with the student teacher. If the student teacher perceives that the university supervisor is unhappy with him or her as a person, the result may be a tendency for the student teacher to refuse to participate. He or she may withdraw to try to please the university supervisor by becoming subservient, may become aggressive and alienate other members of the triad, or do only what must be done to prevent retaliation by others in the triad.

The final activity of the postobservation conference is to use the information obtained in the preobservation conference for the next cycle. Using the analyzed data, the university supervisor, the cooperating teacher, and the student teacher should be able to develop a much more workable agreement that encourages the student teacher to continue the practices that support a viable learning environment and those instructional practices that appear to be producing the desired results. These desired results may be the objectives of the lesson plans or they may be the incidental learnings that are often the hallmark of a successful teacher. These results should be developed by the student teacher under the tutelage of the university supervisor and the cooperating teacher. As each cycle is completed, it is expected that the active involvement of the university supervisor will diminish, and the student teacher will progressively take charge, improving instructional practices within the classroom.

However, the university supervisor is expected to offer assistance to the student teacher, both in theories that increase the effectiveness of instruction and in assisting the student teacher to develop incentives for professional self-assessment and continual self-evaluation.

Postobservation Analysis

The primary distinguishing characteristic that separates clinical supervision from other types of supervision is the goal of self-assessment by the student teacher instead of being told what to do by others. A second distinguishing characteristic of clinical supervision is the requirement that there be a self-assessment of the supervisory process. The supervisory processes of the university supervisor should be examined with the same rigor as the instructional practices of the student teacher are examined. If a university supervisor truly believes that professional behavior is more likely to be useful if it is carefully examined, instead of just assuming that it is correct and justifiable, then the university supervisor's professional commitment must be to do an analysis of the entire clinical process by critically examining the tape of the most viable and action-oriented part of clinical supervision—the postobservation conference.

Expectations

The university supervisor faces the first postobservation analysis with reluctance and anxiety about inquiry into his or her own practices. Probably the first item of analysis should concern tangible and nonthreatening analytical issues. One of these relates to the time variables involved in completing the first clinical supervision cycle. It would appear that a minimum of two hours would be necessary to complete the first four stages of the clinical supervision cycle. The university supervisor must determine if there was sufficient time, if the hours selected met the schedule of all involved, and what types of time

adjustments should be made to enhance the quality of clinical supervision. Another tangible variable can deal with the physical facilities available for conferencing. Focus should be on privacy, convenience, suitable seating arrangements, and other physical facilities.

Roles

The most difficult role for the university supervisor is assuming an objective view of the supervision process. This means that the university supervisor must view the supervisory actions objectively rather than defensively as though the clinical supervision was completed by someone else.

Activities

Once the university supervisor has ascertained the quality of the simple ingredients in the clinical supervision process, the audiotape from the postobservation conference is analyzed as the topics begin to center on the actions of the university supervisor. The university supervisor must assume that, like the examination of the instructional practices of the student teacher, the repetitive patterns in supervisory behavior constitute its most potent features. These repetitive patterns are the components that are most likely to ensure or impede the success of the clinical supervision process. These repetitive patterns are what should be sought by the university supervisor as the audiotape is examined for consistent behavior patterns that influence the effectiveness of the clinical supervision cycle.

It is suggested that the university supervisor listen to the tape several times and pay special attention to portions of the tape that convey somewhat intense positive or negative feelings. These portions of the tape may tend to discolor the entire tape and alter the objectivity of the university supervisor. This is especially true if there was disagreement on an issue or issues, and it is apparent that the members of the triad were unable to successfully interact without becoming hostile. Lack of agreement among the members of the triad should be the type that allows professionals to engage in inquiry and seek common solutions without destructive behavior toward other members of the group.

The university supervisor can analyze the audiotape for evidence of successful completion of his or her role, responsibility, and activities in clinical supervision. The first analysis must be on the understanding of the clinical supervision cycle. The university supervisor should determine from the tape whether the other members of the triad understood the clinical supervision cycle and assumed the role of colleagues rather than any type of ascendent or descendent role. The university supervisor should be able to find examples of role fulfillment in anxiety abatement and expressions of mutual respect among members of the triad. From the audiotape, the university supervisor's role to provide democratic facilitative service by providing an external criteria check should be evident.

The university supervisor should be able to find evidence that certain supervisory roles in clinical supervision were fulfilled. There should be evidence that the university supervisor kept to the areas of agreement throughout the entire cycle and did not abuse the situation by including information from areas outside the agreement. The attitude of the university supervisor, one of an empathetic, sympathetic, and rational supervisor, should be reflected throughout the audiotape. Any suggestions made by the university supervisor should be ones reflecting a complete and thorough understanding of the events within the classroom. Fulfilling these responsibilities is an essential part of clinical supervision, and the university supervisor should be certain that these responsibilities were met.

The audiotape should offer evidence that the university supervisor's activities were supportive of the activities essential to successful implementation of clinical supervision. The audiotape should demonstrate the university supervisor's understanding of the strong relationship among lesson plans, the objectives of the lesson, and the data obtained in the observation. There should be evidence that the university supervisor was cognizant of the feelings of the student teacher. This means that the central theme of the conference was to build the self-confidence of the student teacher to the level where inquiry into his or her own teaching is routine. This requires sensitivity in opening the conference, a limit to the quantity of data, frequent use of morale builder statements, and the use of effective communication strategies that focus on the listening skills of the university supervisor. A sample checklist for these activities and other possible analyses of clinical supervision is provided in Figure 7.5.

The activities listed in Figure 7.5 do not represent a complete list, but rather a list of some of the possible areas a university supervisor might wish to examine to improve the clinical supervision cycle. In addition, the university supervisor should try to examine the audiotape as if the person on the tape were someone else. This provides objectivity that might otherwise not be available.

The most extensive technique that assists the university supervisor is analyzing the university supervisor-student teacher interaction (Blumberg 1984). The university supervisor listens to the tape and every three seconds identifies what is occurring between the student teacher and the university supervisor according to the following numerical scale. Interactions that are between the university supervisor and the cooperating teacher or the student teacher and the cooperating teacher are not identified.

Supervisory behavior

1. Support-inducing communications behavior
2. Praise
3. Accepts or uses student teacher's ideas
4. Asks for information
5. Gives information
6. Asks for opinions
7. Asks for suggestions
8. Gives opinions
9. Gives suggestions
10. Criticism

University supervisor _____

Student teacher _____

Cooperating teacher _____

List date of each of the following

_____ _____ _____ _____
Preconference   Observation   Analysis & Strategy   Postconference

DIRECTIONS: Read each of the supervisory characteristics, which may or may not be evident form the audiotape. Place a check mark in the position you think designates how much emphasis you placed on the specific supervisory characteristic.

The categories for rating your behavior are: (1) heavy emphasis; (2) fairly heavy emphasis; (3) moderate emphasis; (4) very little emphasis; and (5) no emhpasis.

Supervisor Behaviors	Rank				
	1	2	3	4	5
Explains clinical supervision					
Anxiety abatement statements					
Mutual respect statements					
Democratic treatment					
Facilitative					
External criteria check					
Adheres to agreement					
Maintains positive attitude					
Empathetic and rational					
Sensitive					
Understands classroom events					
Relates plans and activities					
Encourages self-confidence					
Encourages reflectivity					
Postitive opening statements					
Limits quantity of data					

Figure 7.5 Postobservation conference analysis

Student teacher behavior

11. Asks for information, opinions, or suggestions
12. Gives information, opinions, or suggestions
13. Positive social emotional behavior
14. Negative social emotional behavior
15. Silence or confusion

Supervisor Behaviors	Rank				
	1	2	3	4	5
Builds morale					
Effective communicator					
Effective listener					
Encourages independence					
Sense of timing					
Effective use of data					
Adequate use of time					
Consistent values					
Positive rewards					
Accepts explicit rationales					
Uses appropriate vocabulary					
Allows for variability					
Accepts others' resources					
Remains indirective					
Communicates patience					
Serves as a resource person					
Student teacher initiates talk					

Figure 7.5—Continued

Once the university supervisor has this long list of numbers, the numbers are sequentially paired, and the numbers mark the vertical and horizontal location on the matrix in Figure 7.6. Tallies are kept, and then the matrix is completed with the total number of tallies in each cell. Then Figure 7.6 is analyzed.

Areas A, B, C, D, E, and F are identified as ''steady state'' areas of behavior. A heavy concentration indicates that the university supervisor is exhibiting a specific kind of behavior.

A heavy loading	Indicates a concern for
A	Building and maintaining interpersonal relationships
B	Using the ideas of the student teacher
C	Working on the informational-data level
D	Working on the opinion-data level

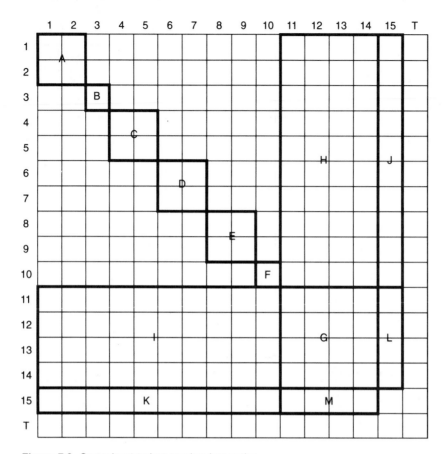

Figure 7.6 Supervisor/student teacher interaction

E	Methodology and/or control
F	Controlling the teacher's behavior

Other areas and implications are:

Area	*Indication*
G	Extended teacher talk
H	Student teacher reactions
I	Supervisor reactions
J	Supervisor behavior that produces silence or confusion
K	Supervisor reactions to silence or confusion
L	Student teacher behavior that produces silence or confusion
M	Student teacher reactions to silence or confusion

This analysis can provide a wealth of information to the university supervisor. Once the university supervisor becomes proficient at using this analysis, further analysis is possible. A university supervisor should analyze his or her behavior with respect to gender, content area, public schools, or any variety of possible concerns. Each of these provides additional information to the university supervisor about how he or she performed in the conferences.

The university supervisor should also find a colleague with expertise in clinical supervision to assist in the postconference analysis. One additional activity might be for university supervisors to view the videotapes on clinical supervision by Droeschers (1988) or be Reed and Gaglione (1977). These tapes review the clinical supervision cycle and provide examples for the university supervisor to compare with the recently completed clinical supervision cycle. These tapes could provide the opportunity for the university supervisor to improve knowledge and techniques before repeating the clinical supervision cycle.

Summary

The expected leadership of the university supervisor makes him or her the pivotal member of the triad involved in clinical supervision of a student teacher. The university supervisor should assume leadership in such a manner that it encourages the growth and self-assessment of the student teacher rather than makes the student teacher dependent on other members of the triad.

The steps in clinical supervision require the university supervisor to develop interpersonal skills beyond the level normally found among university supervisors. The university supervisor should remember that the goal of clinical supervision is improvement of the instructional techniques used in classrooms. These techniques, which are part of an agreement among members of the triad, are analyzed by the classroom observation, seeking specific student teacher behaviors and resultant student behaviors. This data pro-

vides the basis for assisting the student teacher in reflecting about his or her own teaching behaviors. The university supervisor should analyze the supervisory behaviors in the clinical supervision cycle before repeating the cycle.

Questions and Discussion Topics

1. Discuss how a university supervisor should function in implementing clinical supervision with a student teacher. How is this different from the usual supervisory activities in student teaching?

2. Which part of clinical supervision do you think is most difficult for a university supervisor? What makes the identified part so difficult and what type of specialized preparation could assist the university supervisor?

3. Discuss the relationship among the preobservation agreement, the lesson plans, and the data. How should a university supervisor ensure that this relationship exists?

4. Describe the limiting factors of clinical supervision from the view of a university supervisor. How can a university supervisor overcome limitations without altering the function of clinical supervision?

5. What type of specialized activities could a university supervisor do to assist in self-analysis of the supervisor's role in clinical supervision? What specific things should be implemented to require some type of self-analysis on the part of the university supervisor?

CHAPTER 8

Applications for Public School Personnel

CHAPTER KEY CONCEPTS

Analysis and Strategy
Modeling
Observation

Postobservation Analysis
Postobservation Conference
Preobservation Conference

Overview

The public school personnel assigned to work with the student teacher, who is called the cooperating teacher (Glickman and Bey 1990), is identified as being a key figure in student teaching with major responsibility for creating, guiding, evaluating, and adjusting the environment for growth of the student teacher. The day-to-day interaction between the cooperating teacher and the student teacher places the cooperating teacher in a position of greatest influence on the student teacher. Although clinical supervision involves all members of the triad, Funk, Long, Bruce, Keithley, and Hoffman (1982) found that 70 percent of the student teachers ranked the cooperating teacher as the "most significant" influence on their performance as student teachers. This supported an earlier study by Yee (1969) who found that a student teacher's attitudes toward young people shifts toward the predominant influence of the cooperating teacher. The cooperating teacher, who has practical knowledge of successful classroom activity, the ability to evaluate students, and a functional educational philosophy should blend support, constructive criticism, and new ideas into comprehensive techniques to assist the student teacher in achieving self-analysis while functioning at the maximum level. The development of the student teacher into a reflective teacher requires wisdom, wit, dedication, and a sense of humor on the part of the cooperating teacher.

The cooperating teacher must use an affective understanding of pupils as well as rapport with other team members to assist the student teacher in developing reflective teaching. This chapter focuses on the interdependent relationship among the triad members as well as the unique bond formed between the cooperating teacher and the student teacher. This collegiality is the hallmark of clinical supervision and is one of its distinguishing characteristics.

Objectives

Upon completing your study of chapter 8, you should be able to:

1. Describe the importance of the cooperating teacher in clinical supervision.
2. Describe the cooperating teacher's responsibilities as they relate to establishing a suitable relationship with the student teacher.
3. Describe the cooperating teacher as a pivotal member of the triad and the specific tasks required of a cooperating teacher.
4. Describe the stages of clinical supervision and the primary function of the cooperating teacher at each stage.
5. Describe reflective student teaching and how the cooperating teacher can promote reflectivity in a student teaching experience.

The cooperating teacher assumes the major responsibility for the direction of the day-to-day experiences of the student teacher. As such, the cooperating teacher has a central role in implementing the clinical supervision model.

Preobservation Conference

The cooperating teacher must prepare for the preobservation conference with the same intensity and amount of preparation that goes into preparation for teaching classes. Just as the cooperating teacher makes long-range and short-range plans, so it is with planning the preobservation conference. The primary emphasis may be upon the immediate conference, but just as a lesson is more important as part of a larger unit, so the preconference is only the beginning of the clinical supervision cycle. The initial conference provides clarification of the clinical supervision process as well as provides baseline information regarding the student teacher by determining a list of strengths and concerns. Although the word "conference" is most often used in describing this meeting of the university supervisor, the cooperating teacher, and the student teacher, this term

may prescribe an atmosphere, structure, and length that could cause a student teacher to become so anxiety-laden as to become inhibiting. If the student teacher also thinks of the word "clinical," the anxiety can surely rise to a level to make the relationship between the cooperating teacher and the student teacher one that does not foster collegiality. Therefore, one of the preparatory tasks of the cooperating teacher may be to describe the initial preobservation conference with such nonthreatening words as dialogue, interaction, discussion, or planning session. The use of these terms may better conjure up the image of cooperation and support necessary in a successful preobservation conference.

Before the cooperating teacher can initiate the procedural activities of the preobservation conference, it is essential that the participants establish a relationship that fosters clinical supervision. The cooperating teacher should prepare for the preobservation conference by developing personal skills that help promote understanding of self and others. These five skills are as follows:

1. **Listening skills.** Listening involves more than passively taking in the content of the student teacher's communication; listening actually involves the active process of responding to total messages (see chapter 3). Attending skills of nonverbal behaviors, such as eye contact, distance, posture, and gesture should be emphasized. Paraphrasing, clarifying, and perception checking are types of verbal activities that offer evidence of listening skills.
2. **Leading skills.** Although it is important for the cooperating teacher to encourage the student teacher to respond to open communication, it is especially important during the opening phases of a relationship. Indirect leading is useful during the initial stages of a conference, and then the cooperating teacher can use direct leading to help elaborate upon ideas or concepts. Focusing, especially in the

form of questions that cannot be answered with a single word, can be used to prevent ramblings or discussions about unrelated topics during the conference.

3. **Reflecting.** Expressing in different words the student teacher's comments allows an emphasis on these feelings and indicates approval for the student teacher to have these feelings. Equal reflecting emphasis should be placed on such areas as experience and content. The cooperating teacher should make every attempt to avoid stereotypical statements and avoid the habit of making reflecting statements after each student teacher statement. The cooperating teacher must wait for the student teacher's confirming or denying response as a cue for how to proceed.

4. **Interpreting.** The explanation of the meaning of events so problems can be seen in a new way is the goal of this step in the preobservation conference. This process may require some type of questioning that focuses on the base message of the student teacher. There is an opportunity for cooperating teacher input, although the message should be very close to the message of the student teacher. There is also opportunity for the student teacher to do interpreting, especially after completing at least one cycle in clinical supervision. This interpretation is essential to establish the relationship between student teacher actions and the resultant student behaviors.

5. **Summarizing**. Tying together the variety of ideas and feelings is essential to establishing a successful relationship. Summarizing provides movement and direction to the conference; thus, the participants will not feel that an enjoyable hour of discussion passed with no direction or resolution of any issues paramount to clinical supervision. Preferably, the student teacher should do the summarizing. This may require the cooperating teacher to put together some basic ideas and their meanings and to present these to the student teacher. The cooperating teacher should take care to avoid taking over the conference by adding new ideas or creating an environment wherein the student teacher will become agreeable only to bring the conference to a close.

The creation of an ideal personal relationship with a student teacher is difficult and dependent on the personalities involved in the relationship. Henry (1990) offered the following suggestions to the cooperating teacher to produce a conference environment that is tension free:

- Avoid criticizing the student teacher in the presence of others.
- Focus criticism on growth rather than evaluation.
- Build collaborative approach of working together on a problem which may be more productive than an evaluative approach that is dominated by the cooperating teacher.
- Focus on ideas rather than criticism of an individual.
- Be flexible in responding to changing needs and concerns of the student teacher.
- Be a good listener.
- Maintain consistency between instructions to the student teacher and your own behaviors.
- Think ahead and prevent problems rather than wait to react to them.
- Make feedback clear, concrete, and specific.
- Explain the reasons behind decisions and suggestions.

Each of these suggestions allows the cooperating teacher to focus on developing and maintaining a collegial relationship that is essential if the student teacher is to assume more responsibility and become an effective decision maker in the classroom through the process of reflective teaching.

Expectations

The cooperating teacher enters into the clinical supervision cycle—with the preobservation conference—with certain expectations. One of the more common expectations for a public school teacher becoming a cooperating teacher is that all rewards will be intrinsic. Stout (1982) found that 73 percent of the cooperating teachers accept a student teacher for intrinsic reasons, while less than 2 percent of cooperating teachers discount any type of professional responsibility and accept the student teacher for monetary reasons. This indicates that the cooperating teacher may be aware that there is the possibility of more work and fewer rewards, but out of a sense of commitment and expectations of the profession, he or she accepts a student teacher. The acceptance of a student teacher requires a commitment unlike any other phase of teaching. The long hours of preparation and weeks of tedious effort are worth it when the cooperating teacher sees the student teacher gain the self-analysis skills necessary to become a successful teacher. Cooperating teachers are reinforced by the idea of intrinsic service, a vital part of a teacher education program, which may be combined with the knowledge that the cooperating teacher helped a neophyte become an excellent teacher.

Cooperating teachers accept student teachers with certain predispositions. Some cooperating teachers view the student teacher as a source of information in the form of creative ideas that the cooperating teacher can take and use in class once the student teacher leaves. Many student teachers have received instruction in the latest techniques and ideas, and student teachers frequently have a zest and creative spirit not found in experienced teachers. One list of anticipated personal and professional benefits of working with a student teacher (Trois 1959) posited the following reasons why cooperating teachers accept student teachers:

1. **Keep up with trends.** Working with student teachers offers the cooperating teacher the opportunity to become acquainted with recent pedagogical trends through the latest research on teaching and learning. A student teacher will have been exposed to these ideas, techniques, and methodologies during recent classroom instruction at a university or college. He or she can demonstrate these ideas as well as provide supporting information that the cooperating teacher can incorporate.

2. **Work to capacity.** Working with a student teacher requires the cooperating teacher to increase the level of personal performance closer to a maximum level. This provides rejuvenation for the cooperating teacher. A new zest for teaching will be felt long after the student teacher is gone and the cooperating teacher returns to accepting full responsibility for the classroom.

3. **Improve academic background.** Just as student teachers possess new pedagogical techniques, they also have subject matter knowledge that may or may not have been part of the cooperating teacher's repertoire. Much of this information is ancillary and provides support for questions that may arise or to make subject matter more interesting. Reacquainting or introducing a cooperating teacher with this information provides additional information that may be used later in the cooperating teacher's instructional strategies.

4. **Appreciate resource person.** A student teacher can serve as a valuable resource person for a cooperating teacher. This may be in the form of extra instructional assistance, clerical assistance, opportunity to do classroom experimentation, extra time to work with those who need special attention, or just to have another teacher with whom to discuss problems, hopes, and aspirations.

5. **Change attitude.** Working with a student teacher may provide the impetus for an attitude change in the cooperating teacher.

The cooperating teacher quickly discovers that another adult needs assistance, and this idea appeals to most cooperating teachers who enjoy working with others. As with all types of assisting others, the most benefit comes to the person who appears to have the least need, in this case, the cooperating teacher. By entering into a collegial dialogue with another adult, when there is no externally imposed requirement, the attitude of the cooperating teacher becomes more positive and outgoing.

Cooperating teachers frequently engage in a sharing relationship with the student teacher. This allows the student teacher to glean from the years of experience of the cooperating teacher and the cooperating teacher to grow from the ideas of the student teacher. Cooperating teachers also hope to individualize instruction, increase the time for noninstructional duties such as bulletin boards, observe students from a different perspective, and form new professional friendships that may last a lifetime. In a survey of cooperating teachers' expectations, Roberts (1978) found that one of the primary anticipated benefits of a student teacher is that the presence of a student teacher improves the classroom environment. Cooperating teachers also hoped to spend more time reading professional materials, thinking about new ideas in education, and developing good interpersonal relationships among pupils. Follow-up studies indicate that cooperating teachers were successful in meeting these aspirations, as well as spending more time working individually with pupils, spending more time in reflection, and being able to develop and improve new instructional techniques. However, they were unsuccessful in improving teacher activities such as devising new evaluation techniques or attempting innovative techniques such as educational games. This indicates that cooperating teachers are, or at least claim to be, altruistic, and they willingly accept student teachers when there will certainly be more work involved, especially at the beginning of the student teach-

ing experience. These aspirations are similar to those stated by the Michigan Council of State College Presidents (1970) who found that cooperating teachers hope for more individual contact with students, more small-group instruction, and better provisions for make-up work. Despite the aspirations of these cooperating teachers, the multifaceted demands of daily instructional practices caused the advantages of working with a student teacher to be more limited than had been anticipated. The amount of covered material decreased by as much as 40 percent, discipline deteriorated, and motivation of pupils declined.

Another concern of cooperating teachers is the different expectations from various members of the triad. The area of greatest agreement about what is expected of the cooperating teacher is the involvement of the student teacher in planning (Garland 1982). All members of the triad agreed that this requires the cooperating teacher to have the same attitude in planning with the student teacher as is required in the rest of the clinical supervision cycle. The cooperating teacher cannot merely serve as a source of knowledge and tell the student teacher how things should happen but rather should serve in a collegial role. Other areas of agreement among the triad is that the cooperating teacher should expect to hold conferences with the student teacher and provide feedback that enhances the student teaching experience and assists in providing some type of feedback to the university or the public schools. One expectation disagreement is the amount of freedom for the student teacher. The university supervisor and the student teacher felt more strongly than the cooperating teacher that there should be maximum freedom for the student teacher as he or she demonstrates the capability to assume more responsibility. This last concept is an integral part of clinical supervision. If student teachers are to achieve the goals of clinical supervision, it is essential that the cooperating teacher allows them the maximum freedom without disrupting the instructional program. It is essential that a student teacher be allowed to make mistakes and analyze these mistakes through inquiry, reflection, and discussion with the cooperating teacher and the university supervisor. A student teacher will not achieve growth as long as the lesson and responsibility for evaluating the lesson come directly from the cooperating teacher. Freedom to make mistakes within limited parameters is essential for maximum student teacher growth, based on an analysis of instructional activities.

Another expectation of the cooperating teacher is anxieties. Cooperating teachers take their responsibilities very seriously and are often very anxious about accepting the responsibility for preparing a novice to enter the profession. There is a sense of professional commitment when the cooperating teacher realizes that, in addition to providing learning for pupils, an extra responsibility is to offer necessary guidance in helping the student teacher. This may cause the cooperating teacher to question professional and personal adequacy. Questions such as, "What will happen if I am unable to adequately prepare this student teacher for a successful first year of teaching?" "Will my colleagues be jealous if I am successful?" "If this student teacher doesn't become successful, will I be viewed as being responsible?" "Will I be able to relate successfully with the university supervisor?" Other concerns focus on the relationship between the student teacher and the cooperating teacher. Questions such as, "What if we don't have compatible teaching styles?" "What if we cannot communicate effectively?" "What if personal beliefs interfere with our functioning as a team?" An equal concern has to do with the relationship between the students and the cooperating teacher. The cooperating teacher is very aware that the student teacher will leave, and the cooperating teacher will be left with the responsibility of teaching the class for the remainder of the term. Therefore, there is much concern about what type of activities the student teacher will design and what the classroom environment will be when the student teacher leaves. Questions such as, "What if the amount of learning decreases because of ineffec-

tive instructional techniques of the student teacher?" "What if the students do not like the student teacher, and it causes problems with the administration or the parents?" "What if the students like the student teacher better than they like me?" "How do I help the student teacher establish the proper type of rapport with the class?" Cooperating teachers should expect such anxieties, each one indicating what types of things must be addressed to establish a warm empathetic relationship.

Roles

In examining the role of the cooperating teacher, it is essential to remember that he or she, like all members of the triad, has a set of specific roles. In this situation, the word *role* is defined as a set of expectations applied to an occupant of a particular position. This definition should not limit the role of the cooperating teacher to one of isolation, but rather expand it to one of interaction. Each and every role assumed by the cooperating teacher acts on the roles of other members of the triad. Consequently, the roles assumed by other members of the triad affect the role assumed by the cooperating teacher. This interrelationship is one of the strengths of clinical supervision. Even a set of expectations may be altered by the interaction of others with whom the cooperating teacher comes into contact.

The cooperating teacher must assume the role of a collective participant. This refers to a collaborative relationship among the members of the triad. The cooperating teacher, the university supervisor, and the student teacher place a commitment on sharing and valuing the opinions expressed by the other members of the triad. To be a collective participant in such an arrangement, it is necessary for the cooperating teacher, as well as other members of the triad, to accept the following statement: "I believe that you understand my point of view, and I understand your point of view; I accept and support any decision from this group because it was arrived at in an open and fair manner," (Chandler 1982). This statement means that the cooperating teacher may not agree with a decision, but if it was developed and arrived at in an open meeting with input from each member of the triad, the decision is agreeable and acceptable to the cooperating teacher. This attitude emphasizes the concept of shared authority and decision making and establishes the necessary foundation for clinical supervision, as well as providing an emotionally safe environment so the student teacher can engage in open, honest, and reflective discussion of teaching strategies.

The role of the cooperating teachers requires that they remove certain predispositions that they may have about teaching to successfully implement reflective teaching with a student teacher. No longer can the cooperating teachers assume the possession of superior knowledge of teaching but rather must be willing to co-explore with student teachers the best in teaching practice. Cooperating teachers also remove from their belief system the existence of a generic definition of teaching practices that can be universally applied. There must be a transition to an acceptance of conflicting and situational knowledge bases that inform rather than control any type of decision about what is appropriate for specific students in a specific location. Another predisposition that must be removed is the cooperating teachers' belief that the main learning for student teachers is to become efficient at doing what they are told. This needs to be replaced with a belief that the main learning for student teachers is to make educationally sound decisions about their own teaching and practices by reflecting on the relationship among objectives, decisions, actions, and reactions.

A cooperating teacher should assume the role of a facilitator who wants the student teacher to be as successful as possible. To enhance the possibility of maximum success, it is the cooperating teacher's responsibility to be as effective a supervisor as possible. Barnes and Edwards (1984) studied cooperating teacher styles and were able to identify characteristics that distinguished be-tween the most effective and the least effective cooperating teachers. Cooperating teachers who were more effective in working with student teachers believed that learning by experience is essential but not sufficient unless accompanied by direct reflection on the experience; teaching includes the enculturation of morals and values as well as community mores to include awareness of and respect for varying group and individual beliefs and perspectives; motivation is better than discipline, but teachers should be aware of the relationship between pupil and teacher; the workplace norms that must be attended to include recognition of organizational complexity and requirements; and professionalism means assuming responsibility to include the right to make decisions and have a degree of control over circumstances as well as acceptance of blame.

Furthermore, Barnes and Edwards (1984) found that those cooperating teachers who were ineffective did not display the identified characteristics. In addition, certain practices of interaction were determined to be factors if the student teacher successfully assumed the responsibility of a teaching position. The cooperating teachers in the more effective experience were more proactive than reactive, successful in modeling the desired behaviors, excellent communicators through feedback, consistent in the relationship between behaviors and verbal comments, adaptable and flexible, able to provide rationale for actions and suggestions, able to practice self-reflection as an active learner, and able to enjoy positive problem-solving approaches in most situations.

Cooperating teachers must be sufficient role models for student teachers. Kuehl (1976) identified this as the critical role of the cooperating teacher. This means that the cooperating teacher must exhibit the skills, attitudes, and actions expected of the student teacher. The cooperating teacher's movements, questions, responses, techniques, attitudes, relationships, degrees of participation, and leadership impact the student teacher by demonstrating the correct way for the student to approach similar processes. No longer is the

Public school personnel should model the desired behavior for the student teacher.

cooperating teacher able to dictate specific actions to the student teacher but, through modeling, serves as a person who can help the student teacher grow as a professional and become a viable member of the teaching profession.

The best way for the cooperating teacher to fully commit to the clinical supervision idea of a role model is to reverse roles with the student teacher during the early stages of the student teaching experience. This "mock exercise" creates a feeling of true empathy; the student teacher totally accepts the idea of nonthreatening feedback regarding instructional strategy if he or she has been the observer and provided nonthreatening feedback to the cooperating teacher. Such role reversal not only creates an excellent role model for the cooperating teacher, but it also provides the student teacher with a better transition from the university classroom to the public classroom and greater gains in positive student teacher experiences (Mills 1980). This also provides an opportunity for the student teacher to learn what to expect before the observation. The student teacher should be provided the necessary structure regarding the observation by the cooperating teacher. A student teacher gains more from an observation that has specific goals. Observing and recording specific data regarding the cooperating teacher's questioning is much more beneficial to the student teacher than being told to

"observe" and see what can be learned. In addition, this provides a frame of reference indicating that the observation by the cooperating teacher has a structure provided by the student teacher. Research by Kerr (1976) indicated that student teachers imitate styles and behaviors found in cooperating teachers. This role model requires the cooperating teacher to develop some type of self-assessment, just as the student teacher should develop self-assessment during the student teaching experience. Discussion of what the student teacher observed is an excellent opportunity for the cooperating teacher to model reflective teaching for the student teacher. Using this reflective model of self-assessment, the cooperating teacher can demonstrate reflectivity as a technique to improve classroom instruction.

Another role for cooperating teachers is to demonstrate the nuances of teaching. That is, the cooperating teacher should model those techniques of teacher judgments regarding the amount of instructional time devoted to specific subject areas, direction giving, when to respond and when to ignore undesirable behavior, and other related skills. Integration of these techniques, which often are the foundation of successful pupil learning, are essential skills for the repertoire of the student teacher. While these behaviors may seem simple, the cooperating teacher should help the student teacher focus on individual thinking patterns. It is these patterns of planning, teaching, evaluating, and analyzing that encourage a teacher to continue growth efforts that separate the mediocre teacher from the superior teacher.

One issue involving the role model is the relationship between the teaching styles of student teachers and those of their cooperating teachers. While there has been some support for the contention that cooperating teachers have little influence on the teaching styles of student teachers, student teachers commonly adopt beliefs about discipline that conform with those held by the cooperating teacher, adopt many of the practices of the cooperating teacher, and emulate the classroom style displayed by the cooperating teacher (Seperson and Joyce 1973). This indicates that one of the primary roles of the cooperating teacher is to serve as a suitable model of desired teacher behavior. This idea is reinforced by a research study (Browne and Hoover 1990) that found that student teachers use more instructional strategies valued by the cooperating teacher than the instructional strategies valued by the university supervisor. The cooperating teacher should be aware of serving as a role model and develop the type and frequency of instructional activities that are desirable for student teacher use. Because the goal of clinical supervision is selfassessment and continual inquiry toward improvement of teacher actions, which result in desired student behavior and improved learning, exhibiting role model behaviors that would support improvement of instruction should be a major role of the cooperating teacher. It is much more important that cooperating teachers assume this type of role rather than teaching student teachers "tricks of the trade" and telling them this is the "real world," while protecting student teachers from the responsibility of their own mistakes.

To provide maximum opportunities for student teachers to practice the types of instructional strategies advocated by the university, the cooperating teacher must do more than merely provide a sufficient role model. Observing a cooperating teacher use a specific instructional strategy would most likely incline a student teacher to use the specific skill in the classroom. However, demonstrating a specific instructional strategy or skill may not be sufficient to provide the student teacher with an opportunity to successfully incorporate the skill or strategy into a personal teaching repertoire. Copeland (1980) described the classroom as an ecological system into which patterns of teaching and learning may or may not function as a part of an interrelated network. The success of a student teacher attempting to use a teaching technique is a factor of past use of that technique in that specific classroom. Therefore, if the cooperating teacher wishes to provide maxi-

mum opportunities for the student teacher to be successful, it is essential that the ecological environment of the classroom is congruent with the teaching strategies and techniques to be used by the student teacher. Therefore, the role of the cooperating teacher is to provide a classroom ecology consistent with the techniques or skills that the student teacher is expected to use.

Activities

One activity that must be accomplished before the onset of the clinical supervision cycle is the acclimation of the student teacher to the classroom, the school, and the community. Although this is not an official step in the clinical supervision process, it is an essential activity that has tremendous impact on the relationship between the student teacher and the cooperating teacher. It is an initial step in the orientation, observation, planning, teaching, and conferencing processes that are part of the cooperating teacher's activities. The orientation is not a specific time set aside for discussion of all topics at one time, but rather it is an ongoing dialogue between the student teacher and the cooperating teacher that starts with their first meeting. Initially, student teacher questions and topics require about 42 percent of the discussion time between the cooperating teacher and the student teacher during the first week of the student teaching experience but decline to about 8 percent after the seventh week (Johnson, Cox, and Wood 1982). During the early stages of this relationship, the focus is on providing information, and most of the talk is cooperating teacher talk of a directive nature or a list of expectations regarding a variety of topics. Some possible topics include orientation to the school through a discussion of the rules of the classroom and school, as well as a discussion of the relationship between the school and the community; an explanation of the student teacher role, including activity expectations during these few days; determining a long range plan for the student teacher, which should include a schedule for assuming full responsibility for the classroom and a discussion of the university's student teaching requirements. Information about supplies and equipment, a brief description of the classes, personal factors that could impact the student teaching experience, expectations regarding extracurricular activities, and other types of logistical information are other topics for discussion in the student teacher orientation. This type of discussion is essential and necessary at the beginning of the student teaching experience. However, the cooperating teacher must be aware that as the student teacher becomes more familiar with the student teaching environment, the relationship should change to that of a colleague, and the dialogue becomes much less directive and much more a two-way conversation.

The first preobservation conference should occur early in the student teacher experience. The cooperating teacher should have successfully completed all the tasks necessary for the student teacher to become acclimated to the classroom routine, and it is now time to discuss the instructional activities of the student teacher and specific plans regarding these activities. The cooperating teacher should enter the preobservation conference with the idea that much of the student teacher's success will be determined by how well the student teacher is able to obtain a self-evaluative teaching posture that results in improved instructional strategies and increased student learning. The focus of professional growth through verbal interaction makes the conference one of the most important sources of feedback; the conference also provides an opportunity for the student teacher to engage in reflective thinking about the instructional activities within the classroom. The cooperating teacher should designate an agenda that focuses on the improvement of instruction. This involves setting the goals to provide information to later analyze verbal and nonverbal behaviors and how these behaviors influence the classroom instruction.

The cooperating teacher should provide some type of direction for the initial preobservation

One of the initial roles of the classroom teacher is to assist the student teacher.

conference. This involves setting an environment conducive to effective dialogue. All procedural items must be discussed, and a special conference content must be determined by the cooperating teacher. Before the start of the conference, the cooperating teacher should establish the affective climate that is so critical in clinical supervision. The most effective way to establish this tone is for the cooperating teacher to involve the student teacher, both formally and informally, in as much of the instructional activities as possible. One technique that might be useful is for a cooperating teacher to sit down with a student teacher and develop a list of supplementary activities that the student teacher can accomplish. In addition to soliciting input from the student teacher, this technique indicates to the student teacher a total involvement in the school rather than a specific classroom only. This begins to establish the necessary type of relationship because it indicates to the student teacher that this school and cooperating teacher value the student teacher as a colleague and not as someone external to the school. A checksheet could be developed such as that shown in Figure 8.1.

This list can be as extensive as the cooperating teacher and the student teacher wish to make it. Although the most important thing about this list is the process involved in developing it, the list

Activity	Date Completed
Observe in other grades	
Work with the librarian	
Work with the guidance counselor	
Visit a special education class	
Visit specialty classes such as music or art	
Learn how to operate audio-visual or instructional machines	
Review and discuss school policies or manuals	
Identify specific instructional strategies to implement	
Identify specific teacher behaviors to avoid	
Identify specific teacher behaviors to be used	
Develop and construct a sociogram	
Discuss ways to evaluate and improve the physical arrangement of the classroom	
Discuss plans to develop and organize a resource file, including bulletin board ideas	

Figure 8.1 Checksheet for supplementary activities

should be kept nearby; as an activity is completed, it should be so indicated on the form.

In the event that the student teacher is not at a sufficient development level to provide input into the preobservation conference to provide structure to the initial observation, the cooperating teacher may elect to provide a list of generic topics for the initial data collection. A possible list could include the following:

1. **Lesson planning.** The cooperating teacher can initiate a discussion of the possibility of examining the student teacher's lesson plans and the implementation of these plans. This would include the usual type of format, with special emphasis on creativity and making allowance for individual differences.

2. **Teaching techniques.** This topic could focus on areas of teaching techniques such as the variety of instructional strategies used by the student teacher. Another area that might be examined is a focus on the availability, selection, and use of materials in instructional activities.

3. **Interpersonal skills.** One topic of interest is the human relations skills exhibited during the lesson. The rapport of the student teacher, especially when dealing with students with special needs, is an area of possible focus during the observation.

4. **Evaluation as feedback and guide.** Another area of focus by the cooperating teacher could be how well the student teacher adjusts the instructional strategies to student responses and other types of student information that should be used to modify the lesson.

5. **Classroom management.** The ability of the student teacher to maintain the type of classroom environment that would be conducive to the lesson being taught is always of interest to the cooperating teacher. Certain types of lessons require different amounts and different types of student participation. Of special interest to the cooperating teacher would be to see if the student teacher possesses adequate classroom management skills (for example, moving desks for discussion or group projects). Regardless of the type of environment desired, the student teacher should be able to organize the instruction to obtain the type of environment most suitable for the lesson.

The specific type of data to be collected determines the method of recording the data. The triad should agree on a plan of action for recording the data. As suggested in chapter 4, some typical methods of collecting data are:

1. **Tallying.** This method shows the frequency of certain events and focuses on this frequency in the postobservation conference. In examining the frequency of positive reinforcement, the number of times the positive reinforcement was used can be determined by the frequency of tally marks. This serves as the basis for further discussion such as the number per minute, the student behaviors that elicited these remarks, and whether the positive reinforcement was the same or different in all situations.

2. **Listing.** One- or two-word descriptors can be used to identify consistent patterns. These patterns can be either verbal use of the same word or mannerisms that detract from the lesson.

3. **Coding.** The use of a predetermined set of abbreviations has limited use unless all members of the triad have extensive preparation in some type of system such as (1) coding patterns for nonverbal communication patterns (Galloway 1966), (2) interaction analysis (Flanders 1970), or (3) instructional analysis (Hough and Duncan 1970).

4. **Verbatim.** This involves the actual writing or taping of word-for-word accounts. Often this is selective verbatim on a topic such as questioning where the cooperating teacher writes only the questioning activity of the student teacher. This method requires the cooperating teacher to be psychomotorally proficient, but it can provide a tremendous amount of data for later analysis.

5. **Anecdotal.** The cooperating teacher writes short narrative accounts of what happened in the classroom. Care must be taken to avoid biases or writing toward a particular slant or viewpoint.

6. **Timing.** Timing is often used to illustrate the frequency or lack of frequency of an event. The cooperating teacher can use a watch to determine the exact time that something occurred or to note student behavior or teacher behavior at specific intervals. Often time records are used to select a sample behavior within a specific time frame with the idea that the specific behavior selected is typical of behavior over a longer time. The task analysis described in this chapter is an example of timing as a method of recording data.

7. **Combination.** Several of these methods can be combined to produce even more relevant and specific data.

Whatever the plan of action for recording data, the cooperating teacher should be certain that the data is ample and varied and that the events are described precisely, without vague or value-laden language.

A cooperating teacher should make a special effort to avoid dominating the conference. O'Neal (1983) found that cooperating teachers talk 72 percent of the time during a conference. Furthermore, the most frequent types of activities were "review" (commenting on previous events) for 37 percent of the time and direction-giving for 24 percent of the time. These types of cooperating teacher activities resulted in most student teacher comments to merely acknowledge what was said by the cooperating teacher. Also, only 3 percent of the conversation was in the affective domain. The cooperating teacher is more knowledgeable and should provide direction for the conference; however, he or she should take care to avoid excluding the student teacher from input in a conference. This requires encouragement from the cooperating teacher during the conference, even telling the student teacher that input is expected on topics of concern or questions. The cooperating teacher can provide the opportunity and the situations where student teacher input is essential to the success of the conference.

Once the triad has established the affective tone of the preobservation conference, they can progress toward the establishment of guidelines for all subsequent activities, especially classroom observation. It is anticipated that the student teacher is able to provide some suggestions regarding the initial observation. To provide examples of how this process works, we will assume that the triad reached consensus that the cooperating teacher should observe the lesson and focus on the questioning of the student teacher, an analysis of student-at-task activity, and the movement patterns of students and the student teacher. It will be impossible for the cooperating teacher and university supervisor to focus on all three of these during the same lesson, so the focus of both observers should be limited to only one—such as questioning during the lesson—and the other two observations can be completed at a time agreeable to all members of the triad.

The analysis of the questioning should be accomplished by using selective verbatim through script-taping during the brief lesson taught by the student teacher. The cooperating teacher can script-tape the same lesson observed by the university supervisor. This dialogue can be analyzed for questioning techniques and presented to the student teacher in the postobservation conference.

Task analysis consists of a chart (see Figure 8.2) of the room with a random selection of one-half of the students' desks identified. The other one-half of the students will be selected for a subsequent task analysis during the next cycle if the triad agrees to focus on another student-at-task activity. During each two-minute interval of a twenty-minute observation cycle, the cooperating teacher will indicate the specific activities of the selected students.

Task analysis is a viable technique for recording behaviors and classroom actions.

It is not necessary to have a schematic of the room but rather only an indication of where each student desk is located. The specific behaviors that are to be coded should also be part of the consensus of the triad. This allows the collection

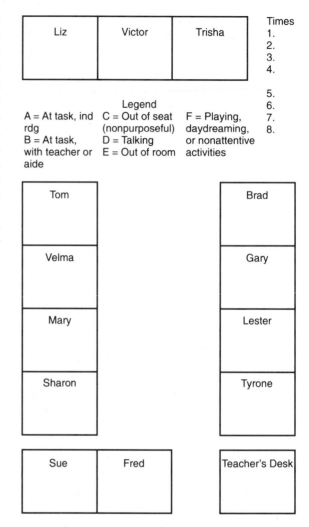

Figure 8.2 Task analysis

of the data to be analyzed and later discussed in the postobservation conference.

The movement patterns of students can also be recorded on a brief schematic of the room (see Figure 8.3), indicating student movements during a twenty-minute period. The focus should be on interaction among the students within the classroom and whatever other factors the cooperating teacher might identify as being pertinent in analyzing the student movement. If an object (such as a book) played a significant part in student

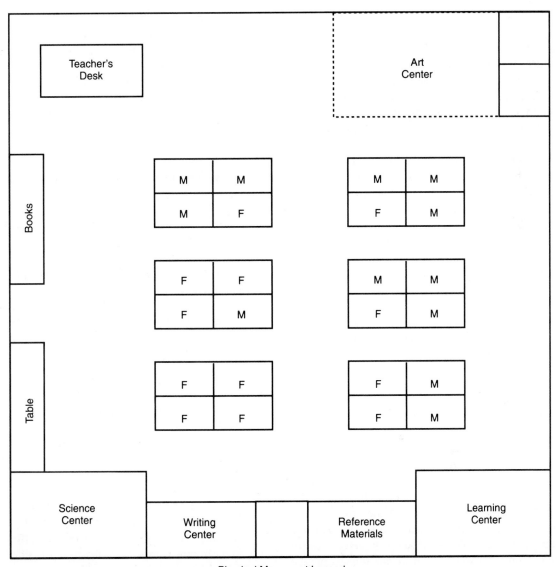

Physical Movement Legend

X X X X X X Directed student movement
– – – – – – – Purposeful student movement (nondirected)
⟶ Teacher movement (arrow indicates direction)
OOOOOOO Nonpurposeful student movement
O Student-student teacher conference (number
   indicates sequential order)

Figure 8.3 Physical movement form

movement, the cooperating teacher could add this to the schematic. Most cooperating teachers cannot examine other activities at the same time as student movement, so an additional activity could be completed following the student movement. This might require examination over a longer period to obtain suitable data, depending on the grade level of the students and the subject being taught.

An analysis of the student teacher's movements during instruction could also be made by designing a form similar to that shown in Figure 8.3. This would require a schematic of the classroom, with identification of the items in the room, that reflects the pattern of the student teacher's movement. There would also be some student movements indicated, especially those that are in response to events that may or may not be under the direct control of the student teacher. This identification of physical movements should occur during direct instruction, providing additional information to the student teacher regarding factors that influence instruction.

Observation

The purpose of the observation of the student teacher is to gather data in accordance with the agreements established in the preobservation conference. Like the university supervisor, the cooperating teacher is limited to these agreements. The fulfillment of the agreements allows the continuation and strengthening of the trustful relationship between the cooperating teacher and the student teacher. To focus on any other type of event, unless it has a significant impact on the agreed-upon areas, will be detrimental to the long-term relationship that is essential for the success of the student teacher.

Many cooperating teachers are not prepared to observe a student teacher. Although these cooperating teachers may work effectively with the student teacher in a variety of situations using a variety of techniques, they do not possess the skills necessary to collect the objective data necessary for implementation of the clinical supervision process. Observations should be systematic and made by a trained observer who records classroom behaviors according to an observation system. The system, as used in this text, is a scheme that specifies both the events that the observer is to record and the recording procedure to be used. This classifies the cooperating teacher as a *recorder,* that is, someone who visits a classroom to record behavior. This distinguishes a *recorder* from a *rater,* whose task it is to observe and rate a student teacher on a performance scale, or a *coder* who uses a category system that requires the observer to classify or code each event according to the set of categories that make up the system.

Observation should provide accurate, objective, and quantifiable records of student teacher and pupil actions and behaviors in the classroom. The following are suggested guidelines for cooperating teachers to use in preparing for an observation:

1. **Keep recording simple and easy.** An observation system should be simple to understand and easy to use in recording data. While complex coding systems may yield valuable data regarding interrelationships and provide more information than a simple and easy observation system, those systems require extensive, specialized training and are beyond the technical expertise of a cooperating teacher who may have a student teacher on an infrequent basis.

2. **Be objective and stick to preobservation agreement.** Cooperating teachers should avoid biases. The purpose of the observation is to provide objective data for use in the postobservation conference. Any type of information that fails to be objective or is not in agreement with the type of data the cooperating teacher should be seeking is detrimental to the spirit and intent of clinical supervision and will surely do harm to the relationship necessary for clinical supervision.

3. **Use clear terms.** The data should be reported in terms that will not be misunderstood by the other members of the triad. It is essential that educationese or other types of jargon that are vocabulary- or experience-dependent should be avoided. If the postobservation conference requires that there should be a focus on the types of positive reinforcement provided by the student teacher, then the data should clearly indicate which specific student teacher behaviors are being discussed.
4. **Avoid personality characteristics.** Cooperating teachers should focus on the student teacher behavior rather than the personality characteristics that may be within the confines of the agreement. Rather than say, "Your voice is too high," it is much better to say "Students would respond better if you were able to lower the pitch of your voice." This puts the focus on the student behaviors rather than on the pitch of the student teacher's voice. The message is the same without being as threatening to the student teacher.

These guidelines allow the cooperating teacher and the student teacher to engage in dialogue about the teaching and learning process. This "language of teacher behavior" (Medley 1971) is far superior to any type of rating of pupils and/or teacher characteristics and can be used to provide a baseline and to reflect on any changes in student or student teacher behavior.

The use of mechanical techniques to collect data appears to offer a valid technique for recording data. In addition, since the presence of the cooperating teacher is a constant in the classroom of most student teachers, students will most likely pay very little or no attention to what the cooperating teacher is doing. This allows the cooperating teacher, as part of the observation process, to collect the data agreed on in the preobservation conference. This can be accomplished while remaining inconspicuous and unobtrusive in the classroom. However, if a recording device is used, it should not make noise or require changing a tape or other unusual circumstances that interrupt the flow of the lesson. Such an interruption can cause an unusual atmosphere that could alter the sampling techniques inherent in systematic observation.

Analysis and Strategy

The cooperating teacher takes the data collected from the observation and begins an analysis of the classroom interactions that occurred during the observation. The first item to be examined is the at-task information based on the cooperating teacher's recording of activities of one-half the students during a specific time. Figure 8.4 reflects the activities of students during a fourteen-minute observation cycle.

A cursory examination of the data presented in Figure 8.4 seems to indicate that several students are not spending sufficient time in activities consistent with maximum student achievement. To succinctly and accurately determine whether this is true, an at-task summary (Table 8.1) is constructed that collects the information in groups and allows all members of the triad the opportunity to quantitatively determine how student time is spent.

The at-task summary should be given to the student teacher without any type of comment that places a value judgment on the information. However, the cooperating teacher would have written some analytical notes that revealed that these selected students spend about one-fourth (26 percent) of their time at task. They also spend one-half as much time playing as they do at task. They also spend almost as much time talking as they do at task. The student teacher should be concerned because for almost one-third of the classroom time (32 percent) the students are not in the room. This may be a factor beyond the control of the student teacher, but it deserves further analysis. Once these analyses are determined, then the triad can begin to develop

Liz		Victor		Trisha		Times
1.F	2.D	1.D	2.D	1.D	2.D	1. 9:20
3.B	4.B	3.D	4.F	3.D	4.A	2. 9:22
5.B	6.A	5.A	6.A	5.A	6.A	3. 9:24
7.D	8.D	7.D	8.D	7.A	8.D	4. 9:26
						5. 9:28
						6. 9:30
						7. 9:32
						8. 9:34

Legend

A = At task, ind rdg
B = At task, with teacher or aide
C = Out of seat (nonpurposeful)
D = Talking
E = Out of room
F = Playing, daydreaming, or nonattentive activities

Tom			Brad	
Absent			1.A	2.D
			3.E	4.E
			5.E	6.E
			7.E	8.E

Velma			Gary	
1.D	2.D		1.C	2.D
3.E	4.E		3.A	4.C
5.E	6.E		5.F	6.D
7.E	8.E		7.F	8.F

Mary			Lester	
1.F	2.C		1.A	2.F
3.E	4.E		3.C	4.C
5.E	6.E		5.F	6.D
7.E	8.E		7.A	8.C

Sharon			Tyrone	
1.D	2.A		1.D	2.D
3.A	4.A		3.C	4.C
5.B	6.B		5.F	6.D
7.B	8.B		7.A	8.C

Sue		Fred		Teacher's Desk
1.A	2.D	1.A	2.E	
3.E	4.E	3.E	4.E	
5.E	6.E	5.E	6.E	
7.E	8.E	7.E	8.E	

Figure 8.4 Task analysis information

strategies that would help the students spend more time on task and less time that is incongruent with task accomplishment.

An analysis of physical movement, such as that shown in Figure 8.5 reveals the movement patterns of the student teacher and some student movement as follows:

1. Student movement appears to be appropriate. There were ten instances of students possessing the maturity and self-confidence to initiate purposeful student movement, two instances of nonpurposeful student movement, and three instances of the student teacher providing impetus for directed student movement.

2. There was good student teacher movement. During the time of the observation, the student teacher moved and interacted with fifteen students. While the pattern of student teacher movement appears somewhat random, there is no movement near one cluster of desks and only a partial circle around another cluster of desks. Each of these two clusters is dominated by male members of the class. The student teacher appears to focus movement on the students on the same side of the room as the teacher's desk.

An examination of the data presented in Figure 8.6 related to student movement reveals the following patterns:

1. There seems to be movement in and out of the classroom. Three students left and three returned during the observation. As revealed in the task analysis, there seems to be a consistent pattern of students being out of the room. These movements may be outside the responsibility of the student teacher (trips to the speech therapist, to the office, and so on), but the triad should discuss this factor.

2. There seems to be frequent movement toward the supply cabinet. Supplies could be distributed before the start of the lesson to control the number of students (6) who went to the supply cabinet.

3. One student (Kathy) seemed to have several visitors (4). Unless this student movement was associated with the lesson, the triad should discuss the relationship between these visits and the lesson.

Table 8.1
At-Task Summary

Behavior	9:20	9:22	9:24	9:26	9:28	9:30	9:32	9:34	Total	%
A. At-task-ind reading	4	1	2	2	2	4	2	0	17	18
B. At-task-rdng teacher or aide	0	0	1	1	2	1	1	2	8	8
C. Out of seat (nonpurposeful)	1	1	1	2	0	0	0	1	8	8
D. Talking	5	8	2	0	0	2	2	3	22	23
E. Out of room	0	1	5	5	5	5	5	5	31	32
F. Playing	2	1	1	2	3	0	2	1	12	13

The cooperating teacher next takes the selected verbatim and analyzes it with respect to the classroom questioning. The resultant analysis is shown in Figure 8.7. It is important to remember that the comments about questions are statements, and the cooperating teacher gives these comments to the student teacher. The cooperating teacher should also make notes about strengths and weaknesses of the questioning, but those comments are not given to the student teacher at this time.

The cooperating teacher may identify suggestions for the student teacher to improve questioning by stating the way students should respond to the questions—wave their hands, shout out the answer, or wait for the student teacher to call on them. The student teacher should also avoid the same reinforcement response, "Very good." This type of repeated response destroys the impact of the phrase as well as limits the effectiveness of all types of reinforcement. Its most common use is to give the student teacher a second or two to conceptualize the next question. Another area of concern is the domination of the questioning process by the student teacher. Rather than have a desired pupil-pupil interaction, each pupil statement was followed by a student teacher statement; each student answer was preceded by a student teacher question. Much more student involvement in the discussion, even some questions from the students, would have occurred if the student teacher had not insisted on being the dominant force in the classroom discussion. As reported by Sadker and Sadker (1982), the student teacher asked more questions of males, and the males received the questions that required higher cognitive thinking skills. All ideas gleaned from the data should be recorded by the cooperating teacher, to have them available for use during the postobservation conference.

Postobservation Conference

The postobservation conference is the step in the clinical supervision cycle where once again there is interaction among all of the members of the triad. The role of the cooperating teacher is to present the data to the student teacher. This requires that an analysis of the data provides the structure for interpreting what happened in the classroom. However, the cooperating teacher should not tell the student teacher what the specific data means. For example, the cooperating teacher could present the at-task information and the at-task summary to the student teacher. The physical movement legend and the analysis of questioning would be given to the student teacher to reflect on what happened and what strategies should be developed in response to the data.

Glickman (1981) proposes that a collaborative orientation toward the postobservation conference may be necessary in the initial postobservation conferences. This orientation would require that

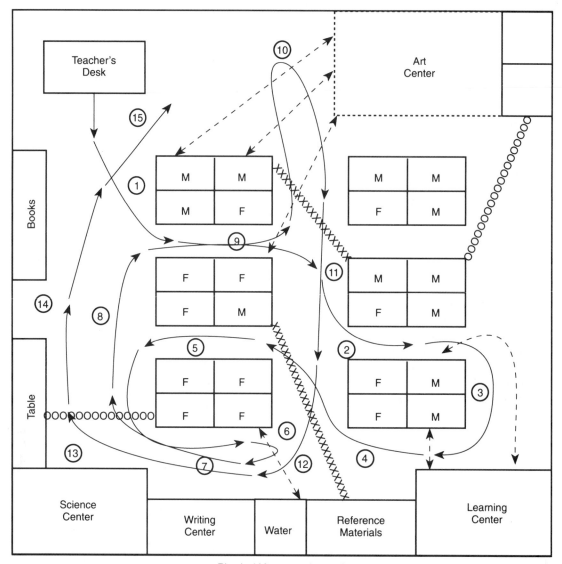

Physical Movement Legend

X X X X X X X Directed student movement
— — — — — — Purposeful student movement (nondirected)
———————▶ Teacher movement (arrow indicates direction)
OOOOOOO Nonpurposeful student movement
O Student-student teacher conference (number
indicates sequential order)

Figure 8.5 Physical movement analysis

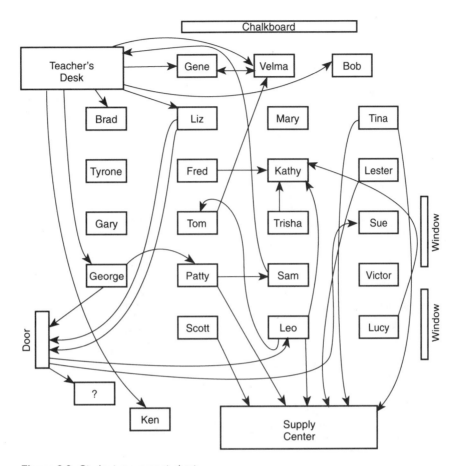

Figure 8.6 Student movement chart

the cooperating teacher initiate the presentation and negotiating of identified weaknesses instead of having the student teacher initiate them as in a nondirective orientation. The cooperating teacher must detect the developmental level of the student teacher and determine the appropriate orientation for the postobservation conference. This requires the cooperating teacher to be a flexible, changing, human person instead of one who operates in a routine, machine-like sequence that uses the same techniques in all situations.

Applying the postobservation conference processes of Hunter (1980) to the student postobservation conference, the emphasis should be on the following four processes:

1. To identify, label, and explain the student teacher's effective instructional behaviors by providing research-based rationale for their success so that the student teacher is able to identify teaching decisions and state why they were effective.

2. To discuss, identify, and develop a group of instructional responses that all members of the triad feel are effective, so the student teacher is not limited to those most frequently used. The triad should also develop a list of alternative student teacher responses to student behavior in case the ones previously used cease to be effective.

Script Tape of Classroom Questioning	Cooperating Teacher Comments
Teacher: (2 minutes of talk.)	
Teacher: Who discovered America?	Test of recall.
Class: (In unison) Columbus!!	
Teacher: Very good. *****Who can tell me the name of Columbus' three ships? Susan?	Another recall with student's name near the end of the question.
Susan: Nina, Pinta, and Santa Maria.	
Teacher: Very good, Susan. *** Patty, when did Columbus sail to the New World?	The use of student's name near the beginning of a question.
Patty: 1942, I mean 1492!	
Teacher: Very good, Patty. **********In your own words, tell me why you think sailing and navigation developed during the time of Columbus, Fred?	You allowed student to correct herself. You asked a student to tell something in his own words.
Fred: There was a desire of many people to make money through trading. Since there were no trains or highways, the best way to move goods, especially items that must be imported, was with the use of ships. There was no other source of power for ships except the wind.	
Teacher: Very good, Fred. *******Why did Columbus come to the New World, Mary?	
Mary: I don't know.	
Teacher: What do you mean you don't know? Haven't you been paying attention to what went on in class?	This is a disciplinary question.

Figure 8.7 Selective verbatim and cooperating teacher comments

3. To assist the student teacher in identifying the teaching activities that did not meet his or her expectations so that additional strategies can be developed for reducing future limiting experiences.

4. To assist the student teacher, through reflective analysis of the teaching events, in identifying and labeling those instructional acts that were not obvious to the student teacher. Subsequently, the triad will select

Script Tape of Classroom Questioning	Cooperating Teacher Comments
Mary: (Silence) Teacher: Very well, you may just sit there. Please answer the question, Trisha. Trisha: Please repeat the question. Teacher: Please listen when I ask the question! Don't you think I have better things to do than repeat the question? Tyrone, do you have any idea what the answer to the question is? Tyrone: He was seeking spices. Teacher: Very good, Tyrone. It is nice to have someone pay attention. *********Robert, where did Columbus land, where did he think he landed, and what name did he give the inhabitants? In other words, why did he do what he did and what words are still in our culture from the time of Columbus? It is the name of a race of people and we still use the terms for people from two different continents? Robert: He landed in the Caribbean, but he thought he was in the East Indies so he named the inhabitants, Indians. Teacher: George, what would you suppose the people of Columbus' day gave him as a nickname? George: The Great Explorer?	This is a rhetorical question. Sarcasm. This is a multiple question. No response to Robert's answer.

Figure 8.7—Continued

alternative behaviors that might be more effective for the student teacher to use in future lessons.

To maintain the balance between a conference that accomplishes nothing and a conference that becomes too intense, Borinstein (1982) has suggested a systems approach designed to maintain interpersonal skills on the job. As applied to the postobservation conference, this process involves the use of the following critical skills.

1. **Maintain self-esteem and standards.** Information presented from the collected data must be sufficiently rigorous to maintain the standards established by the

Script Tape of Classroom Questioning	Cooperating Teacher Comments
Teacher: Let's try to analyze what he did and see if we can put together a good name for him. Where did Columbus do his most famous work?	Refocusing questions that allow the students to be guided toward the correct answer.
Sam: In the New World.	
Teacher: What type of terrain did he do his most famous work?	Additional focus.
Mary: He did it at sea or in the ocean?	
Teacher: Very good. What official title does a person have who has great command of the sea?	Not directed toward any student.
Several Students: Captain!	
Teacher: What rank is held by a person who tells a captain what to do?	Not directed toward any student.
Gary: (Waving his hand wildly) I know!! I know!! Admiral!	
Teacher: Let's put these together and you will find out that he was called the "Admiral of the Ocean". (Writes on chalkboard) Now, tell us, George, of the explorers Columbus, Magellan, and Vespucci, which do you think was most influential in establishing the new world and why?	Reinforced answers of several students by using their answers. This question was not redirected.
George: I think Amerigo Vespucci was because he knew what he had discovered and that is why we are called America instead of Magellan or Columbus.	

*10 seconds of teacher talk for each *

Figure 8.7—Continued

triad without destroying the self-esteem of the student teacher. During the initial postobservation conference, the emphasis must be on the self-esteem of the student teacher. As the student teaching experience progresses, the emphasis can move from a primary emphasis on self-esteem to a primary emphasis on the standards established by the triad.

2. **Be specific about behavior.** The behaviors, whether they describe the student teacher or the students, should be described in clear and lucid terms. If the cooperating teacher is not clear about the behavior, the

entire process may be muddled, and there will be a lack of communication among members of the triad.

3. **Manage the consequence of behavior.** The focus must be on the appropriate response to undesirable behavior. If the student teacher exhibits undesirable behavior, the situation can be managed much more effectively than if it is undesirable student behavior. It may be necessary to design several student teacher behaviors to alter undesirable student behaviors. Also, the student teacher should be encouraged to have patience and not expect immediate changes in student behavior.

4. **Communicate effectively.** The cooperating teacher is responsible for ensuring that other members of the triad understand comments, suggestions, and descriptions. These interpersonal communication skills must be part of the cooperating teacher's skills.

5. **Organize for results.** Nothing defeats the effectiveness of a group like the lack of an agenda. Although taking care not to dominate the conference, the cooperating teacher should approach the post-observation conference with an agenda that ensures that the conference is organized and functions smoothly.

This Borinstein list is somewhat similar to a list by Moorehead, Foyle, and Lyman (1990) who developed a series of instructional videotapes on how cooperating teachers should confer with student teachers. These tapes, which provide specific examples on conferring with the incompetent student teacher as well as conferring with the excellent student teacher, established six principles for successful conferences:

1. **Be positive.** A positive tone indicates a posture of assistance, mutual support, and respect.

2. **Be in charge.** This does not mean to dominate the conference but rather to direct the conference toward its goal, not allowing it to flounder around aimlessly.

3. **Limit focus.** The focus should be on what was agreed on in the previous conference. If there were too many issues agreed on during the preobservation conference, it may be necessary to schedule another conference. Focusing on too many issues creates burnout and overload, which dilutes the effectiveness of the data.

4. **Be positive.** Try to include three or four positive comments for each weakness discussed. Just as there should be supporting data for each weakness, there should also be sufficient data to provide positive comments.

5. **Plan.** Develop a plan of action until the next conference. Depending on where this conference fits into the total student teaching experience, it may be necessary to view this conference as the preobservation conference for the next clinical supervision cycle.

6. **Summarize.** At the end of the conference, the triad should summarize the strengths and weaknesses of the student teacher and the plan of action. This closure is essential to be certain that everyone understands the processes and the products involved in the conferencing.

In all cycles of the clinical supervision process except the last cycle, the postobservaiton conference is combined with the preobservation conference of the next cycle.

This may be viewed as a developmental conference that allows the student teacher to discuss steps for improving the choice and implementation of the instructional strategies used in the classroom. The members of the triad will use this data as a baseline for suggestions during the next cycle. This discussion of the data indicates strengths and weaknesses and will allow the triad to decide where to continue the focus, which areas to continue monitoring to provide evidence of continued student teacher strength, and new areas that may require observation data in the next cycle.

A summary conference is the final conference at the end of the student teaching experience. It should start with a review of the data that was obtained in the observation and analyzed in the analysis and strategy stage. Then the conference progresses to a discussion of future directions for the student teacher. Rather than discuss the items for the next preobservation conference, the focus should move to positive discussions of newly acquired skills and behaviors of the student teacher. After a review of the positive experiences of the student teacher, especially the reflective teaching strategies that have become part of the student teacher's repertoire, the cooperating teacher should provide the student teacher time to clarify his or her own thinking. The role of the cooperating teacher is that of a listener, clarifier, and encourager. This encourages the student teacher to accept the challenge of future growth opportunities as well as to declare individual competency in improving his or her own instruction, as a result of the reflective practices inherent in the clinical supervision process.

Postconference Analysis

In an attempt to improve the clinical supervision process, especially the parts under the direct control of the cooperating teacher, it is essential that the cooperating teacher reflect on personal performance. This requires an analysis of the overall function of the cooperating teacher as a provider of specific information and cooperating teacher actions. A cooperating teacher evaluation, which could be completed by the cooperating teacher and the student teacher, could be designed to provide specific feedback about cooperating teacher actions. An example of a cooperating teacher evaluation form is shown in Figure 8.8. The cooperating teacher should use this form to compare how well the planned activities were accom-

plished. Of special interest to the cooperating teacher should be an analysis of the discrepancy between the opinion of the cooperating teacher and the student teacher.

Just as the cooperating teacher expects the student teacher to reflect on the instructional activities within the classroom, the cooperating teacher must reflect on his or her own actions. This requires that the cooperating teacher, just as the university supervisor did, audiotape the postobservation conference and analyze the tape. The cooperating teacher can use the supervisory-student teacher interaction techniques (Figure 7.6) presented in chapter 7. This will help the cooperating teacher critically analyze the effectiveness of the entire clinical supervision cycle, determining the level of success of the experience and the impact that the cooperating teacher had upon improving the instructional activities of the student teacher.

Summary

The cooperating teacher is the ''most significant other'' during a student teaching experience. If the clinical supervision process is to be successful, the cooperating teacher must remember that a student teacher cannot achieve maximum self-development in a subordinate role. Reflectivity about teaching, and the resultant changes in instructional strategies, can occur only in an environment where differences in personality and teaching style are treated as an asset rather than a problem.

The cooperating teacher should provide the structure and support to allow the student teacher to achieve at a maximum level, while maintaining acceptance as a colleague in the profession. Interpersonal skills, leadership, self-confidence, and sensitivity to the needs of others are the key characteristics of cooperating teachers who are able to successfully implement the clinical supervision cycle to its fullest potential—the improvement of instruction through self-analysis by the student teacher.

DIRECTIONS: Evaluate your performance as a cooperating teacher and have your student teacher also evaluate your role as a cooperating teacher. These should be independent and for your use to determine how you could become a better cooperating teacher. Use the following scale:

5 = This was accomplished to a very high degree
4 = This was accomplished to a high degree
3 = This was accomplished at an average level
2 = This was accomplished at a low level
1 = This was not accomplished

Cooperating Teacher Activity	Cooperating Teacher Evaluation	Student Teacher Evaluation
Demonstrated and explained the function of the classroom as related to the grade, the subject, the school, the community, and the total educational picture.		
Explained the principles of clinical supervision to the student teacher.		
Created an atmosphere where the student teacher was treated as a professional colleague.		
Developed a positive relationship to improve the effectiveness of the student teacher/cooperating teacher relationship.		
Provided student teacher with information about the school that would help the student teacher become self-confident.		
Provided support and nurture to the student teacher to help the student teacher achieve in accordance with abilities.		
Focused all assistance on the improvement of instruction within the classroom.		
Communicated effectively, including suggestions, without reducing the self-concept of the student teacher.		
Provided opportunity and situations where the student teacher could reflect on own instructional activities.		
Held frequent conferences to provide necessary feedback.		
Encouraged the development of an individual teaching style rather than emulating the teaching style of the cooperating teacher.		

Figure 8.8 Cooperating teacher analysis form

Questions and Discussion Topics

1. Which stage of clinical supervision has the most responsibilities for the cooperating teacher? Why? Which stage has the most opportunities for the cooperating teacher? Why?

2. If you were a cooperating teacher and your student teacher was so unsure that he or she would not offer suggestions about observation topics, what would you do?

3. If a student teacher was determined to control the preobservation conference so that the focus would be only on areas of strength, what should a cooperating teacher do?

4. Assume that the cooperating teacher and the university supervisor collect contradictory data from the same observation. What are the implications? What should the cooperating teacher do?

5. Assume that the developmental level of the student teacher was such that self-analysis and reflectivity were impossible. What should the cooperating teacher do?

CHAPTER 9

Applications for Student Teachers

Chapter Key Concepts

Analysis and Strategy
Filtering
Masking
Observation

Postobservation Analysis
Postobservation Conference
Preobservation Conference
Wandering

Overview

The most important part of any teacher preparation program is the student teaching experience. This experience is based on the premise that student teaching behavior can be understood and modified and that instructional improvement can be achieved only by changing or modifying certain student teacher behaviors. Student teaching provides the opportunity to synthesize techniques, methods, and skills learned in university courses to the real world of teaching. However, this opportunity can be threatening to a student teacher whose key to success has been by doing what university teachers have suggested.

The challenges of a new experience wherein the student teacher is expected to be involved in decision-making activities, which will be an ingredient in the student teacher's successes or failures, may be one of the chief sources of anxiety in student teachers. While clinical supervision provides opportunities for the student teacher to engage in reflective teaching and enhance self-evaluation skills, these opportunities require the student teacher to actively participate in the improvement of instructional strategies through self-analysis of instructional techniques. Unless the student teacher is properly prepared for the responsibilities of clinical supervision, anxiety may increase when the requirements go beyond the role traditionally expected of student teachers. However, properly implemented, the process of developing self-analysis and working as a member of a triad provides a structure to the student teaching experience, provides the student teacher with experience working as a member of an educational team, and increases the student teacher's self-concept by empowering him or her with a sense of destiny control. The intense, sometimes threatening, involvement of the student teacher in providing input into a professional decision about his or her performance is the focus of this chapter.

Objectives

Upon completing your study of chapter 9, you should be able to:

1. Describe the changing role of the student teacher in clinical supervision.
2. Describe how the role of the student teacher in clinical supervision differs from the role of the student teacher in more traditional types of supervision.
3. Describe the advantages and disadvantages of a student teacher engaging in reflective teaching through clinical supervision; list some specific techniques that are essential in clinical supervision but not required in traditional student teaching experiences.
4. Describe some of the characteristics of the student teacher who successfully engages in clinical supervision that are not essential characteristics of traditional supervision. Explain which ones are the hardest for student teachers to develop.
5. Describe the most difficult clinical supervision characteristics for student teachers to develop. Explain why you think these characteristics are the most difficult.

Student teachers enter the classroom to apply the theory of the university classroom to the practical world of teaching. The groundwork has been laid, and it is time to find out what really works. The clinical supervision model, with its cyclic process, is designed to help the student teacher develop and refine the skills necessary to become an effective teacher.

Preobservation Conference

The student teacher enters the first preobservation conference with much anticipation and many questions about the future and what is going to occur in the conference. It is best if the student teacher has been introduced to the classroom and has begun to develop an understanding of the classroom environment and how the teacher must plan, organize, and implement learning activities in the classroom. The student teacher is prepared to synthesize all the individual professional skills that have been gleaned from previous coursework and field experiences into a consistent, logical program of instruction that functions within the parameters of the goals and objectives of the classroom.

To clarify the understanding of the information essential to implementing instructional plans for the students, the student teacher should receive a completed form somewhat like Figure 9.1. Additional space, or attached sheets of additional information, may be required to provide the needed information to the student teacher.

Reading and integrating information like that used to complete the cooperating teacher information sheet helps establish the sharing of information essential to the colleagueship necessary for a successful triad. Traditionally, this process is one-way with all the information going from the student teacher; therefore, the student teacher may know nothing about the community or the school unless he or she has had personal or professional experiences with the school or the community. Reading and integrating the information on this form also helps the student teacher synthesize what information has been provided regarding the human essentials of the environment where the student teaching experience will occur.

Subsequently, the student teacher should provide information to the cooperating teacher. Figure 9.2 offers a framework for the type of information that should be given to the cooperating teacher before the start of the student teaching experience.

The student teacher should complete the information sheet and deliver it to the cooperating teacher during one of the introductory visits to the school. This provides professional information that helps the triad prepare for the initial stage of clinical supervision. Depending on the previous experiences of the university supervisor with the student teacher, this information may not be essential for the university supervisor. However, there will probably be some information

Areas of Interest	Information
Personal	
Education	
Family	
Hobbies	
Other	
Professional	
Pupils	
Classroom	
School	
Community	
Other	
Professional	
Pupils	
Classroom	
School	
Community	
Other	

(Attach additional sheets if needed)

Figure 9.1 Cooperating teacher information sheet

Areas of Interest	Information
Personal	
Education	
Family	
Hobbies	
Other	
Professional	
Previous field experiences (locations)	
Previous field experiences (students)	
Previous community experiences	
University goals for student teaching*	
Personal goals for student teaching	

*Please provide a Student Teacher Handbook or other university publications listing university goals, knowledge base and relevant university requirements.

Figure 9.2 Student teacher information sheet

that was not included in the biographical information requested by the university and provided to the university supervisor and the cooperating teacher. Therefore, the student teacher should also be responsible for providing this information to the other member of the triad—the university supervisor. Some of the information, which may appear somewhat personal to the student teacher, may be essential to the functioning of the triad. Of special interest would be health problems that may affect the performance of the student teacher or such specialized interest areas as extracurricular activities and previous experiences with children beyond those required in the university's teacher education program. If the student teacher has lived and/or worked in the community, that information is essential to gauge the time needed to acquaint the student teacher with the community. Also, this information may be helpful in acquainting the student teacher with available community resource persons to be involved in the learning experiences planned by the student teacher.

The requirement that the student teacher list personal goals for the student teaching experience indicates an early commitment of the triad to characteristics of reflective teaching as applicable at the student teaching level. For student teachers, reflectivity is a way of encouraging them to think about educational matters that involve the ability to make rational choices and to assume responsibility for those choices (Zeichner & Liston 1987). The identification of these goals is initiated by the student teacher, independent of the goals of the university supervisor or the cooperating teacher. These goals should address problems, strengths, and weaknesses that may influence the objectives in the planning phase of the clinical supervision cycle. These goals should be shaped to be congruent with the student teacher's internal values and what is expected by himself or herself. This requirement indicates that the student teacher may have personal goals that are different from the university's goals for student teaching, although it is hoped that any individual goals are congruent with or subsets of university goals. The student teacher will most likely focus on issues dealing with growth—issues such as being encouraged to examine the intended and unintended consequences of a teaching strategy and to determine whether the consequences are desirable or not. Other possible goals might include opportunities to develop the ability to view teaching situations from different perspectives, the opportunity to search for alternative explanations of classroom events, and opportunities to develop decision-making skills through careful examination of the incidents that led to the classroom events.

Just as there is certain information that should be shared among the members of the triad, especially between the cooperating teacher and the student teacher, there are certain predispositions that are essential for an effective conference to occur. An essential ingredient in clinical supervision is the establishment of effective communication that helps alleviate anxiety, especially within the student teacher. Hennings (1975) suggests

three elements that can become barriers to effective communication: masking, filtering, and wandering.

Masking is the use of words or nonverbal signs to hide an individual's thoughts and feelings. Agreeing to participate in something, which a participant would rather not be involved in, is an example of masking. Appearing, through facial or other gestures, to be interested in a speaker's message is another form of masking that allows a person to project an image consistent with the image being expected. A student teacher is likely to use masking behaviors in a potentially offensive situation to avoid the threatening aspects of the situation. Rather than becoming subservient and agreeing with whatever is said by the cooperating teacher or the university supervisor, the student teacher should be honest, establishing a personal commitment to an environment of open communication that avoids having to mask true feelings. This process must be an open sharing of those involved without fear or anxiety about how the message will be received by the other members of the triad.

Filtering, another technique that may be used by a student teacher, results in a lack of communication with the other members of the triad. The attitudes, values, and beliefs of a student teacher can alter the messages sent during meetings of the triad or in meeting with any member of the triad. Personal insecurity, or excessive anxiety, may cause the student teacher to feel threatened when a message sent by the other members of the triad is not a threat. This filtering can be fostered by dialectical differences, cultural differences, or by personal preferences regarding nonverbal communication patterns. Such behaviors as distance, physical contact, gestures, facial expressions, and posture or stance may become a filtering agent that inhibits communication among members of the triad. The student teacher should be careful to avoid any type of filtering elements that alter communication among members of the triad.

Wandering, which is defined as a lack of focus on the speaker's message, may also inhibit communication. Often, personal problems may cause a listener to shift attention between what the speaker is saying and pressing personal problems. Anticipating is another form of wandering in which people are so confident that they know what the speaker is going to say that they feel it is not necessary to focus on the message of the speaker. Mental waiting, which may be caused by conversation between other members of the triad, or focusing on what is going to be said next also causes wandering. The type of wandering that is often the most difficult to overcome is that of the mind going totally blank. External factors such as fatigue or preoccupation with external thoughts or ideas can cause a listener to receive none of the speaker's message. Student teachers should be aware of these factors before trying to engage in meaningful communication with other members of the triad. It is important for the student teacher to remember that forms of these inhibitors can affect speakers as well as listeners. Although the cooperating teacher has often been identified as the member of the triad who must assume primary responsibility for overcoming the barriers to effective communication (Lang, Quick, and Johnson 1982), the student teacher can help by (1) avoiding those behaviors that interfere with communication and (2) promoting an environment, through personal action and commitment, that frees others of the need to engage in activities that are barriers to one of the essential ingredients of clinical supervision—effective communication.

Expectations

The student teacher enters into the student teaching experience with certain expectations regarding the initial involvement in clinical supervision. The student teacher should expect the clinical supervision experience to provide opportunities for growth that are not usually found in traditional student teaching experiences. As part of preparation for working with the student teacher using the clinical supervision model, the cooperating teacher and university supervisor receive specialized instructions regarding the correct use of

clinical supervision techniques with student teachers. Whitehead (1984) found that cooperating teachers with specialized preparation in clinical supervision used a supervisory style that was indirect, interpersonal behaviors that were freeing, conferencing that was information-based, and feedback that was restricted to what was specified by the student teacher. These types of behaviors provide the type of environment in which the student teacher is free to express personal opinions and to take risks, openly discussing and analyzing instructional acts from the classroom interactions.

The student teacher also has certain expectations based upon what has been learned in university coursework, as well as experiences from previous activities in the public schools. One of the basic premises of student teaching is that it should be the capstone experience in a series of planned experiences in the public schools. These experiences should be hierarchical and sequential. The early experiences should be exploratory, with students engaged in classroom observation as they contemplate a teaching career. This experience is followed by subsequent field experiences and progresses to student teaching where the student teacher assists the cooperating teacher, works with individual pupils as a tutor, teaches small groups, and eventually assumes full responsibility as a novice teacher. The expectations of the student teacher may depend on the information that has been conveyed to the cooperating teacher regarding the experiences and the amount of responsibility that should be given to the student teacher. Figure 9.3 offers a recommended sequence of involvement of the student teacher in moving toward total responsibility. The student teacher is slowly acclimated to the teaching role; after about three weeks of experience the student teacher should assume full responsibility for the class. All the duties of a teacher, including routine noninstructional duties, are included under the heading "teaching" because those duties are part of the responsibility of the person who is in charge of the classroom. Upon completion of

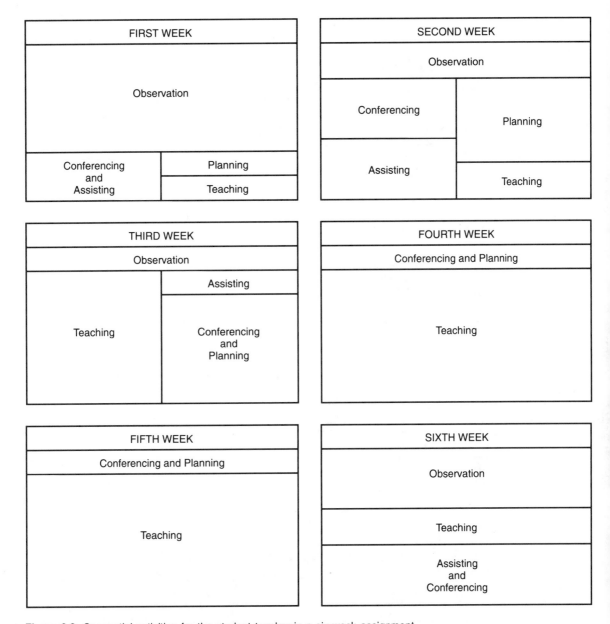

Figure 9.3 Sequential activities for the student teacher in a six-week assignment

about two weeks of full responsibility, it is assumed that the student teacher has sufficient experience to further profit from additional observation.

Figure 9.4 represents the same type of expectations of a student teacher involved in a twelve-week student teaching assignment. Note that during this experience, the student has total teaching responsibility during weeks 8 through 11. Once again, the student teacher observes during the latter stages of the student teaching experience to

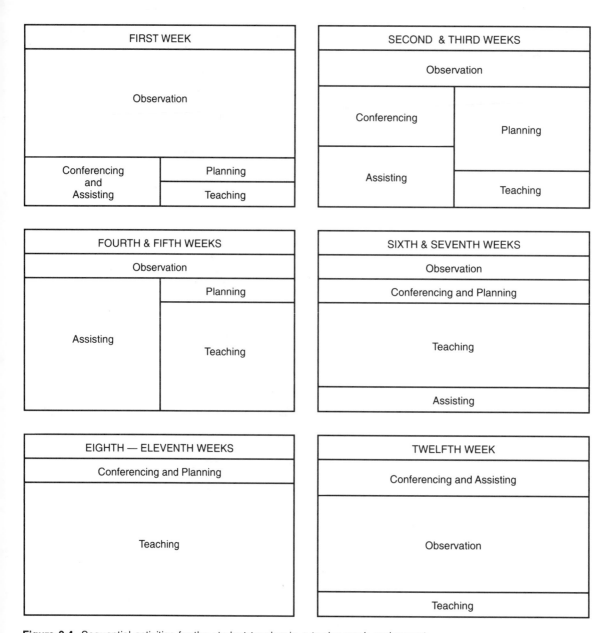

Figure 9.4 Sequential activities for the student teacher in a twelve-week assignment

learn additional skills that can be added to a personal teaching repertoire.

Another expectation of the student teacher is that of being reflective during the student teaching experience. Reflectivity means more than

being able to learn from one's own experiences. Gore (1987) indicated that reflective teaching focuses on how one teaches a given lesson with the intent of improving delivery of instruction. For a student teacher, reflectivity means becoming aware of the inconsistencies between intentions and the outcomes of teaching and, thus, searching for an explanation and alternative instructional strategies that will more likely make intended outcomes and actual outcomes more congruent.

Reflectivity in student teaching involves the freedom of choice necessary to make a decision on a theoretical base, and one based on research. This means that the student teacher is able to exercise the freedom of choice, using the careful consideration of the knowledge that supports an action and the resultant consequence of the action. This allows the student teacher to be involved in choice rather than in a routine guided by tradition, by the external authority of the university supervisor and the cooperating teacher, and by the tradition that has dictated what actions are appropriate for student teachers. Through the process of learning and teaching as a responsible professional, the student teacher can begin to move into the arena of learning how to learn rather than to adhering to a checklist of guidelines or activities on how to perform in a prescribed manner. Thus, the student teacher is able to incorporate inquiry, personal relevance, diverse thinking, and psychological influences into multiple approaches to teaching rather than attempt to perform in a predetermined manner that is, itself, an end.

Entering into the initial preobservation conference, the student teacher should expect that the relationship that will be established with the cooperating teacher will be closer than the relationship with the university supervisor. This may be partly due to the fact that a student teacher will spend more time with the cooperating teacher than with the university supervisor. This closeness is exhibited not only in characteristics of the affective domain but is also prevalent in characteristics of the cognitive domain. Morrow and Lane (1983) found that although there was some agreement among the members of the triad regarding potential instructional difficulties of student teachers, there was a much closer agreement between the student teacher and the cooperating teacher than between any other two members of

the triad. Although the areas of agreement among all members of the triad—organizing and managing classrooms, selecting appropriate material, and interaction or communication with students— were as expected, the congruence of the cooperating teacher and the student teacher on difficult areas such as providing for individual differences and motivation suggest a parallel commitment that may be based on long hours of close personal and professional interaction.

Another expectation of the student teacher regarding the initial preobservation conference relates to areas of anxiety. One of the major concerns of student teachers as they begin their student teaching experience is high concern about subject matter competency (Evans and Tribble 1986). Student teachers are very concerned that their knowledge of the subject matter is not sufficient to provide the foundation for instruction. They hope that they will not be "academically embarrassed" by a lack of content knowledge. Part of this concern may be due to the media expressing concern that teachers are not academically competent and a push for more coursework from the arts and sciences, especially for elementary teachers. As the student teaching experience develops, content concern wanes as student teachers begin to recognize that subject matter knowledge alone does not guarantee teaching success, and other areas such as classroom management and interaction with students may be almost as important as subject matter knowledge. Unfortunately, the anxieties of student teachers are often misdirected. In comparing the anxieties of student teachers with the realities for first-year teachers, Evans and Tribble (1986) also found that assessing students' work and dealing with parents were the two areas of greatest concern of practicing teachers that are of little concern to student teachers.

Roles

The primary role of the student teacher is that of an equal partner in the triad. This requires the student teacher become an equal partner in a three-way dialogue with the goal being the development of independent problem-solving and self-analysis on the part of the student teacher. To achieve this colleagueship, the student teacher must have a total understanding of his or her role as expected by other members of the triad. If the student teacher assumes one role and the other members of the triad assume that the student teacher has a different role, the potential for success in the clinical supervision situation will be limited, and valuable time that could be spent on growth activities will be spent determining the role of the student teacher. A simple form such as that shown in Figure 9.5 can be used to identify the role expected of the student teacher. This form should be completed by the university supervisor and the cooperating teacher prior to the first preobservation conference.

Once the role expectation form is completed and returned to the student teacher, initial discussion of the role of the student teacher can begin. This does not mean that the student teacher must agree with the role identified by other members of the triad, but rather that the student teacher knows the other members' role definitions. This will allow clarification and refinement to start during the initial preobservation conference without spending time and becoming frustrated because of an unknown or unsatisfactory role expectation.

Activities

The student teacher should come to the preobservation conference prepared to discuss the agenda for the focus during the observation. The student teacher should offer evidence of completion of some preobservation activities. Figure 9.6 offers guidance regarding the types of activities that might have been completed by the student teacher before the preobservation conference.

Once the student teacher has reflectively completed the activities listed in Figure 9.6, it is time for the triad to reach agreement on the focus of the observation. Following the guidelines of clinical supervision, it is assumed that the areas of questioning, classroom management (effective transition and effective classroom praise), and lesson characteristics will be selected. Although these topics may be too numerous for an initial observation, it clearly demonstrates the types of topics that may be selected by members of the triad.

Observation

Collecting objective data presents more of a problem to the student teacher than it presents to other members of the triad. Since it is impossible for the student teacher to observe the teaching act, it becomes necessary to audiotape or videotape the lesson and use a series of carefully designed self-analysis devices. These devices allow the student teacher to engage in the clinical supervision process and also provide opportunity to be reflective about the instructional activities that occur in the classroom.

Expectations

The primary expectation of the student teacher is one of extreme nervousness. For perhaps the first time since beginning in a teacher education program, the student teacher expects to be observed by the one person who knows all about the student teacher—himself or herself. Excuses or other face-saving devices will not be tolerated by a person who has total knowledge of the student teacher.

Roles

The primary role of the student teacher is to be objective about the classroom instructional activities. This requires student teachers to assume the role of an observer with no biases and do everything possible to study and learn from their experiences. This also requires the role of being a student of teaching. Rather than assume the role of mindlessness (Siberman 1971), where teachers are unable to find anything wrong with what they

Topic Area	Cooperating Teacher	University Supervisor
Observing		
Planning		
Small group instruction		
Large group instruction		
Evaluating students		
Range of instructional planning and teaching		
Tentative growth plan		
Goals for student teacher		
Additional anticipated roles		

Figure 9.5 Role expectations

Activity	Completed	Date
Planning		
Examine cooperating teacher's plans		
Work cooperatively with the cooperating teacher		
Develop written lesson plans		
Present evidence of planning		
Adjust plans based on the recommendation of the cooperating teacher		
Discuss planning with students		
Observation		
Study cooperating teacher's plans before observing a lesson		
Take notes while the cooperating teacher is teaching		
Share and discuss notes with the cooperating teacher		
Observe other teachers		
Student/Community Observation		
Identify characteristics of community		
Observe students above and below grade level of assignment		
Visit community activity and observe students there		
Use a sociogram in classroom		
Selected Learning Activities		
Work with an individual student		
Work with a small group of students		
Construct, give, and interpret an evaluation (both test and nontest methods)		
Other Activities		
Visit special teachers		
Attend faculty meetings		
Do routine task such as attendance and money collection		
Have conferences with the cooperating teacher		
Keep reflective log of experiences		
Initiate a file of activites and bulletin board ideas		

Figure 9.6 Preobservation student teacher checklist

Student teachers should use all possible resources in preparing for teaching.

do and continually repeat their errors, this role requires an intensity and accuracy in the collection of observation data. This new intensity and focus on data that might be germane to the agreement of the triad is an initial step toward the empowerment of teachers through reflective teaching during clinical supervision.

Activities

Using a tape recording of the planned lesson, the student teacher listens and script-tapes all activities related to questioning. The advantage of the student teacher doing the scripting is that by listening to a tape instead of attempting to script-tape during the lesson, it is possible to replay sections and to listen to the tape more than once. This allows an improved reliability over what might be obtained from scripting in the classroom. The cooperating teacher and the university supervisor have practiced and developed this skill to a high degree of proficiency, but the student teacher has most likely never attempted to script-tape and does not possess the same skills. However, through perseverance and dedication, the student teacher is able to develop a script-tape of the same lesson as the other members of the triad. This is the objective part of the observation, and the student teacher must take the script-tape and analyze, for questioning techniques, the

same lesson that other members of the triad chose. Questioning is such a broad topic that the student teacher may select different strategies to analyze and bring back to the triad, along with the analyses and strategies to be developed by the triad. An example of a student teacher script tape is listed in Figure 9.7. Notice that there is space beside each question for the student teacher to write objective, data-laden comments. This script tape, with the comments in the appropriate column, should be brought to the postobservation conference by the student teacher.

Observation is a complex activity. Student teachers should be given direction and assistance in learning how to record objective data and how to construct analyses based on that data. One technique that can be used to collect this data and to help structure the analyses is that of focused observation. Everton and Green (1986) say that the purpose of the observation influences what is observed, how it is observed, who gets observed, when observation takes place, where it takes place, how observations are recorded, how data is analyzed, and how data is used. Focused observations provide the structure to allow the specific behaviors to be assessed and analyzed. This approach allows the student teacher to attend to only the areas identified by the triad and to consciously disregard other extraneous events in the room. An example of a focused observation on questioning is presented in Figure 9.8. This approach provides structure as the student teacher listens to the tape and indicates the frequencies of specific student teacher questioning events.

Another pertinent area that was selected for observation in this example is classroom management. By listening to the tape and completing Figure 9.9, the student teacher can obtain observational data based on classroom management skills used during instruction.

Another variable that may be a determiner of classroom management success is effective praise of students. Effective praise in the classroom does more than just control students. It can be used to bring attention to student efforts and accomplishments and bring favorable responses from students. The quality of genuine, spontaneous praise is more important than the frequency of praise. Good and Brophy (1987) maintain that effective praise can be an effective intrinsic motivator because it leads students to believe that success is based on their own abilities and efforts. By completing Figure 9.10, the student teacher can determine the frequency and specific examples of effective praise.

Keeping students' attention during a lesson is necessary to facilitate learning. Students are much more attentive when they are involved in the learning process. By focusing on the transitions in Figure 9.11, the student teacher can gather specific observational data regarding this aspect of the instructional activities in a specific lesson.

Specific student-teacher lesson characteristics that may affect the lesson but not be identified by other observational techniques should be part of the observational techniques. Although there is a variety of lesson characteristics that could be selected by the members of the triad, Figure 9.12 provides the student teacher with a structure to identify specific lesson characteristics so that the triad can develop alternative strategies to improve instructional techniques.

Script Tape of Classroom Questioning	Student Teacher Comments
Teacher: (2 minutes of talk.)	
Teacher: Who discovered America?	No person identified
Class: (In unison) Columbus!!	
Teacher: Very good. *****Who can tell me the name of Columbus' three ships? Susan?	Halting time?
Susan: Nina, Pinta, and Santa Maria.	
Teacher: Very good, Susan. *** Patty, when did Columbus sail to the New World?	Halting time
Patty: 1942, I mean 1492!	
Teacher: Very good, Patty. **********In your own words, tell me why you think sailing and navigation developed during the time of Columbus, Fred?	Same reinforcement
Fred: There was a desire of many people to make money through trading. Since there were no trains or highways, the best way to move goods, especially items that must be imported, was with the use of ships. There was no other source of power for ships except the wind.	

Figure 9.7 Student teacher questioning script tape

Script Tape of Classroom Questioning	Student Teacher Comments
Teacher: Very good, Fred. *******Why did Columbus come to the New World, Mary?	Very good again
Mary: I don't know.	
Teacher: What do you mean you don't know? Haven't you been paying attention to what went on in class?	Rhetorical Question
Mary: (Silence)	
Teacher: Very well, you may just sit there. Please answer the question, Trisha.	
Trisha: Please repeat the question.	
Teacher: Please listen when I ask the question! Don't you think I have better things to do than repeat the question? Tyrone, do you have any idea what the answer to the question is?	Ignored student's request and turned situation into a disciplinary situation Name too early in the question
Tyrone: He was seeking spices.	
Teacher: Very good, Tyrone. It is nice to have someone pay attention. *********Robert, where did Columbus land, where did he think he landed, and what name did he give the inhabitants? In other words, why did he do what he did and what words are still in our culture from the time of Columbus? It is the name of a race of people and we still use the terms for people from two different continents?	Student's name early in the question Multiple question Good clue to answer
Robert: He landed in the Caribbean, but he thought he was in the East Indies so he named the inhabitants, Indians.	No response to student
Teacher: George, what would you suppose the people of Columbus' day gave him as a nickname?	Name early
George: The Great Explorer?	No response

Figure 9.7—Continued

Script Tape of Classroom Questioning	Student Teacher Comments
Teacher: Let's try to analyze what he did and see if we can put together a good name for him. Where did Columbus do his most famous work?	
Sam: In the New World.	No response
Teacher: What type of terrain did he do his most famous work?	
Mary: He did it at sea or in the ocean?	
Teacher: Very good. What official title does a person have who has great command of the sea?	Used very good Not directed
Several Students: Captain!	
Teacher: What rank is held by a person who tells a captain what to do?	Providing focus
Gary: (Waving his hand wildly) I know!! I know!! Admiral!	
Teacher: Let's put these together and you will find out that he was called the "Admiral of the Ocean". (Writes on chalkboard) Now, tell us, George, of the explorers Columbus, Magellan, and Vespucci, which do you think was most influential in establishing the new world and why?	Builds on answers to develop another question Early identification of student, but encourages thought by asking student to state an opinion and provide a rationale for his opinion
George: I think Amerigo Vespucci was because he knew what he had discovered and that is why we are called America instead of Magellan or Columbus.	

Figure 9.7—Continued

Questioning Event	Frequencies
Teacher Questions	
Seeks specific factual responses	
Questioning encourages thinking and/or problem solving	
Response to a question is yes or no	
Question deals with personal, directional, or disciplinary matters rather than curriculum	
Repeats or rephrases questions	
Asks multiple questions or two questions at once	
Student	
Names student before asking question	
Calls on volunteer	
Calls on nonvolunteer	
Selects a variety of students to answer	
Feedback	
Verbal praise	
Provides positive nonverbal feedback through voice tone or voice inflection	
No feedback	
Ambiguous or inconsistent feedback	
Asks students to respond to other students	
Asks another question to the same student	
Critical of a student's answer	
Negative response to a student's answer	
Fails to provide any type of feedback	
Asks class or another student if the response given was correct	
Provides clues in question	
Provides "prompts"	
Gives explanation	
Asks student to provide explanation	
Explains why student response was incorrect	
Encourages guessing by providing praise for good attempt or guess	

Figure 9.8 Recorded focused observation (questioning)

Student Teacher Actions	Check if Heard on Tape
Student Motivation	
Establishes importance of learning	
Relates new information to prior student experiences and knowledge	
Respects students by using his/her name and positively interacting with students	
Gives verbal responses that indicate active listening to students	
Encourages and praises appropriately	
Encourages student involvement	
Classroom Management	
Presents an appropriate lesson	
Presents a lesson that contains skills new or not mastered by the students	
Establishes a climate for learning by gaining student's attention and stating what is to be learned	
Organizes materials and equipment prior to beginning the lesson	
Uses voice as a teaching tool	
States suggestions or directions positively	
Gives directions at the time they will be most effective and reinforces understanding	
Defines limits clearly and maintains them constantly	
Paces activities during a lesson	
Models acceptable/desirable behavior	

Figure 9.9 Classroom management

Analysis and Strategy

The student teacher should engage in activities to determine individual effectiveness of professional activities in the clinical supervision process. This requires that the student teacher examine his or her individual role in the entire clinical supervision process. This examination helps the student teacher to determine how well his or her participation in the clinical process contributed to the success or limited the success of the clinical supervision cycle.

Expectations

The student teacher may feel a certain amount of defensiveness in analyzing his or her professional role in the clinical supervision cycle. One of the more difficult tasks in reflective teaching is to examine the discrepancy between what one claims is a belief and what belief systems are

Type of Remark	Frequency	Specific Examples
Good behavior of the class		
Inteligence or ability		
Work habits		
Thinking skills		
Willingness to learn		
Steady progress toward goal		
General improvement		
Mature or responsible		
Achievement or success		
Cooperativeness		
Positive social behaviors		

Figure 9.10 Effective classroom praise

supported by behaviors. Too often a person may claim a certain belief and at the same time exhibit instructional acts that are inconsistent with the stated belief system. In clinical supervision, one task of the analysis and strategy stage is to identify any discrepancy and to develop strategies that allow a student teacher to exhibit behaviors consistent with stated belief systems.

Student teachers, like other students in teacher education programs, have preconceived notions about what teaching is like and how their own performance will compare with the performance of others. In analyzing his or her own behavior, a student teacher may tend to analyze behavior in light of how successful one thinks a performance will be. Often, preservice teachers assume a self-serving attitude about their individual performance. This means that they enter student teaching with a great deal of opinion about what is important. They are confident that the attributes they themselves possess are important and the attributes they may not possess are of lesser value.

This view is typified especially among elementary preservice teachers who believe that enhancing students' self-esteem is more important than maximizing student achievement (Book, Byers, & Freeman 1983). Therefore, the student teacher should make special effort to avoid giving extra emphasis to areas of personal strength or to personal beliefs. Objectivity is an essential ingredient if clinical supervision is to achieve its goal of teacher empowerment through reflective teaching.

Roles

The role of the student teacher is to identify the specific behaviors agreed on in the preobservation conference and to adhere to an analysis of these behaviors. Just as other members of the triad should not decide that something is more or less important and adjust the criteria, the student teacher must take care not to (1) omit or de-emphasize areas of needed growth or (2) select additional student teacher behaviors that enhance the review of the classroom activities.

Transition Activity	Present Yes/No	Specific Example
Student teacher gives advance signals or reminders		
Students are aware of expected behavior when moving from activity to activity		
Materials are stored with sufficient lead time to indicate a transition		
Evidence that the student teacher has established adequate traffic patterns		
Evidence of an overall view of the class and potential problem areas or locations are identified		
Evidence of appropriate student seating arrangement		
Adequate preparation of charts, materials, equipment, illustrations, and directions		
Evidence of student teacher movement throughout the room		
Evidence of courtesy and organization		
The student teacher has everyone's attention before beginning an activity		

Figure 9.11 Transition classroom management

Activities

The primary activities of the student teacher are to complete the charts as shown in Figure 9.7 through 9.12. This is the objective data that will be presented to the triad. In addition, the student teacher should plan strategies based on this data. These strategies should be written on the back of the charts for sharing with the members whenever needed. After completing these charts and developing strategies based on the data, the student teacher should complete the chart in Figure 9.13 so that it can be presented and discussed during the postobservation conference.

Completion of this chart provides an opportunity for the student teacher to be reflective about teaching, to focus on improving the instructional activities within the classroom, and to improve his or her function as a member of the triad.

Postobservation Conference

At this phase, the student teacher has already completed an independent self-analysis of the data obtained during the observation phase of clinical supervision. It is time for another meeting of the triad to discuss the topics agreed on and focused on by each member of the triad. During the observation phase, the data was collected and analyzed during the analysis and strategy stage. This data, and its resultant conclusions and recommendations, forms the framework of the postobservation conference.

Expectations

The student teacher enters with the expectation that the discussion will focus on the items agreed on in the preobservation conference and that all discussion will be honest and sincere. Any

Lesson Characteristics	Present Yes/No	Course of Action
Activity is too lengthy		
Level is inappropriate to student needs		
Lack of student involvement; too much teacher talk		
Ineffective monitoring		
Needless repetition or rephrasing		
Predictable patterns of questioning		
Lack of continuity in lesson		
Teacher interruptions		
Lack of variety		

Figure 9.12 Student teacher instructional actions

changes or suggestions that emerge shall come from an agreement that will be reached by members of the triad.

The student teacher expects to have an opportunity to examine the process of teaching and the impact of the content upon the students. The opportunity to become reflective through experience should be made available to the student teacher. This reflectivity involves both pedagogical techniques and philosophical commitment. If the student teacher focuses only on pedagogical techniques, the teaching act becomes the act of a technician who is interested only in technological practice. Conversely, focus only on a philosophical commitment leads to poor practices that may be zealously pursued by the student teacher but result in decreased student learning. Only through the combination of pedagogical techniques and philosophical commitment can reflectivity result in effective techniques that lead to improvement of instruction.

The student teacher should expect a different emphasis among the various members of the triad. Tanner and Tanner (1986) found that the difference among members of the triad was consistent and fit logical patterns. The cooperating teacher most often focused on pragmatic ideas that worked within the classroom. The cooperating teacher would not be as concerned with ideas that were research-based or founded on the knowledge base of the university. If the consequences of a student teacher behavior were consistent with desired outcomes, even if there were a lack of planning of this relationship between actions and outcomes, the cooperating teacher will most likely indicate that this type of behavior is desired and should be considered by the student teacher as a type of teacher action that should be desired. However, the university supervisor is more likely to focus on more theoretical applications. This means that the university supervisor is interested in student teacher behaviors that allow the student teacher to develop reflective teaching habits while exhibiting behaviors that are consistent with the knowledge base of the teacher education program that the student teacher attended.

Roles

During the postobservation conference, the student teacher should assume the role of a reflective teacher who seeks improvement in the

DIRECTIONS: The student teacher will complete Part I and Part II as part of the Analysis and Strategy. Part III will be completed by the members of the triad during the Postobservation Conference.

I. Areas of strength identified during Analysis and Strategy.

1. _____
_____
_____

2. _____
_____
_____

3. _____
_____
_____

II. Areas of needed growth.

1. _____
_____
_____

2. _____
_____
_____

3. _____
_____
_____

4. _____
_____
_____

III. Plans for implementing growth activities.

1. _____
_____
_____

2. _____
_____
_____

3. _____
_____
_____

4. _____
_____
_____

_____   _____   _____
  (Student Teacher)   (Cooperating Teacher)   (University Supervisor)

_____   _____
Date of Postobservation Conference   Date of Next Observation

Figure 9.13 Student teacher postobservation conference self-evaluation and planning

Student teachers should enter into open discussion with other members of the triad.

classroom instruction. To achieve improvement in instructional processes, it is the student teacher's responsibility to avoid ego-involved processes where the main goal is to protect one's ego. If the student teacher has a defensive attitude or an attitude that indicates a disdain for constructive ideas, the postobservation conference may develop into a tense situation with disagreement or with the coolness of the sounds of silence. A careful and reflective practitioner always seeks improvement through input from others. This is the role that the student teacher should assume.

Objectivity is often difficult for professionals at any level. Weinstein (1989) found that student teachers have unrealistic optimism about their own teaching. In an examination of their own performance and the competencies that consisted of their overall rating, student teachers rated their overall teaching performance higher than any one of the twenty-nine competencies that contributed to their overall teaching skills. Therefore, the student teacher needs to remember that objectivity is somewhat difficult to determine and often is not a strength of the beginning student teacher.

Activities

The agenda consists of each member of the triad placing on the table the objective data represented by the observation and analysis for discus-

sion by the other members. This will be the real test of the atmosphere of trust and colleagueship created in the earlier stages of clinical supervision. Each member should have the collected data available for discussion by other members of the triad. It is imperative that this process be limited, objective data. As a part of this objective data, there will be some analyses of the data. Several of the forms used by the student teacher have analyses sections that can be used by the triad to help formulate the analyses. It would be helpful if the student teacher brought the audiotape of the lesson to the conference in the event there is any discussion about what occurred during the lesson.

Following a discussion of the data, the triad should reach some agreement on recommendations for future lessons. This requires that they discuss and determine future strategies. These strategies can be listed on the reverse side of the charts. The student teacher should be careful not to focus on so many topics that it will be impossible for success in the next cycle. The student teacher should remember that the postobservation conference is also the preobservation conference for the next cycle. It is the responsibility of the triad to focus on initial success in fewer areas rather than to try to improve in so many areas that it will be impossible for the student teacher to succeed in all of the areas listed.

Postobservation Analysis

A major responsibility for growth in the student teaching experience rests with the student teacher. Although the cooperating teacher and the university supervisor can thwart the growth of the student teacher, the actual growth depends on the student teacher seizing the opportunity to be reflective and achieving at a maximum level. This requires a student teacher whose self-concept is sufficiently strong and whose professional acumen is sufficient to provide the inner strength to develop into a reflective teacher. Just as the student teacher must be reflective about instructional strategies to achieve maximum student growth,

Behavior	Scale
Planning and Implementation	
Plans were appropriate for the lesson	
Plans were properly implemented	
Student response was as anticipated	
Student teacher response was appropriate	
Conferencing	
Asked for opinion of other triad members	
Asked for clarification of opinions	
Accepted suggestions of triad	
Positive in dealing with triad	
Objective in my own opinion	
Offered suggestions	
Practiced reflective thought and action	
Strength Areas	
Areas of Needed Growth	

Figure 9.14 Student teacher perceptions of own behavior

reflectivity regarding the clinical supervision process is also essential to maximize student teacher growth.

Figure 9.14 provides the student teacher with the structure to analyze his or her own behavior during part of the lesson as well as during the postobservation conference. By initially focusing on some of the basics of the lesson, the figure provides the student with a starting point to focus on behavior during the postobservation conference and resulting analysis. The student teacher analyzes behavior on a scale of 1 to 10 (with 10 being the highest rating). After the initial postobservation analysis, there should be a comparison by arranging these sheets in sequential order. This should indicate the growth of the student as

Growth Areas	Scale
More congruent and less defensive with the triad	
More objective about teaching skills	
Less anxious	
More accepting of others	
Less imitative of the triad	
More reflective about my own teaching	
Have a more realistic self-perception	
Have developed an adaptive teaching style	
Adjusts teaching based on experience	
Improved skill in meeting objectives of lesson	

Figure 9.15 Personal and professional growth

measured by higher ratings and improvements in the areas of needed growth identified in earlier cycles.

Just as the student teacher must be reflective about teaching, it is also essential that he or she be reflective about personal and professional growth. The chart in Figure 9.15 should be completed by the student teacher at the end of each clinical supervision cycle. Again, each item should be given a rating from 1 to 10.

Likewise, Figure 9.14 and Figure 9.15 should be kept in sequential order and examined for growth during the entire clinical supervision process.

Summary

The student teacher must approach clinical supervision with the attitude that maximum growth during the student teaching experience will be achieved only if he or she is successful in participating in a relationship that encourages reflectivity about teaching. The student teacher must be able to function as a triad member who is willing to incorporate the knowledge base of the teacher education program into a successful student teaching experience.

During the clinical supervision cycle, the student teacher must be willing to communicate with other members of the triad in a way unlike any other previous experience at the university or in previous field experience courses. The ability to participate in a meeting of independent professionals to achieve a common good allows the student teacher to experience the initial level of teacher empowerment. Once this communication level has been achieved, the student teacher should feel confident enough to engage in reflective teaching and to openly and honestly discuss instructional strategies with other members of the triad.

The focus on the instructional process provides clinical supervision with its strength and its hope for improving the schools. Instruction is the central theme of the schools, and the focus should be on improving instruction through the formative evaluation of the student teacher's instructional techniques.

Questions and Discussion Topics

1. What can a student teacher do to help establish the climate necessary for clinical supervision?
2. Describe the attitudes of the student teacher that lead toward successful student teaching in a clinical supervision setting.
3. How can a student teacher be reflective and meet the external demands of the university supervisor, the cooperating teacher, the students, and the school system?
4. Describe the inherent problems in being a reflective student teacher. How does a student teacher overcome these problems?
5. From a student teaching viewpoint, what parts of integrating reflective teaching into clinical supervision represent the greatest challenges to the student teacher? How does the student teacher prepare to meet these challenges?

CHAPTER 10

Evaluating Student Teachers

CHAPTER KEY CONCEPTS

Basic Principles

Effective Evaluation Systems

Formative Evaluation

Summative Evaluation

Overview

Evaluation is a vital function in clinical supervision. If reflective teaching is to be operational through the process of clinical supervision, it is essential that the evaluation component associated with student teaching be a consistent and viable part of the student teaching experience. If the evaluation component is not consistent with the rest of the experience, the process of clinical supervision is not functional because an inconsistent evaluation process that is externally imposed upon the student teacher.

During the initial cycle of clinical supervision, the student teacher learns evaluation is an integral function of learning and that, through reflective teaching, the evaluation process becomes much less threatening—aimed at assisting the student teacher in improving the instructional activities within the classroom. Also, the student teacher accepts his or her role in evaluation and recognizes that the evaluation process will fail without his or her input. Therefore, it is in the student teacher's professional interest to fully participate in the evaluation process. The student teacher can begin to realize the potential of teacher empowerment through reflective teaching in a clinical supervision setting.

Objectives

Upon completing your study of chapter 10, you should be able to:

1. Name the principles of evaluation and tell how they apply to student teaching, and to clinical supervision.
2. Name the characteristics of effective student teacher evaluation systems and tell how they may be implemented in clinical supervision.
3. Explain the differences between formative and summative evaluation and explain how to use each in clinical supervision of student teaching.
4. Describe how evaluation is different when applied to clinical supervision as compared with traditional supervision.

The entire program of teacher education is designed to help the prospective teacher grow in the understandings, attitudes, and skills basic to a professional educator. While courses and other parts of a university program contribute to this development, student teaching provides the most complete opportunity to evaluate progress toward desired goals.

Basic Principles

Evaluation is a consistent part of life and growth. Throughout our lives, each of us has received evaluative feedback about our performance. This evaluation may have been in an informal setting, a reminder from our parents, a mark on a paper, a grade on a report card, or a verbal or written evaluation in the world of work. Whatever the environment or the circumstance, consistent evaluation is a part of all professions. As a participant in clinical supervision in the culminating field experience, the student teacher discovers that he or she can have input into this process and develop the types of instructional strategies that enhance the evaluation process.

Anxiety often accompanies evaluation. This is true of all members of the evaluation process—the evaluators and the person being evaluated. The cooperating teacher enjoys the opportunities and challenges afforded by working with the student teacher. However, the time for evaluation is often viewed as traumatic (Lang, Quick, and Johnson 1975). Evaluation, which is viewed as the least desirable part of working with student teachers, puts the cooperating teacher in the position of having decisive input regarding the professional advancement of another adult. A cooperating teacher can be an excellent designer of instructional strategies for students and still be very willing and capable in the evaluation of public school students. However, this willingness and skill may not transfer into an environment where the person being evaluated is another adult; the relationship is that of a colleague rather than that of a teacher to student. Anxiety may be compounded if the cooperating teacher is not knowledgeable about the knowledge base and the objectives of the student teaching program of the university where the student teacher attended. Lack of extensive knowledge about and formulation of input into the objectives may put the cooperating teacher in the somewhat difficult situation where with limited input, he or she is evaluating a student teacher.

University supervisors also suffer from anxiety as they face the difficulty of providing input into a process that is designed to assess the competence of student teachers. Although university supervisors are the representatives of the university that has the ultimate responsibility for the student teacher, the university supervisor may have had limited contact, if any, with the student teacher before the student teaching experience. This lack of input into the preparation of the student teacher may leave the university supervisor with a feeling of limited input until the initial preobservation conference. In contrast, the university supervisor may have had extensive contact with the student teacher and, despite completing the clinical supervision cycle, has a predisposition about the student teacher. This is reflected by McNeil (1971) who felt that the lack of objectivity of evaluating student teachers, despite agreement of the triad, may reflect characteristics and prejudices of the university supervisor rather than give an accurate description of the student teacher's instructional strategies within the classroom.

Among the members of the triad, the student teacher feels the most anxiety. Despite having participated in the entire clinical supervision process from the beginning, the external pressures associated with student teaching may not support reflectivity and involvement in evaluation. The most anxiety-laden aspect of student teaching is the expectation of trying to be reflective from the beginning of the student teaching experience. Although the student teacher has most likely received much information about reflective practices and is very aware of the terminology and techniques of reflective teaching, information about reflective practice is not to be confused with the experience of reflective practice (Wellington 1991). This lack of experience may make it very difficult for the student teacher to effectively participate in reflective teaching from the beginning of the student teaching experience.

To minimize the anxieties of all members of the triad, it is essential that effective, honest, and open communication exists among the members.

During the initial preobservation conference, the triad members should discuss the principles of evaluation, its role in the student teaching process, and the implementation of this role. If there is a required university form that is to be completed by any member of the triad, this form should be distributed and discussed during the initial preobservation conference. This requires more than merely an overview with perfunctory attention given to the terminology. An example of this discussion would be a university form that focuses on the student teacher's "use of resources outside the normal avenue of the teaching assignment. Equally confusing are statements that describe multiple characteristics. In the above example, if the statement said, "prepares and effectively uses resources," and the student teacher was not effective in both preparation and use, any statement other than a narrative statement that specifically addresses each area would add to the confusion instead of providing information to the student teacher.

Evaluation should reflect all aspects of clinical supervision. One unique aspect of clinical supervision is the relationship that should exist among the members of the triad. Part of evaluation includes the student teacher evaluating other members of the triad. Figure 10.1 is an example of the type of information that the student teacher should provide to the other members of the triad.

The supervisory actions listed in Figure 10.1 are not intended to be a complete list, but rather they provide the idea that the evaluation must involve all members of the triad. This is an informal evaluation and should be completed by the student teacher and brought to the postobservation conference. This open discussion of the effectiveness of the university supervisor and the cooperating teacher is a unique characteristic of clinical supervision and must exist for maximum growth of the student teacher.

A narrative statement is essential in providing information to the student teacher. Regardless of the quality and construction of a rating scale that uses any type of numerical indicators, an effective evaluation must have some narrative. One purpose of a narrative is to provide explicit interpretation about what is meant by the person completing the scale. In addition to providing more information than can be provided with some type of checksheet, a narrative provides the student teacher with specific directions for improvement and dialogue. If a student teacher wishes to engage in further dialogue, based on the information provided in some type of written evaluation, a narrative provides more information and provides a springboard for such dialogue. This dialogue is essential for the growth of the student teacher and is also essential to effective communication.

It is the triad's responsibility to identify specific techniques that the student teacher could use to help alleviate shortcomings. If the student teacher is unable to develop and adequately use resources, the narrative part of the evaluation should indicate the reasons for this deficit. If, for example, the student teacher has had limited background in preparing resources and feels that the resources prepared were not properly integrated into instructional activities, the university supervisor and cooperating teacher should provide appropriate suggestions to assist the student teacher. In the above example, they might assist the student teacher in working with the university's audiovisual lab or with the resource center of the school district to provide direction to the student teacher's efforts. Other activities might include (1) providing the student teacher with references and sources for developing materials in curricular areas, (2) allowing the student teacher to visit with a cooperating teacher who consistently develops a wide variety of teacher-made materials to assist in the instructional process, or (3) reviewing the student teacher's future lesson plans to ensure that there are adequate resources to enhance instruction. This commitment to assisting the student teacher enhances the evaluation process and makes it less threatening for the student teacher to admit weaknesses.

Another basic principle is sequential growth. During the initial preobservation conference, the

DIRECTIONS: Complete this chart and take it with you to the final postobservation conference during the student teaching experience. Discuss this completed chart with your university supervisor and your cooperating teacher. Complete the chart by placing a checkmark in the N column for never, the U column for usually, and the A column for always. Provide clarification in the narrative column.

Supervisory Action	N	U	A	Narrative
1. My cooperating teacher and I plan together.				
2. My cooperating teacher is helpful when I have problems or difficulties.				
3. My cooperating teacher keeps me informed of my progress.				
4. My cooperating teacher has frequent conferences with me.				
5. My university supervisor is available when I need assistance.				
6. My university supervisor conducts conferences that help me improve my teaching skills.				
7. My cooperating teacher and my university supervisor encourage reflective teaching.				

Figure 10.1 Effectiveness of the university supervisor and the cooperating teacher

triad should agree on a specific hierarchy of objectives throughout the student teaching experience. This means that just as there should be sequential growth of the student teacher throughout the student teaching experience, there should be sequential expectations in the evaluation processes. Just as reflectivity should increase, the skills of the student teacher should increase with experience. The evaluation expectations of the triad should also increase, and these sequential expectations must be communicated to the student teacher.

Setting Goals and Objectives

Goals serve two basic purposes. The primary purpose of goals is to provide direction for activities. The goals of student teaching should develop from the knowledge base of the teacher education program of the university. Out of these goals come the objectives that are listed in the student teacher handbook of the university. Based on

these objectives, the triad establishes objectives for the specific student teaching experience. Figure 10.2 indicates the process used by the members of the triad as they develop goals and objectives for the student teaching experience. Notice that each member of the triad has input into the goal-setting process. However, the only member of the triad with identified goals is the student teacher who listed his or her goals in Figure 10.2. These objectives are based on the university's goals and objectives, the school system's goals and objectives, the specific school's goals and objectives, and the cooperating teacher's goals and objectives.

Once established, the goals and objectives serve as benchmarks of accomplishments for the student teacher. The triad uses the goals and objectives as it tries to identify the objectives during the initial preobservation conference. In addition, these goals and objectives are hierarchically organized and are used throughout the student teaching experience to provide appropriate

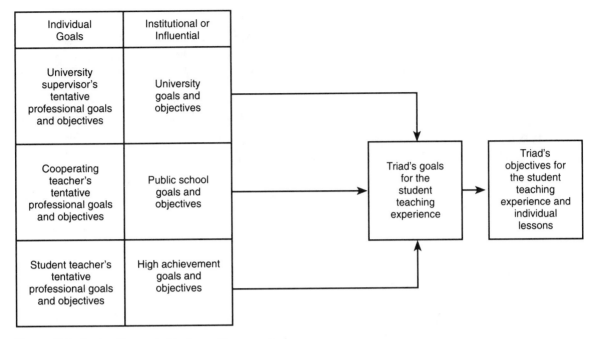

Individual Goals	Institutional or Influential
University supervisor's tentative professional goals and objectives	University goals and objectives
Cooperating teacher's tentative professional goals and objectives	Public school goals and objectives
Student teacher's tentative professional goals and objectives	High achievement goals and objectives

Triad's goals for the student teaching experience

Triad's objectives for the student teaching experience and individual lessons

Figure 10.2 Goal-setting and objective-setting process

growth sequences to the student teaching experience.

Gathering Data

Data gathering is crucial to the evaluation process. In all types of evaluation, the time to plan the data gathering is at the beginning of the process. If the clinical supervision stages have been correctly completed and the cycle repeated several times, the observational data, the reflective process of the student teacher, the successful involvement of the student teacher in clinical supervision, and the growth of the student teacher as measured by improved instructional activity have provided sufficient data for evaluation. Likewise, a lack of progress in any of the areas can also be indicated by the data. The members of the triad gather data to reflect the objectives established in the initial preconference observation of the triad.

Interpreting Data

Once the data has been collected and collated into related categories, it is time to interpret the data. Using the recommendations of Clements and Evertson (1981), the members of the triad should write a descriptive narrative citing specific student teacher behaviors during the experience, communicating in nonjudgmental language. This provides a holistic examination of what occurred and provides a basis for discussion. Using nonjudgmental language such as, "It took you four lessons to make improvement in your questioning skills," instead of saying, "You didn't improve much in your questioning skills," provides an objective view of what happened instead of a value-laden statement in judgmental language.

Following this process, the triad examines these narratives in light of the objectives selected for focus. Rather than selecting numerical indications of success or failures, the emphasis is on broad generalizations. The interpretations should answer such questions as, "What do the results mean?'', ''What patterns seem to emerge?'', and ''Are these patterns consistent with the objectives stated in the initial preobservation conference?'' Answering these questions provides the type of interpretation that is most consistent with the structure of the activities that produced the data.

Effective Evaluation Systems

Any type of evaluation is defined by the type of system used. Too frequently, evaluation systems become too specific or too broad to have a worthwhile process or a worthwhile product. To establish some type of guidelines for evaluation, the Joint Commission of Evaluation Standards (Stufflebeam 1988) established criteria for any type of evaluation system. These criteria were designed to give structure and a framework to the process of evaluation. Although these standards offer more constructs for evaluation of programs rather than the evaluation of specific student teachers, these guidelines provide descriptors of what an evaluation system should contain. There are four large categories with a total of 30 standards under the larger categories. The first of these categories is *utility,* or serving the practical needs of the student teacher, the university, and the public schools. The category of *feasibility* requires that the evaluation be realistic, prudent, diplomatic, and frugal. *Propriety* requires that student teacher evaluation be legal, ethical, and with due regard to those affected by the process or its results. *Accuracy,* the last of the standards, focuses on the need for evaluation to convey technically adequate information.

Another characteristic of effective evaluation systems is that the system should facilitate self-evaluation. Clinical supervision, with its emphasis on reflective teaching and the involvement of the student teacher in the supervision cycle, focuses on what happens within the student teacher. This process should assist the student teacher to develop as an empowered teacher by increasing self-image. This is made possible by enhancing the vision of the student teacher regarding the available choices. This expansion not only enlightens him or her about choices previously thought to be unobtainable but also assists the student teacher in realistically appraising residual weaknesses and realistic limitations. This process allows the student teacher to determine reasons for successes and failures and establish plans of action that are positive in nature, building on strengths and helping to minimize weaknesses.

An effective evaluation system should encompass the objectives of the knowledge base of the university and the objectives of the site where the student teaching occurred. The student teacher provides the cooperating teacher with the objectives of the teacher education program of the university, which provided the professional education coursework essential to success of the student teacher. These objectives, which should focus on mastery of skills, attitudes, and integration of reflective teaching into the student teaching process, should provide the structure for evaluation. The evaluation process should focus on ancillary activities essential for total success in the clinical supervision cycle. The willingness of the student teacher to develop the attitude necessary to successfully participate in clinical supervision is an example of the type of activity that should be included in the evaluation process. In addition to providing feedback to the student teacher, the inclusion of this type of activities provides information to the university about how well it is meeting its obligation to prepare its student teachers to be successful. This feedback also relates to the larger issue of curriculum and can be a guide as an institution continually modifies its teacher education program. The aim is to prepare student teachers who are capable of successfully designing instructional strategies that produce expected student learnings.

The evaluation process must facilitate learning and teaching. Instructional improvement is the heart of clinical supervision. Through the process of collecting evaluative data, the triad, especially the student teacher, learns to recognize a good learning experience and the factors that made it good. By providing feedback regarding the instructional acts within the classroom, evaluation provides opportunities for the student teacher to analyze instructional activities and determine the components of a good lesson. This focus firmly reinforces the basic premise of clinical supervision—learning is a function of teaching, and the focus of supervision is the improvement of instruction.

An effective evaluation system should produce records that area appropriate for the activities. All student teaching experiences should provide some type of documentation that indicates completion of the student teaching experience. Universities and licensing agencies require documentation, expressed in a single letter, to indicate successful completion of student teaching. However, while this may be one record that is required of the evaluation process, the larger and much more important record is feedback to the student teacher. Records, often in the form of comments and narrative accounts focusing on strengths and weaknesses, should be provided to the student teacher to assist him or her to move toward becoming more reflective and more able to provide quality instruction to students.

Formative Evaluation

Formative evaluation is characterized as evaluation that focuses on analyzing instruction and providing feedback to improve that instruction. This means that formative evaluation is proactive and aimed at the needs of the student teacher during the instructional process. Scriven (1967) first distinguished this characteristic as being a difference between formative evaluation and other types of evaluation. Another distinctive characteristic of formative evaluation is that the evaluation is collected during the student teaching experience to provide improvement while the student teaching experience is still in progress. This intermittent feedback concerning the quality of instructional activities provided by the student teacher should be incorporated in subsequent in-

Formative evaluation, which focuses on growth potential, is essential in achieving maximum growth.

structional activities and lead to progressively better instruction. This continual improvement of instruction through feedback to the student teacher encourages him or her to achieve at a maximum level.

In achieving the function of a systematic collection of information that can be used to improve teaching, formative evaluation moves through three distinct phases. Figure 10.3 indicates the relationship among these phases, the evaluation function, and the stage of clinical supervision represented by the activity.

The *design* phase builds on the conceptualization of the planning phase and ends with plans to collect data. The *production* phase focuses on gathering formative evaluation through observation, while the *implementation* phase tests the effectiveness of the feedback in subsequent cycles. During this cycle, the members of the triad meet, and they provide feedback based upon the observation data. The other members of the triad elicit the student teacher's opinions, feelings, and inferences about the observational data. The student teacher analyzes what was happening during the lesson as evidenced by the data. The other members of the triad provide clarification regarding the behaviors represented by the recorded data. The student teacher, with the help of the other members of the triad, integrates the feedback

Phase	Evaluation Process	Clinical Supervision Stage
Design	Preteaching formative	Preobservation conference
Production	Gathering formative evaluation data	Observation
Implementation, maintenance, and growth	Effectiveness testing	Analysis and strategy postobservation conference

Figure 10.3 Phases of formative evaluation

and considers alternative objectives, methods, and reasons. Based on this process, the cycle starts again, and the student teacher practices the decisions made as a result of feedback and compares instructional practices for examples of growth. As the cycle is repeated, the focus is to continually strive for improvement in the instructional strategies.

Summative Evaluation

Summative evaluation, a function entirely different from formative evaluation, focuses on retroactive decisions. It is designed to meet the needs of those interested in accountability. The function of summative evaluation is to categorize, weigh, and discriminate concerning whatever is being evaluated. In other words, the goal of summative evaluation is to categorize, weigh, and discriminate concerning the competency of the student teacher. The goal of summative evaluation is the product, which may range from a completed evaluation sheet to a letter grade. The processes whereby the student teacher learns or grows is not important; only the final result of the evaluation is important. This sorting of student teachers into various categories, whether they be categories of licensing, pass or fail grades, or letter grades representing some type of value, is the purpose of summative evaluation.

Establishing some type of summative evaluation as a result of student teaching does not preclude the use of clinical supervision and formative evaluation. Manatt (1987) suggests that

evaluation can include several formative evaluations that would ultimately become part of the summative phase. In such a process, the triad ensures that the formative data, which provides direction for student teacher instructional improvement, becomes a vital part of the summative evaluation that results in some type of recommendation regarding a grade or licensure. This relationship is strengthened by Duke and Stiggins (1986) who advocate the construction of an evaluation system that is highly individualized and personally productive. This means the individualization of evaluation would come from the establishment of an agenda in the clinical supervision, and continual feedback as the cycle was repeated would increase the productivity (instructional improvement) of the student teacher. They further suggest that the success of evaluation would be based on the interaction among the student teacher and the other members of the triad, the observational data, the feedback, and the context in which the feedback was provided.

Although formative evaluation is the consistent type of evaluation used throughout the clinical supervision process, as long as admission to the profession is controlled by a bureaucracy such as the state, there will always be some type of summative evaluation required to provide documentation relative to the successful completion of the student teaching experience. Until the licensing of teachers is no longer a function of the state, as advocated by Goodlad (1990), summative evaluation will be required. However, if the clinical supervision process is implemented as designed, the involvement of the student teacher in reflective teaching, the involvement of the student teacher in determining the evaluation criteria, and the feedback through formative evaluation will make summative evaluation a simple process rather than a hurdle to be overcome.

Self-Analysis

Just as each of us receives feedback, we also engage in some level of self-analysis. Bailey (1981) indicates that this self-analysis is self-examination in which the student teacher uses a series of sequential feedback strategies for the purpose of instructional improvement. The purposes are to enable the student teacher to become self-directed in improvement of all activities associated with instruction. This definition indicates that the improvement of instruction should encourage the student teacher to focus on more than the specific activities that occur during the actual teaching of the lesson. The totality of this concept is presented in figure 10.4. This is not an attempt to totally define all possible areas that might be applicable, but rather to limit the information to what was agreed on by the triad. In ad-

dition, the student teacher has the option to reflect and carefully reconsider belief systems in the light of what actions support them and the consequences to which they lead. This option allows the student teacher, based on experiences, to add areas that he or she feels are essential determinants in the instructional process. However, the student teacher may not delete any areas to enhance self-analysis.

Once completed, the self-analysis form is brought to the last postobservation conference as another piece of data that is examined by the triad. Hopefully, this information indicates the ability of the student teacher to objectively identify characteristics of effective instruction, the importance of student teacher activities that are not visible in instructional activities, and the interrelationship among all of these areas.

Summary

The evaluation phase of student teaching is always one of anxiety and uncertainty. While part of this anxiety may be due to the importance of the experience, a larger share of the anxiety is caused by the lack of communication and structure found in many student teaching experiences. Clinical supervision, with its emphasis on communication among the members of the triad, and the structure provided by the preobservation conference help evaluation become another phase that can be successfully completed by the members of the triad.

The student teacher has input into the process through determining the criteria for evaluation and interpreting the evaluative data. Although it is difficult to use a checksheet from an external source, such as a university, evaluation in clinical supervision is meaningful and appropriate, and it contributes to reflectivity and lifelong improvement of instructional strategies.

Student teachers should reflect on classroom events to improve teaching.

Questions and Discussion Topics

1. How should a student teacher incorporate professional goals into the evaluation process for student teaching? How should the student teacher act if these goals are not warmly received by other members of the triad?

2. Should the triad avoid developing a checksheet of skills as part of the evaluation process? What are some of the strengths and weaknesses of checksheet evaluations?

3. What anxiety abatement activities should be part of the triad's activities? When should these be introduced? Who has the responsibility to bring up the topic?

4. Is there a role conflict between the formative and summative evaluation requirements of the university supervisor and the cooperating teacher? How should these be addressed? When? Whose responsibility is it to initiate this discussion?

DIRECTIONS: Identify your abilities in each of the following areas. Mark O for outstanding, C for competent, N for needs improvement, and D for does not apply. Please provide a very brief statement in the example column.

Characteristic	O	C	N	D	Example
Personal					
1. Dress appropriately					
2. Pleasant voice with an adequate vocabulary					
3. Good health and vitality					
4. Punctual					
Interpersonal Relationships					
1. Show poise, enthusiasm and confidence in working with students					
2. Ability to develop effective teacher-student rapport					
3. Ability to develop effective student-student relationships					
4. Ability to work effectively with staff as a team member					
5. Express empathy for students' point of view					
Professional					
1. Demonstrate sincere interest in teaching					
2. Involved in school activities					
3. Respect confidential matters					
4. Accept and implement suggestions for self-improvement					
5. Able to function effectively as a member of the triad					

Figure 10.4 Student teacher self-analysis

Characteristic	O	C	N	D	Example
School Management					
1. Know students' names					
2. Demonstrate awareness of students' strengths and weaknesses					
3. Well-prepared					
4. Use appropriate materials					
5. Prompt in submitting plans and reports					
Management and Learning Environment					
1. Demonstrates skill in fostering self-reliance in students					
2. Perceive emerging problems and solve them quickly					
3. Able to direct large group activities					
4. Able to direct small group activities					
Instruction					
1. Knowledgeable in subject areas					
2. Willing to experiment and use new ideas					
3. Able to formulate objectives from curriculum					
4. Teach to objectives					
5. Utilize suggestions from the triad in future lessons					
6. Engage in reflective teaching after a lesson					

Figure 10.4—*Continued*

Characteristic	O	C	N	D	Example
7. Provide effective explanations and demonstrations					
8. Have good questioning skills					
9. Adjust to pupil needs following evaluation					
10. Encourage student participation in lessons					
11. Have evidence of student learnings related to lesson taught					
12. Provide correct model in writing, spelling, and grammar					
13. Effective at integrating student feedback during a lesson					
Management-Special Learning					
1. Worked effectively with mainstreamed students					
2. Worked effectively with gifted/talented					
3. Worked effectively with students from a variety of cultures					
4. Worked effectively with bilingual students					
5. Avoided sterotyping students					

My greatest strengths are:

My areas of needed growth are:

Figure 10.4—Continued

PART 3
THE FUTURE

American education is undergoing change. The public is voicing concerns about the quality of public education and teacher preparation. Teachers tomorrow must be prepared to address the effects of the changing American family and the needs of students. The student population in the twenty-first century will be more diverse racially and ethnically than that of the present society. Thus, the successful supervisor must be adaptive to innovations in education. Although it is often diffi-cult to forecast the precise future, it is essential that we continually try to improve supervision.

Part 3 examines change and educational re-form and their impact on student teaching and su-pervision, thus, providing insight into changes in the future. Chapter 11 focuses on the call for re-structuring teacher education. In effect, it ad-dresses proposed changes in the way teachers are prepared.

CHAPTER 11

Changing Functions

CHAPTER KEY CONCEPTS

Entry-Year
Faculty Associate
Induction

Internship
Mentor
Professional Development Schools

Overview

There has been a national call for the restructuring of teacher education. This restructuring includes agendas such as (1) internships, (2) extended programs, (3) professional and school development, (4) mentoring, and (5) induction programs.

Moreover, with the movement toward teacher empowerment, teaching will continue to evolve to a higher level of professional status in the future. Virtually everyone sees teachers as the most critical variable in improving teacher preparation. Thus, we will most likely see more active teacher involvement in the preparation of the next generation of teachers.

Because of the increasing complexity of teaching, teachers in the future must be more competent in more diverse ways. To meet this demand, there will be a need for reform in the way teachers are prepared. Most educators—public schools and higher education—see teachers taking a more active role in the decision-making related to education at the public school and higher education levels.

This chapter focuses on proposed changes in the way teachers are prepared and the continued empowerment and professionalism of teachers.

Objectives

Upon completing your study of chapter 11, you should be able to:

1. Explain reasons for the national call for the restructuring of teacher education.
2. Discuss the national proposals for improving the preparation of teachers.
3. Describe the major characteristics of internship programs, five- and six-year plans, Goodlad's postulates, professional development schools, mentoring programs, and teacher induction programs.
4. Describe the changing roles of school and university faculty that will likely result from the restructuring of teacher education.
5. Explain why time constraints are a major issue in reform efforts.

6. List and describe teacher preparation that will be needed to implement the various reform efforts.
7. Compare and contrast the clinical supervision approach with the coaching and modeling approaches to supervision.

Teachers are presently being prepared for the twenty-first century. Needless to say, the demand put on teachers will be much different from the present. Futurists forecast that tomorrow's society will be: (1) an information-based society, (2) a microelectronics society, (3) a society with changing values and morality, (4) a population of elderly, and (5) a society with a rapidly changing job market.

Professionalism

Teaching must become increasingly more professionalized to meet the changing needs of society. This increased professionalism will result in expanded roles for teachers in educational policymaking, more lengthy and rigorous professional training programs, and much more teacher involvement and responsibility in the preparation of future teachers.

In 1986, the Holmes Group report (1986), which was written by deans of research-oriented schools of education and the Task Force on Teaching as a Profession of the Carnegie Forum on Education and the Economy report (1986), called for restructuring teacher education. In addition, a more recent five-year study report by John Goodlad (1990) presents nineteen postulates for the improvement of teacher education. Among the proposals called for by these national reports are requiring:

1. A bachelor's degree in arts and sciences as a prerequisite to the professional study of teaching.
2. A new master's degree professional program of study for all teachers that includes internships and residencies in schools.

3. More collaboration between universities and public schools with the establishment of professional development schools where most teacher training takes place.
4. Restructuring the teaching force, with master teachers being in charge of newer teachers.

Internships

Internships are generally viewed as concentrated, postbaccalaureate teaching experiences. Denemark and Nutter (1980) believe that internships are needed because teachers do not receive a fully professional preservice education.

Bents and Howey (1979) suggest that the following be characteristic of internships:

1. Internships should occur only after student teaching.
2. Internships should be planned and coordinated by higher education institutions and public school districts.
3. Interns should be paid and under contract.
4. Interns should be given carefully planned, limited teaching responsibilities (loads).
5. Interns should be simultaneously enrolled in university courses related to their teaching responsibilities.
6. Internships should have a duration of one year.
7. Interns should be supervised by master teachers who are given release time for supervisory responsibilities.
8. Interns should also be supervised by university supervisors.

Basically, internships can be viewed as five-year programs: four years of campus-based, but field-orientated preparation, followed by a year of supervised internship. The intern concept is relatively new in the United States. Indeed, few existed prior to 1980. However, by the late 1980s, at least 31 states plus the District of Columbia had either implemented or were piloting such programs (Huling-Austin 1990). Among the most noteworthy of the successful internship programs have been the Kentucky Beginning Teacher Internship Program, the California Mentor Teacher Program, the Georgia Teacher Certification Program, the Oklahoma Entry Year Assistance Program, and the North Carolina Initial Certification Program. These internship programs have proven useful as a transition between teacher preparation and independent teaching. Needless to say, internships put more of the training responsibilities on experienced practitioners.

Five- and Six-Year Plans

To meet the demands of our continually changing society, more knowledgeable and better prepared teachers are needed. In other words, teaching is becoming more demanding because of the expansion of knowledge that has resulted in the past century. To stay abreast, teaching should become more professional by requiring higher standards for entering and staying in teaching and by the use of more viable evaluation systems so that only quality teachers are trained. This goal has resulted in university teacher preparation programs becoming longer, more selective, and more demanding.

A number of institutions now require four years of study in the liberal arts and sciences followed by a subsequent year of professional study that includes student teaching. Indeed, some universities now require that all prospective teachers have a degree in the liberal arts and sciences, a one-year internship operated by a university and a school district, and one or more years of apprentice teaching supervised by a mentor teacher.

Instead of simply adding another year to existing preservice programs, some critics of present teacher preparation programs suggest shifting to a continuous five-year program that would culminate in the Master of Teaching degree. Students would begin the program in the junior year, and it would include a series of university and school-based teaching and learning activities

spanning development from novice to beginning teacher.

Again, five- and six-year programs with extended apprentice teaching puts additional supervisory responsibilities on experienced practitioners.

Goodlad Postulates

Goodlad (1990) suggests the formation of Centers of Pedagogy that work closely with schools in the preparation of teachers. Representatives from fields such as English, biology, history, and art would join education personnel to form the faculty of these centers. The centers would stand apart from existing colleges of education, would have their own budget, design their own curriculum, develop their own reward system, control field settings in collaboration with school districts, and limit program admission (Olson 1990). It is suggested that these centers implement five-year programs leading to a new bachelor's degree in pedagogy or create two-year post-baccalaureate programs that culminate in the same degree. However, Goodlad does not recommend that the bulk of teacher training be moved to the graduate level. In fact, he does not recommend the reduction or elimination of the traditional undergraduate routes to teacher certification.

According to Goodlad (Skelly 1991), the desired improvement in teacher preparation will come only when the practical part of teacher preparation is carried out in good schools with good supervising teachers. These schools would be practice schools for prospective teachers and would be operated jointly by universities and school districts. At least half of the prospective teacher training would take place in the practice schools with several different teachers working with each prospective teacher.

Professional Development Schools

Critics of present teacher education programs maintain that the professional education components of programs based in the public schools do not prepare prospective teachers to adequately cope with the myriad of problems encountered in the schools. These experiences are often supervised by university faculty who are not actively coping with public school students.

Reform advocates urge the formation of partnerships between the public schools and universities to better prepare teachers for the nation's schools. These professional development schools would be established and operated through a collaborative effort of school systems and universities. The idea is to have the school system and university faculty work together in clinical school settings toward the common goal of providing better preparation of prospective teachers. By combining the knowledge that university personnel bring with the experience and the practical knowledge that teachers possess, an innovative, totally new educational approach to teacher preparation is provided.

While traditional schools and universities are characterized by working with prospective teachers in isolation, professional development schools would be characterized by collegiality between schools and universities. Classroom teachers would hold joint appointments at both the school and the university and would be given the title of Faculty Associates. These Faculty Associates would team-teach some school-site courses with university personnel, and both would guide and carry out supervisory functions in school classrooms. Moreover, the Faculty Associates would occasionally teach courses at the university.

Mentors

As universities narrow the gap between theory and practice and provide a smoother transition between university coursework and student teaching, an increase in collaboration between universities and public schools should develop. Supervising field experiences, including student teaching, continues to be an expensive and difficult undertaking. Indeed, many university faculty members lack the training or knowledge of teaching skills to be effective supervisors. In most cases, university faculty are not hired for their supervisory skills; but rather, most are hired for their content expertise or their research skills. Inasmuch as the expenses continue to climb and it is becoming more difficult to find university supervisory faculty, universities are investigating the feasibility of using a form of mentoring program in the student teaching phase of their preparatory programs. That is, universities are giving cooperating teachers total responsibility for the guidance and refinement of teaching skills, as well as evaluation responsibilities.

Mentoring programs require that the public school teacher assume the role of mentor—a wise and trusted teacher who assumes responsibility for instructing, supervising, and evaluating the person completing preservice teaching experiences. The preservice teacher, known as an intern, is an advanced student in a professional field who is getting practical experience under the supervision of an experienced teacher. The idea of a novice entering a career under the guidance and direction of a wise, experienced mentor is not new. Mentor programs, for example, have been successfully implemented in business and in providing support for new teachers through teacher induction programs (discussed later).

The mentoring process is more than a change in names. The mentor's need specialized preparation that enables them to provide successful experiences for the university and the public schools. This specialized preparation should focus on the philosophy, model, delivery system, and knowledge base of the university teacher education program. This process, which more thoroughly involves public school personnel in the essentials of teacher preparation, enhances the likelihood of success by having public school personnel buy into the program.

Mentor teachers must be leaders, committed to improvement of the profession, who share the dispositions of openness and concern for others (Futrell 1988). In addition, mentors need the wisdom to be effective with student teachers. In short, they need a knowledge of the stages of development as the novice moves toward becoming an experienced teacher, a knowledge of the needs of student teachers, and a knowledge of effective instructional strategies, as well as knowledge of supervisory techniques (reflective strategies, communication, observational strategies, conferencing strategies, and evaluation techniques).

Clearly, mentors also need to deal with the survival anxieties, self-concept issues, and the reality shock surrounding student teaching. Thus, training in interpersonal skills such as active listening, questioning, conflict resolution, problem solving, and decision making are essential elements of a successful mentoring program.

As university budgets become more restrictive and public schools demand more involvement in teacher preparation, collaboration between universities and public schools is desirable and inevitable. It is the responsibility of university personnel to assume a proactive approach to provide the best type of preparation for preservice teachers who are involved in collaborative efforts.

Teacher Induction

The first year (entry year) of teaching is the toughest. Thus, beginning teachers should be given assistance in this first year to further improve their teaching performance and develop additional teacher effectiveness knowledge. An induction program represents an effective technique to keep promising beginning teachers in the profession by providing the personal and professional well-being that is so essential to first-year teachers. An effective induction program would be a collaborative effort between higher education and the public schools with a consultant (sometimes called a mentor teacher) and a higher education person assigned to provide personal support, continuing educative experiences, and further development of identified teaching skills. Of course, the consultant teacher would have most of the supervisory responsibility to provide

needed personal support, teaching assistance, and constructive feedback.

Teacher consultants should be experienced teachers who have mastered their craft and are dedicated to helping inexperienced teachers achieve excellence in the profession. To be effective teacher consultants should be: (1) skilled teachers, (2) conscientious role models, (3) skilled supervisors, and (4) not overly judgmental. Clearly, consultant teachers need to provide the guidance to help beginning teachers analyze their teaching reflectively. That is, they must guide the new teachers to be self-analytic, reflective, and independent learners about the teaching process.

Changing Roles

Extensive participation of classroom teachers is central to most efforts to reform teacher education and to restructure teacher preparation. Teachers who are participating in these efforts are providing rich insights on the concept of teacher preparation. In effect, most educational reform has been directed toward the formation of partnership between universities and public schools who work together to bring improvement to teacher preparation.

The focus of most plans to restructure teacher preparation is on more classroom practice that uses the knowledge and skills of master teachers. The emphasis is on empowering classroom teachers so they can assume more responsibility for the preparation of future teachers.

Some educators propose that much of the preparation of prospective teachers take place in actual classroom environments under the direction of school teachers, school administrators, and university faculty. This arrangement would enable university faculty and practitioners to be integrally involved in a total program. That is, university faculty and practicing teachers would be involved in both the theoretical and practical aspects of teacher preparation.

While the collaboration between universities and public schools in teacher preparation is an excellent start, a number of challenges face the partnership. Chief among these challenges is the change in role expectations, the time demanded of university and school personnel, and the training needs of school personnel.

Role Expectations

Teachers are moving toward a higher, more complex, more demanding plane. They are now expected to have a major role in preparing their replacements; they will have a greater voice in deciding what preparation future teachers need and how it should be delivered. In doing so, they are expected to set high teacher training standards and drive out the weak teachers or those individuals who because of personality factors should not be in the classroom.

With teacher empowerment, the job of teaching will become more complex and more demanding. Teachers will be called upon to teach their own classes while training the teachers of tomorrow. Therefore, today's teachers must be trained to fulfill both of these functions. In other words, the term classroom teacher will evolve into a faculty associate position with public school and university responsibilities.

With the bulk of teacher training taking place in the schools, university faculty must move from the isolated classroom of the university to the public schools. Many of their classes will be team-taught with public school master teachers. That is, they will be taught by university faculty and public school teachers (faculty associates), which will require collaboration and a team approach to instruction. Moreover, the practical application of university classroom theory to public school classrooms will necessitate more university faculty participation in actual classroom situations to carry out supervisory functions. Needless to say, the focus of the university faculty must move from a study of teaching to an involvement in teaching.

Demands placed on classroom teachers have increased as teacher preparation has moved into the schools.

Time Demands

Collaboration and school-based experiences are time-consuming. University and public school personnel should meet regularly and systematically plan the total teacher education curriculum. When this has been done, public school teachers will be asked to (1) teach in many of the school-based courses, (2) hold seminars and conferences with prospective teachers, and (3) carry out supervisory functions. These changes in roles require time out of the usual classroom responsibilities. Therefore, if the restructuring of teacher education is to be successful, involved classroom teachers should be given release time.

The reward system for university faculty should change (see chapter 6). Promotions and tenure should be geared to what teacher educators actually do—prepare teachers. The number of publications (many of which are totally worthless) and research must cease to be the *only* criteria for promotion and tenure. There simply will not be sufficient time for university faculty to be involved in the schools and also to do a great deal of research and publication.

Public School Teacher Preparation

Preparing involved teachers is essential to the success of teacher preparation with major components in the schools. The traditional roles of modeling teaching, observing the student teacher, and offering verbal feedback should be replaced by a more formal system of supervision. This formal system requires specialized preparation. To be viable, teachers need preparation in new teaching methods, new management techniques, and collaborative methods, as well as supervision techniques.

This textbook has focused on the clinical supervision model. However, this is not the only effective supervision model. Another commonly used supervision model is the coaching and modeling approach. Table 11.1 compares clinical supervision with the coaching and modeling approach to supervision. While clinical supervision consists of a three-phase cycle of conferencing, observation, and feedback, the coaching and modeling approach gives student teachers the opportunity to observe new skills in others and then to practice the skill until they are proficient (Joyce and Showers 1981). Unlike the clinical supervision model, attitudes and cooperation skills are important components of the coaching and modeling techniques. Thus, cooperating teachers often need preparation in the modeling of acceptable teaching and nonteaching practices.

Cooperating teachers will assume most of the responsibility for facilitating experiences for university students in their classrooms. These experiences must be planned so they are tied closely to the coursework taught at school sites and are reflective of students' needs and interests. It follows that assessment, including the final evaluation, will be another major responsibility of cooperating teachers. Therefore, cooperating teachers will need more in-depth knowledge of planning and evaluation techniques.

What will teacher preparation be like in five, ten or twenty years? Of course, no one really knows, but we can make some predictions. Most likely, future teacher education programs will be more lengthy and rigorous, and there will be an expanded role for teachers in policy and training decisions. However, these are only predictions. Teacher education may stay the same; only time will tell.

Summary

Although we cannot claim to see the future, the call for reform and the restructuring of teacher preparation is loud. Among the many suggestions, five areas of reform show some promise: internships, extended programs, professional development schools, mentoring, and teacher induction.

Internships and extended programs are similar in that both add one or two years of preparation for full certification. However, the internship differs in that it takes place after student teaching, and the prospective teacher is paid and is under contract. The philosophy undergirding most of the extended programs is that the best way to train better teachers is to require more content and a major in liberal arts and sciences.

Table 11.1
Supervision Models

Model	Key Components
Clinical Supervision	Analysis of instruction; classroom visitations; observation techniques; data gathering techniques; conferencing skills.
Coaching and Modeling	Effective instructional strategies; demonstration teaching; reinforcing teaching effectiveness; modifying instruction; maintaining professionalism.

Although Goodlad's postulates and professional development school show much promise with their partnership arrangements, there are some problems associated with their implementation. Specifically, the feasibility of Goodlad's postulates and the success of the professional development school depends on (1) the ability of public school and university faculty to work together in teaching and supervising prospective teachers in field settings, (2) the likelihood of obtaining release time for classroom teachers, (3) the restricting of the higher education reward system, and (4) the meeting of the retraining needs of school and university faculty.

The use of mentors to supervise student teachers and induction programs to assist beginning teachers also shows a great deal of promise. However, the teachers involved in these programs need specialized preparation. We can't expect them to be agents of change when they are schooled only in the traditional ways of teaching and working with student teachers.

Clearly, the reform and teacher restructuring suggestions need to be investigated carefully. Disagreement abounds on what is best for future teachers. Just more of the same is not the answer to the problems facing this nation's schools.

Questions and Discussion Topics

1. Consider the problems associated with teacher preparation and suggest ways that the programs presented in this chapter could contribute toward their solution.
2. How will teacher preparation in the year 2010 be different from today? Do you think public school classroom teachers will have a significant role in the preparation of teachers?
3. Which reform suggestion presented in this chapter interests you the most? Do you think it represents a significant solution to the problems in teacher preparation? Why?
4. Do you think the formation of partnerships between the public schools and higher education institutions in the preparation of teachers is feasible? What are the advantages? What are the disadvantages?

Bibliography

Acheson, K., and Gall, M. D. 1980. *Techniques in the clinical supervision of teachers-preservice and inservice applications.* New York: Longman, 119–125.

Amidon, E. J.; Casper, I. G.; and Flanders, N. A. 1985. *The role of the teacher in the classroom,* 3rd ed. St. Paul, Minn.: Paul S. Amidon & Associates, Inc.

Arends, R. I. 1991. *Learning to teach,* 2nd ed. New York: McGrawHill.

Bailey, G. D. 1981. *Teacher self-assessment: A means for improving classroom instruction.* Washington, D.C.: National Education Association.

Barker, L. L. 1971. *Listening behavior.* Englewood Cliffs, N.J.: Prentice-Hall.

Barnes, S., and Edwards, S. 1984. Effective student teaching experience: A qualitative and quantitative study. Austin, Tex.: Research and Development for Teacher Education, ERIC, ED 251 441.

Bennie, W. A. 1972. *Supervising clinical experiences in the classroom.* New York: Harper and Row.

Bents, R. A., and Howey, K. R. 1979. A historical perspective. In R. Howey and R. A. Bents, (Eds.), *Toward Meeting the Needs of the Beginning Teacher,* Minneapolis, Minn.: Midwest Teacher Corps Network and University of Minnesota/St. Paul Schools Teacher Corps Project, 7–18.

Blumberg, A. 1984. *Supervisors and teachers: A private cold war.* Berkeley, Calif.: McCutchan.

Blumberg, A., and Amidon, E. 1965. Teacher perceptions of supervisor-teacher interaction. *Administrator's Notebook, 14,* L8, 18.

Blumberg, A., and Weber, W. 1968. Teacher morale as a function of perceived supervisor behavioral style. *Journal of Educational Research, 62*(3), 109–113.

Book, C.; Byers, J.; and Freeman, D. 1983. Student expectations and teacher education traditions with which we can and cannot live. *Journal of Teacher Education, 38*(1), 2–12.

Borinstein, D. 1982. A systematic approach to increasing supervisory skills. *Supervisory Management, 42*(9), 35–39.

Boyan, N. J., and Copeland, W. D. 1978. *Instructional supervision training program.* Columbus, Ohio: Charles E. Merrill.

Brophy, J. E. 1979. Teacher behavior and student learning. *Educational Leadership, 37*(5), 33–38.

Browne, E., and Hoover, J. H. 1990. The degree to which student teachers report using instructional strategies valued by university faculty. *Action in Teacher Education, 12*(1), 20–23.

Calfee, R. 1981. Cognitive psychology and educational practice. In D. C. Berliner (Ed.), *Review of research in education,* 9. Washington, D.C.: American Educational Research Association.

Carnegie Forum Task Force. 1986, May. *A nation prepared: Teachers for the 21st century.* Carnegie Forum on Education and the Economy.

Cartwright, C. A., and Cartwright, G. P. 1974. *Developing observation skills.* New York: McGraw-Hill.

Chandler, T. A. 1982. Can theory Z be applied to the public schools? *Education, 104,* 343–345.

Clements, B., and Evertson, C. 1981. *Developing an effective research team for classroom observation.* (R & D Report Number 6103.) Austin: University of Texas R & D Center for Teacher Education.

Cogan, M. L. 1973. *Clinical supervision.* Dallas, Texas: Houghton Mifflin Company.

Copeland, W. 1980. Student teachers and cooperating teachers: An ecological relationship. *Theory into Practice, 18*(3), 194–199.

Corrigan, L., and Griswold, T. 1974. The effects of the university supervisor on the performance and adjustment of student teachers. *Journal of Educational Research, 50*(10), 358–362.

Curren, J. 1977. An applied behavioral analysis training model for preservice teachers. Unpublished Doctoral Dissertation, Ohio State University.

Denemark, G., and Nutter, N. 1980. The case for extended programs of initial teacher preparation. Washington, D.C.: *ERIC Clearinghouse on Teacher Education,* (ERIC document Reproduction Service No. ED 180 995.)

DeVito, J. A. 1985. *Communication,* 3rd ed. New York: Harper and Row, Publishers.

Droeschers, C. G. 1988. *What is clinical supervision and how can it be applied?* Northridge, Calif.: California State University, Northridge.

Duke, D. L., and Stiggins, R. J. 1986. *Teacher evaluation: Five keys to growth.* Washington, D.C.: National Education Association.

Eisenberg, A. M., and Smith, R. R. Jr. 1971. *Nonverbal communications.* Indianapolis, Ind.: Bobbs-Merrill.

Eisner, E. 1982. An artistic approach to supervision. In T. Sergiovanni (Ed.), *Supervision of Teaching.* Alexandria, Va.: Association for Supervision and Curriculum Development.

Evans, E. D., and Tribble, M. 1986. Perceived teaching problems, self-efficacy, and commitment to teaching among preservice teachers. *Journal of Educational Research, 80*(2), 81–85.

Evertson, C. M., and Green, J. L. 1986. Observation inquiry and method. In M. C. Wintrock (Ed.), *Handbook of Research on Teaching,* (3rd ed., pp. 162–163). New York: Macmillian.

Fensternmacher, G. D. 1978. A philosophical consideration of recent research in teacher effectiveness. In D. C. Berliner (Ed.), *Review of Research in Education,* 6. Washington, D.C.: American Educational Research Association.

Flanders, N. 1970. *Analyzing teacher behavior.* Reading, Mass.: Addison Wesley Publishing Co.

Florida. 1988. *Public education: General provisions.* Section 228.041, 4.

Franco, J. 1985. Supervision: Critical performance link. *Industry Week, 225*(2), 14–18.

Friebus, R. J. 1977. Agents of socialization involved in student teaching. *Journal of Educational Research, 70*(5), 263–268.

Friedman, P. G. 1983. *Listening processes: Attention, understanding, evaluation.* Washington, D.C.: National Education Association.

Funk, F.; Long, B.; Keithley, A.; and Hoffman, J. 1982. The cooperating teacher as a most significant other: A competent humanist. *Action in Teacher Education 4*(2), 57–64.

Futrell, M. H. 1988. Selecting and compensating mentor teachers: A win-win scenario. *Theory into Practice, 27*(3), 223–225.

Galloway, C. 1976. *Silent language in the classroom.* Bloomington, Ind.: Phi Delta Kappa Educational Foundation, Fastback 86.

Galloway, C. M. 1966. Teacher nonverbal communication. *Educational Leadership. 24*(1), 55–63.

Garland, C. 1982. *Guiding clinical experiences in teacher education.* New York: Longman.

Garman, N. B. 1982. The clinical approach to supervision. In T. J. Sergiovanni (Ed.), *Supervision of Teaching.* Alexandria, Va. Association for Supervision and Curriculum Development, 35–52.

Garman, N. B.; Glickman, C. D.; Hunter, M.; and Haggerson, N. L. 1987. Conflicting conceptions of clinical supervision and the enhancement of professional growth and renewal: Point and counterpoint. *Journal of Curriculum and Supervision, 2*(2), 152–177.

Glatthorn, A. 1984. *Differentiated supervision.* Alexandria, Va. Association for Supervision and Curriculum Development.

Glickman, C. 1985. *Supervision of instruction: A developmental approach.* Boston, Mass.: Allyn and Bacon.

Glickman, C. G. 1981. *Developmental supervision: Alternative practices for helping teachers improve instruction.* Alexandria, Va.: Association for supervision and Curriculum Development.

Glickman, C. G., and Bey, T. M. 1990. Supervision. In W. R. Houston (Ed.), *Handbook of research in teacher education.* (pp. 549–566.) New York: Macmillian.

Goldhammer, R. 1969. *Clinical supervision.* New York: Holt, Rinehart and Winston.

Goldsberry, L. 1988. Three functional methods of supervision. *Action in Teacher Education, 10*(1), 1–10.

Good, T. L., and Brophy, J. E. 1984. *Looking in classrooms,* 3rd ed. New York: Harper and Row, Publishers.

Good, T. L., and Brophy, J. E. 1987. *Looking in classrooms,* 4th ed. New York: Harper and Row, Publishers.

Goodall, Jr., H. L. 1983. *Human communication.* Dubuque, Iowa: Wm. C. Brown.

Goodlad, J. I. 1990. *Teachers for our nation's schools.* San Francisco: Jossey-Bass Inc.

Gore, J. M. 1987. Reflecting on reflective teaching. *Journal of Teacher Education, 38*(2), 25–31.

Grambs, J. D., and Carr, J. C. 1991. *Modern methods in secondary education,* 5th ed. Fort Worth: Holt, Rinehart and Winston, Inc.

Guyton, E. 1987. Working with student teachers: incentives, problems, and advantages. *The Professional Educator, 10*(1), 21–28.

Guyton, E. 1989. Guidelines for developing educational programs for cooperating teacher. *Action in Teacher Education, 11*(3), 54–58.

Gwynn, J. M. 1961. *Theory and practice of supervision.* New York: Dodd, Mead & Company.

Haberman, M., and Harris, P. 1982. State requirements for cooperating teachers. *Journal of Teacher Education, 33*(3), 45–47.

Hall, E. T. 1969. *The hidden dimension.* Garden City, N.Y.: Archor, 113–130.

Hansen, J. 1977. Observation skills. In J. M. Cooper et al. *Classroom Teaching Skills: A Handbook.* Lexington, Mass. D.C. Heath and Company.

Harris, B. M. 1976. Limits and supplements to formal clinical supervision. *Journal of Research and Development in Education, 2*(9), 85–89.

Helm, V. 1982. Defamation, due process, and evaluating clinical experiences. *Action in Teacher Education 4*(2), 27–32.

Hennings, D. G. 1975. *Mastering classroom communication: What interaction analysis tells the teacher.* Pacific Palisades, Calif.: Goodyear Publishing Company.

Henry, M. 1990. *Supervising teachers the professional way,* 4th. ed. Terre Haute, Ind.: Sycamore Press.

Henry, M. A., and Beasley, W. W. 1982. *Supervising Student Teachers the Professional Way,* 3rd. ed. Terre Haute, Ind.: Sycamore Press.

Holland, P. E. 1989. Implicit assumptions about the supervisory conference: A review and analysis of literature. *Journal of Curriculum and Supervision. 4*(4), 362–379.

Holmes Group. 1986. *Tomorrow's teachers: A report of the Holmes Group.* East Lansing, Mich.: Author.

Hough, J., and Duncan, J. 1970. *Teaching: Description and analysis.* Reading Mass.: Addison Wesley Publishing Co.

Huling-Austin, L. 1990. Teacher induction programs and internships. In W. R. Houston, M. Haberman, & J. Sikula (Eds.), *Handbook of Research on Teacher Education.* New York: Macmillan.

Hunter, M. 1980. Six types of supervisory conferences, *Educational Leadership, 37*(5), 409–412.

Hunter, M. 1986. Let's eliminate the preobservation conference. *Educational Leadership, 43*(6), 69–70.

Hurt, H. T.; Scott, M. D.; and McCroskey, J. C. 1978. *Communications in the Classroom.* Menlo Park: Calif.: Addison-Wesley.

Indiana. 1969. *Indiana acts 1969.* Chapter 246.

Johnson, W. C.; Cox, B.; and Wood, G. 1982. Communicative patterns and topics of single and paired student teachers. *Action in Teacher Education, 4*(2), 59–60.

Joyce, B. R., and Showers, B. 1981. Transfer of training: The contribution of coaching. *Journal of Education, 162*(1), 163–172.

Katz, R. 1974. Skills of an effective administrator. *Harvard Business Review, 52*(5), 90–102.

Kerr, B. J. 1976. An investigation of the process of using feedback data within the clinical supervision cycle to facilitate teachers' individualization of instruction. Ph.D. diss. University of Pittsburgh, 1976.

Kilbourn, B. 1982. Linda: A case study in clinical supervision. *Canadian Journal of Education, 7*(2), 1–24.

Krajewski, R. J. 1976. Clinical supervision to facilitate selfimprovement. *Journal of Research and Development in Education, 2*(9), 58–66.

Kuehl, R. 1976. A taxonomy of critical tasks for supervising teachers. (ERIC Document Reproduction Service No. ED 179 507.)

Lang, D. C., Quick, A. F., and Johnson, J. A. 1975. *A partnership for the supervision of student teachers.* Mt. Pleasant, Mich.: Great Lakes Publishing Co.

Lang, D. C.; Quick, A. F.; and Johnson, J. A. 1982. A partnership for the supervision of student teachers. DeKalb, Ill.: Creative Educational Materials.

Lanier, J., and Cusick, P. 1985, June. An oath for professional educators. *Phi Delta Kappa, 66*(10), 711–712.

Likert, R. 1967. *The human organization.* New York: McGraw-Hill.

Lordon, J. 1986. In defense of the preobservation conference. *Educational Leadership, 43*(6), 70–71.

Love, A. M., and Roderick, J. A. 1971, October. Teacher nonverbal communication: The development of field testing of an awareness unit. *Theory into Practice,* 295–296.

Lucio, W. H. 1962. Instructional improvement: Considerations for supervision. *Educational Leadership, 20*(3), 211–217.

McCarthy, M. M., and Cambron-McCabe, N. H. 1987. *Public school law: Teachers' and student rights,* 2nd ed. Boston: Allyn and Bacon, Inc.

McGregor, D. 1960. *The human side of enterprise.* New York: McGrawHill.

McIntyre, J. D. 1984. A response to the critics of field experience supervision. *Journal of Teacher Education, 35*(2), 42–45.

McNeil, J. D. 1971. *Toward accountable teachers: Their appraisal and improvement.* New York: Holt, Rinehart and Winston.

Manatt, R. P. 1987. *Evaluating teacher performance.* Association for Supervision and Curriculum Development. (Videotape)

Martin, G. S. 1975. Teacher and administrator attitudes toward evaluation and systematic classroom observation. Ph.D. diss., University of Oregon.

Medley, D. M. 1971. The language of teacher behavior: Communicating the results of structural observations to teachers. *Journal of Teacher Education, 22*(2), 157–165.

Michigan Council of State College Presidents. 1970. *The impact of the student teaching program upon public schools in Michigan.* Lansing, Mich.: Author.

Miller, P. W. 1981. *Nonverbal communications.* Washington, D.C.: National Education Association.

Mills, J. R. 1980. A guide for teaching systematic observation to student teachers. *Journal of Teacher Education, 31*(6), 5–9.

Montana. 1987. *Montana school law.* Section 20–4–101.

Moore, K. D. 1989. *Classroom teaching skills: A primer.* New York: Random House.

Moorehead, M A.; Foyle, H. C.; and Lyman, L. 1990, August. *A videotape model: Conferencing with the incompetent/excellent student teacher.* Paper presented at the Summer Workshop of the Association of Teacher Educators, Baltimore, Md.

Moorehead, M. A.; Lyman, L.; and Waters, S. 1988. A model for improving student supervision. *Action in Teacher Education, 10*(1), 39–42.

Morris, J. K. 1974. The effect of the university supervisor on the performance and adjustment of student teachers. *Journal of Educational Research 58*(8), 358–362.

Morrow, J. E., and Lane, J. M. 1983. Instructional problems of student teachers: Perceptions of student teachers, supervising teachers, and college supervisors. *Action in Teacher Education, 5*(12), 71–78.

Mosher, R. L., and Purpel, D. E. 1972. *Supervision: The reluctant profession.* Boston: Houghton Mifflin.

Newman, N. S. 1979. Teacher perception of supervision: Verbal reinforcement and clarity of presentation under direct and indirect conferencing. Ph.D. diss., Syracuse University, 1979.

Nichols, R. G., and Stevens, L. A. 1957. *Are you listening?* New York: McGraw-Hill.

North Carolina. 1990. *Public school laws of North Carolina.* Section 115C–3001, 203.

North Dakota. 1987. *Teacher certification.* Section 67–02–01–01, 6.

O'Neal, S. 1983. *Supervision of student teachers: Feedback and evaluation.* Austin: University of Texas, Research and Development Center for Teacher Education.

O'Reilly, R. C., and Green, E. T. 1983. *School law for the practitioner.* Westport, Conn.: Greenwood Press, 148–150.

Olson, L. 1990, October 24. Goodlad's teacher-education study urges college 'Center of pedagogy'. *Education Week, 10*(8), 1, 12–13.

Peterson, P. P. 1979. Direct instruction reconsidered. In H. J. Walberg (Ed.), *Research on teaching.* Berkeley, Calif.: McCutchan.

Pfeiffer, I. L., and Dunlap, J. B. 1982. *Supervision of teachers: a guide to improving instruction.* Phoenix, Ariz.: The Oryx Press.

Reed, E. C., and Gaglione, F. 1977. *Student teaching: The clinical supervision practice.* Nashville, Tenn.: Tennessee State University.

Roberts, A. A. 1978. A cooperating teacher's perceptions of the effect of them having a student teacher in the classroom. Ph.D. diss., Syracuse University.

Roe, B. D.; Ross, E. P.; and Burns, P. C. 1984. *Student Teaching and Field Experiences Handbook,* Columbus, Ohio: Charles E. Merrill Publishing Company.

Rogers, C. 1977. *Carl Rogers on personal power.* New York: Delacorte.

Russell, D., and Hunter, M. 1980. *Planning for effective instruction.* Los Angeles: University Elementary School.

Sadker, M., and Sadker, D. 1982. *Sex equity handbook for schools.* New York: Longman.

Scriven, M. 1967. The methodology of evaluation. In R. E. Stake (Ed.), *Curriculum Evaluation.* American Education Research Association Monograph Series on Evaluation. Chicago: Rand McNally.

Seidentop, D. 1976, September. Teacher assessment in physical education. Paper presented at the Professional Preparation Conference in Physical Education, Sponsored by the Midwest District of AAHPERD and NASPF, Pokagon State Park, Angola, Indiana.

Seperson, M. A., and Joyce, B. R. 1973. Teaching styles of student teachers as related to those of their cooperating teachers. *Educational Leadership Research Supplement,* (31) November.

Shinn, J. L. 1976. Teacher perceptions of ideal and actual supervisory procedures used by California elementary principals: The effects of supervisory training programs. Ph.D. diss., University of Oregon.

Silberman, C. 1971. *Crisis in the classroom.* New York: Random House.

Skelly, M. E. 1991, February. Connecting teacher training to school reform. *School and College,* 21–24.

Sokolove, S.; Sadker, D.; and Sadker, M. 1986. Interpersonal communication skills. In J. M. Cooper et al., *Classroom Teaching Skills,* 3rd ed. Lexington, Mass.: D.C. Heath.

Spaulding, R. L. 1982. Generalizability of teacher behavior: Stability of observational data within and across facets of classroom environments. *Journal of Educational Research, 74*(4), 197–216.

Stallings, J. A. 1977. *Learning to look*. Belmont, Calif.: Wadsworth Publishing Company, Inc.

Stout, C. 1982. Why cooperating teachers accept students. *Journal of Teacher Education, 33*(6), 2–24.

Strahan, R. D., and Turner, L C. 1987. *The Courts and the Schools*. New York: Longman.

Stufflebeam, D. L. (Ed.). 1988. *The personnel evaluation standards*. Newbury Park, CA: Sage Publications, Inc.

Tanner, D., and Tanner, L. N. 1986. *Supervision in Education*. New York: Macmillan.

Taylor, J. A. 1983. A college supervisor speaks to student teachers. *Kappa Delta Pi Record, 20*(1), 20.

Taylor, L. K.; Cook, P. F.; Green, E. E.; and Rogers, J. K. 1988. Better interviews: The effects of supervisor training on listening and collaborative skills. *Journal of Educational Research, 82*(2), 85–95.

Tillman, M.; Bersoff, D.; and Dolly, J. 1976. *Learning to Teach*. Lexington, Mass.: D.C. Heath and Company.

Trois, N. 1959. Development of supervisory teacher's role. In E. J. Melvin (Ed.), *The Supervising Teacher 38th yearbook*. Dubuque, Iowa: Association for Student Teaching.

Valente, W. D. 1987. *Law in the schools,* 2nd ed. Columbus, Ohio: Merrill Publishing, 426.

Valverde, L. 1982. The self-evolving supervisor. In T. Sergiovanni (Ed.), *Supervision of teaching* (pp. 81–89). Alexandria, Va.: Association for Supervision and Curriculum.

Weinstein, C. 1989. Teacher education students' perceptions of teaching. *Journal of Teacher Education, 40*(2), 24–37.

Weller, R. (Ed.) 1977. *Humanistic education: Visions and realities*. Berkeley, Calif.: McCutchan.

Wellington, B. 1991. The promise of reflective practice. *Educational Leadership, 48*(6), 4–5.

Whitehead, R. 1984, June. *Practicum students' perceptions of teacher associates' supervisor behaviors*. Paper presented at the annual meeting of the Canadian Society for the Study of Education, Guelph, Canada. (ERIC Document Reproduction Service No. ED 269 856)

Wiles, K. 1967. *Clinical supervision for better schools*. Englewood Cliffs, N.J.: Prentice Hall.

Wolvin, A. D., and Cookley, C. G. 1979. *Listening instruction*. Urbana, Ill.: ERIC Clearinghouse Reading and Communications Skills.

Worchel, S., and Shebilske, W. 1989. *Psychology*. Englewood Cliffs, N. J.: Prentice Hall.

Yee, A. H. 1969. Do cooperating teachers influence the activities of student teachers? *Journal of Educational Psychology, 60*(4), 327–330.

Zeichner, K. M., and Liston, D. P. 1987. Teaching student teachers to reflect. *Harvard Educational Review, 57,* 23–48.

Zimpher, N. L. 1980. A closer look at university student supervision. *Journal of Teacher Education, 31*(4), 11–15.

Index